Bloom's Modern Critical Interpretations

Bloom's Modern Critical Interpretations

William Shakespeare's
Romeo and Juliet
New Edition

Edited and with an introduction by
Harold Bloom
Sterling Professor of the Humanities
Yale University

BLOOM'S
LITERARY CRITICISM
An imprint of Infobase Publishing

Bloom's Modern Critical Interpretations:
William Shakespeare's *Romeo and Juliet*—New Edition

Copyright ©2009 by Infobase Publishing

Introduction ©2009 by Harold Bloom

Bloom's Literary Criticism
An imprint of Infobase Publishing
132 West 31st Street
New York NY 10001

Library of Congress Cataloging-in-Publication Data

William Shakespeare's Romeo and Juliet / edited and with an introduction by Harold Bloom. — New ed.
        p. cm. — (Bloom's modern critical interpretations)
    Includes bibliographical references and index.
    ISBN 978-1-60413-633-3 (alk. paper)
1. Shakespeare, William, 1564–1616. Romeo and Juliet. I. Bloom, Harold. II. Title: Romeo and Juliet.

PR2831.W552 2009
822.3'3—dc22   2009009817

Bloom's Literary Criticism books are available at special discounts when purchased in bulk quantities for businesses, associations, institutions, or sales promotions. Please call our Special Sales Department in New York at (212) 967-8800 or (800) 322-8755.

You can find Bloom's Literary Criticism on the World Wide Web at
http://www.chelseahouse.com.

Cover design by Alicia Post

Printed in the United States of America
MP BCL 10 9 8 7 6 5 4 3 2 1

This book is printed on acid-free paper.

All links and Web addresses were checked and verified to be correct at the time of publication. Because of the dynamic nature of the Web, some addresses and links may have changed since publication and may no longer be valid.

Contents

Editor's Note

My introduction briefly analyzes the drama's four crucial personages: Juliet, Mercutio, the nurse, and Romeo.

"Informal language" in the play is Norman F. Blake's concern, while Tanya Pollard contrasts potions and poisons in *Romeo and Juliet* and the later, more vital tragedy, *Antony and Cleopatra*.

David Salter shrewdly details Shakespearean friars, remarking their pagan quality, after which William M. McKim charts the imaginative difference between Romeo and Juliet.

Images of rape invoked throughout the tragedy are noted by Robert N. Watson and Stephen Dickey, while Jennifer A. Low considers the dialectic of audience and actors in Shakespearean theater.

Memory is the focus of Lina Perkins Wilder, after which the intricacies of the orchard scene are expounded by Thomas Honneger.

This volume concludes with Daryl W. Palmer's Platonic account of the philosophy of motion as embodied in the mercurial Mercutio.

HAROLD BLOOM

Introduction

WILLIAM SHAKESPEARE'S *ROMEO AND JULIET*

Harold C. Goddard, in his *The Meaning of Shakespeare* (1951), remarked upon how much of Shakespeare turns upon the vexed relationships between generations of the same family, which was also one of the burdens of Athenian tragedy. Except for the early *Titus Andronicus,* which I judge to have been a charnel-house parody of Christopher Marlowe, *Romeo and Juliet* was Shakespeare's first venture at composing a tragedy, and also his first deep investigation of generational perplexities. The Montague-Capulet hatred might seem overwrought enough to have its parodistic aspects, but it destroys two immensely valuable, very young lovers, Juliet of the Capulets and Romeo of the Montagues, and Mercutio as well, a far more interesting character than Romeo. Yet Romeo, exalted by the authentic love between the even more vital Juliet and himself, is one of the first instances of the Shakespearean representation of crucial change in a character through self-overhearing and self-reflection. Juliet, an even larger instance, is the play's triumph, since she inaugurates Shakespeare's extraordinary procession of vibrant, life-enhancing women, never matched before or since in all of Western literature, including in Chaucer, who was Shakespeare's truest precursor as the creator of personalities.

Juliet, Mercutio, the nurse, and to a lesser extent Romeo are among the first Shakespearean characters who manifest their author's uncanny genius at inventing persons. Richard III, like Aaron the Moor in *Titus Andronicus,* is a brilliant Marlovian cartoon or grotesque, but lacks all inwardness, which is true also of the figures in the earliest comedies. Faulconbridge the Bastard in *King John* and Richard II were Shakespeare's initial breakthroughs in the forging of personalities, before the composition of *Romeo and Juliet.*

1

After Juliet, Mercutio, and the nurse came Bottom, Shylock, Portia, and most overwhelmingly Falstaff, with whom at last Shakespeare was fully himself. Harold Goddard shrewdly points out that the nurse, who lacks wit, imagination, and above all love, even for Juliet, is no Falstaff, who abounds in cognitive power, creative humor, and (alas) love for the undeserving Hal. The nurse is ferociously lively and funny, but she proves to be exactly what the supremely accurate Juliet eventually calls her: "most wicked fiend," whose care for Juliet has no inward reality. In some sense, the agent of Juliet's tragedy is the nurse, whose failure in loving the child she has raised leads Juliet to the desperate expedient that destroys both Romeo and herself.

Mercutio, a superb and delightful role, nevertheless is inwardly quite as cold as the nurse. Though he is Shakespeare's first sketch of a charismatic individual (Berowne in *Love's Labor's Lost* has brilliant language, but no charisma), Mercutio is a dangerous companion for Romeo, and becomes redundant as soon as Romeo passes from sexual infatuation to sincere love, from Rosaline to Juliet. Age-old directorial wisdom is that Shakespeare killed off Mercutio so quickly, because Romeo is a mere stick in contrast to his exuberant friend. But Mercutio becomes irrelevant once Juliet and Romeo fall profoundly in love with one another. What place has Mercutio in the play once it becomes dominated by Juliet's magnificent avowal of her love's infinitude:

> And yet I wish but for the thing I have.
> My bounty is as boundless as the sea,
> My love as deep; the more I give to thee,
> The more I have, for both are infinite.

Contrast that with Mercutio at his usual bawdry:

> If love be blind, love cannot hit the mark.
> Now will he sit under a medlar tree,
> And wish his mistress were that kind of fruit
> As maids call medlars, when they laugh alone.
> O, Romeo, that she were, O that she were
> An open-arse, thou a poperin pear!

Since Juliet develops from strength to strength, Romeo (who is only partly a convert to love) is inevitably dwarfed by her. Partly this is the consequence of what will be Shakespeare's long career of comparing women to men to men's accurate disadvantage, a career that can be said to commence with precisely this play. But partly the tragic flaw is in Romeo himself, who yields too readily to many fierce emotions: anger, fear, grief, and despair. This yielding leads to the death of Tybalt, to Romeo's own suicide, and to Juliet's own farewell to life. Shakespeare is careful to make Romeo just as culpable, in his way, as Mercutio or Tybalt. Juliet, in total contrast, remains radically free of flaw: she is a saint of love, courageous and trusting, refusing the nurse's evil counsel and attempting to hold on to love's truth, which she incarnates. Though it is "The Tragedy of Romeo and Juliet," the lovers are tragic in wholly different ways. Juliet, in a curious prophecy of Hamlet's charismatic elevation, transcends her self-destruction and dies exalted. Romeo, not of her eminence, dies more pathetically. We are moved by both deaths, but Shakespeare sees to it that our larger loss is the loss of Juliet.

NORMAN F. BLAKE

On Shakespeare's Informal Language*

1. Introduction

When asked to compile a dictionary of Shakespeare's informal English within a series published by Athlone Press (now taken over by Continuum Books), I naturally reviewed what the attraction of compiling such a dictionary might be. Informal language is a neglected topic—at least from a historical standpoint—and it is not well covered in historical dictionaries like the *Oxford English Dictionary* [OED] if only because, to illustrate why a word or phrase may be understood as informal, a much longer context is necessary than most dictionaries provide. There are dictionaries and glossaries devoted to other aspects of Shakespeare's language like legal and military language, sexual innuendo, and neologisms, but his informal language has not been covered though it forms so large a part of conversation. As Shakespeare is primarily a dramatist and he is one of the first dramatists to use informal language for conversation, his informal English should be a major topic of investigation. Indeed, his informal language is often ignored by editors and commentators, who often interpret what could be informal as formal and/or grammatical. I have had an interest in informal language for some time (Blake 1981), and through compiling this dictionary I hope to learn more about Shakespeare, conversational language in the Elizabethan and Jacobean periods, and to what extent we may need to change our views about Shakespeare through studying this aspect of his linguistic usage. However,

Journal of Historical Pragmatics, Volume 3, Number 2 (2002): pp. 179–204. Copyright © 2002 John Benjamin Publishing Company.

although all dictionaries have fuzzy boundaries, topic-based dictionaries are especially problematic because the boundaries of any given topic are less clearly defined than what constitutes the standard forms of a language.

2. The data for a dictionary of Shakespeare's informal English

Shakespeare wrote both poems and plays. It is in the plays, which are conversation based, that one expects to find examples of informal language, because the poems are rhetorical and elevated in their language, dealing as they do with love, and in the longer poems this passion is set in a distant past and treated in an almost epic manner. Although they may contain dialogue, that dialogue is likely to be idealised. Some of the dialogue in the poems is inspired by hate, revenge, fear and other emotions which could readily give rise to less formality in speech. Shakespeare may deliberately set the tone of this language in direct contrast with that which is both more formal and elegant. The lover in the *Sonnets*[1] can exclaim *But out alack, he was but one hour mine* (33.11), where *out* and *alack* are examples of informal language with parallels in the plays. When in *Venus and Adonis* Adonis's stallion sees a mare, he cares little for what his master shouts:

(1) What recketh he his riders angrie sturre,
     His flattering holla, or his stand, I say, (283–284).

Here, *holla, stand,* and *I say* are all examples of informal language—that language which a rider addresses to his horse or which people use to others whom they are trying to command or restrain. There is no reason to exclude poems from the data-base; and it may be that there are interesting parallels between the poems and some of the plays.

These caveats lead naturally to a consideration of the canon of Shakespeare's work. There are two problems here, especially regarding the plays: they may exist in different formats and they may also have been written by more than one author. The plays attributed to Shakespeare in the period c.1582–1608 survive in various copies: (i) the so-called "bad" and "good" quartos [Q], most of which are dated before 1623, (ii) the First Folio [F], the first collected edition of Shakespeare's plays issued by Heminge and Condell in 1623, and (iii) the Second (1632), Third (1663–1664) and Fourth (1685) Folios, which are revised versions of the earlier editions, some of which may have had access to a better text. Although editors of Shakespeare's plays take account of these later folios to support emendations, they contain few genuine readings because their editors were influenced by the wish to make the text intelligible. I do take account of cases where they differ significantly from F, because this could indicate informal English where their editors found F difficult to understand.

A lexicographer should work from the original editions. But here there is a problem arising from the need to fit a dictionary into a publisher's programme. Most publishers want to tie their dictionaries to a modern edition because they assume that a modern edition is authoritative and widely known among students and others, and because they assume sales will be better if their dictionaries are tied to a complete edition of Shakespeare's works which is commonly chosen by teachers at institutions of education as their set text for students, such as the Oxford collected edition (Wells and Taylor 1988). The problem is that any scholarly work which uses one of these editions for its data will both omit much of what might be Shakespeare's language and become outmoded in the not-too-distant future as a new collected edition becomes accepted. Thus Spevack's thesaurus (1993), which is based on the Riverside Shakespeare, omits many words which occur in less favoured texts, especially the bad quartos. It is difficult to accept that it encapsulates the whole of Shakespeare's world vision and intellectual framework (which is its aim), as it fails to evaluate the *whole* of his potential vocabulary. Quite apart from the bad quartos, there are different versions of the same play as for example *Hamlet* and *King Lear*. With *King Lear* older editors often amalgamated Q2 and F to form a conflated modern edition. Nowadays, it is thought that Shakespeare revised the text so that there are two equally valid and authoritative versions of the same play. With *Hamlet* some editors prefer to follow F and others Q2, whereas some try to amalgamate the two. Even with those editions which amalgamate the two texts into a single version, the result is that only additional, and not variant, lines are included in the final edition. Where there are variant lines, the editor has to choose between them, for he or she cannot include them both.

Many of the plays also show evidence of the hands of different authors, for co-operation in the pressurised life of the theatre may have demanded it. When a play is announced, it has to be made ready for the first performance. It is likely that several authors were put to work to get the play ready in time. When a play went into rehearsal, it might have been adapted, as Philip Gaskell (1978:245–262) has shown for the modern theatre, and if the principal author was not available another dramatist might have stepped in to provide revised scenes or lines. The manuscript play of *Sir Thomas More* contains six hands as well as annotations by the Master of the Revels. It is probable that the main part of the play was written by Anthony Munday in association with Thomas Chettle and possibly one further author. The Master of the Revels demanded alterations to the first draft and this is one reason why additional hands are found in the manuscript. Some alterations are Shakespeare's, identified as Hand D in the manuscript. This hand wrote a whole scene (164 lines in Wells and Taylor 1988). In addition, twenty-one lines of a soliloquy by More, in the hand of a professional scribe, are attributed to

Shakespeare. Quite apart from this play, other plays in the Shakespeare canon show signs of joint composition, often with Thomas Middleton. When a play was finished in draft, a fair copy was made to be used as a prompt copy and another copy may have been in the company's archives for future use. When the company travelled, to escape the plague or creditors, they may have taken a smaller number of actors on tour to keep their costs down and then the plays in the repertoire would have been adapted to suit a reduced company. So different versions of the same play may exist, all of which are authoritative to a greater or lesser extent, though Shakespeare may not have been the author of the complete text of these versions. The problem is deciding precisely how much was his—or even if this is something worth trying to establish. By "Shakespeare's English" one has to accept anything in the canon of works attributed to Shakespeare in all their versions up to and including F with the addition of some plays attributed to him which do not appear in F, such as *Pericles* and *Two Noble Kinsmen*.

This decision is significant for a dictionary which records Shakespeare's informal language. Although some informal language may be particularly Shakespearian, such as the malapropisms used by Dogberry or the idiomatic phrases used by Mrs Quickly, informal language by its nature is likely to reflect the colloquialisms and the lower linguistic registers characteristic of its period. The bad quartos may be memorial re-constructions by an actor. Each actor would remember his own part or parts, but other parts could be reproduced in a less authentic form. This could affect examples of informal language, for there is little reason to suppose that this actor would necessarily remember the informal utterances exactly as in the prompt copy. For example, discourse markers express the speaker's emotional response to the situation he or she is involved in, but many such discourse markers are freely interchangeable—and this is as true today as it was in Shakespeare's time. When performing the plays actors might vary the discourse markers or idiomatic expressions without thinking twice about such variation. A discourse marker like "why" could be readily inserted or omitted depending on how much emphasis the actor wanted to put on the following utterance (Blake 1992). Where a character is identified with a particular turn of phrase, as is Nym in the Henry plays and *Merry Wives* with *that is the humour of it,* it is likely that examples of this phrase were added or deleted by the actor playing this role in different places in the text and in different performances. This facility to alter examples of informal English which cannot be detected so easily today may have been freely exercised, and we are unable to tell what actually started out as Shakespeare's own informal English. That is the nature of informal English. In this area of language we can do little more than use Shakespeare as a token of the informal language used at his time without claiming that all examples of informal language actually came from his pen. A dictionary dealing with this topic will be a snapshot of informal language of the time in which Shakespeare lived, who would in any case be recording what was commonly heard at the time rather than necessarily trying to invent new examples of informal language, as he might have done with some specialised example of literary or elevated language. Yet, even with new words, older claims that he introduced so many new ones into the language have been modified by recent scholarship (Schäfer 1980).

3. Different varieties of Early Modern English

To talk about informal English presupposes that there is a formal language against which it is compared, and this naturally assumes that people at the time also understood that there were variations in speech which acted as markers of social status or of a different environment in which the speech is found. There is no problem with this concept, for Shakespeare often highlights differences in language. Prince Hal refers to the language of drawers and tapsters in this way:

> (2) They take it already vpon their confidence that though I be
> but Prince of Wales, yet I am the King of Curtesie: telling me
> flatly I am no proud Iack like Falstaffe, but a Corinthian, a lad
> of mettle, a good boy, (1H4 2.5.8–12).[2]

Similarly, Hotspur rebukes his wife for using oaths which are not appropriate to her status:

> (3) Not yours, in good sooth?
> You sweare like a Comfit-makers Wife:
> Not you, in good sooth; and, as true as I liue;
> And, as God shall mend me; and, as sure as day:
> (1H4 3.1.243–246).

We might, in reference to quotation (3), have assumed that all oaths or asseverations were informal, though we might not so readily accept that ones like *in good sooth* were associated with artisans' wives, i.e. with both a gender and a class association. In fact, in Shakespeare's other plays *in good sooth* is used by Trinculo in *The Tempest* (2.2.146), by Lucio in *Measure for Measure* (3.1.366), and as *Good sooth*, by Pericles in *Pericles* (sc.1.129). Although Trinculo is a lower-class male and Lucio an affected man about town with effeminate attitudes, Pericles is an older man of heroic character. Hotspur's assessment of these oaths does not tally with their use in other plays. Of the examples in quotation (2), *proud Iack, Corinthian, a lad of mettle* and *a good boy*, only the last one occurs elsewhere in Shakespeare and there it appears to have no overtones, for it is used by Mrs Page to compliment the young lad, Robin, for keeping details of her plot secret (MW 3.3.29). Mrs Page would hardly use the language of tapsters, and presumably it is only in certain contexts that this phrase took on a specialised meaning.

At the upper end of the language hierarchy Shakespeare's contemporaries undoubtedly understood that many speakers tried hard to make their language elegant and fashionable. Mercutio expresses it this way:

> (4) The Pox of such antique lisping affecting phantacies, these new tuners of accent: Iesu a very good blade, a very tall man, a very good whore. Why is not this a lamentable thing Grandsire, that we should be thus afflicted with these strange flies: these fashion Mongers, these pardon-mee's, who stand so much on the new form, that they cannot sit at ease on the old bench.
>
> (RJ 2.3.26–33)

Modern affectations are contrasted with old-fashioned values, which are neglected by such fashionable people. There is no doubt people accepted that the English of this time contained different levels of language, for although language at all times is stratified, this is not always readily recognised by the speakers of that language.

The difficulty with tracing informal language from the past is that it does not necessarily consist of a specialised vocabulary in the same way that technical or Latinate words do. The words which make up informal English are likely, for the most part, to be ordinary words which have been given a particular connotation or have been drained of their normal semantic meaning. They do not confine themselves to a particular subject, like technical vocabularies. Equally, one does not expect foreign words to be borrowed for the purpose of creating informal language, though this can happen with witticisms and educated playing with words—and such forms might eventually become informal. In quotation (2) Prince Hal implies that *proud Iack, Corinthian, a lad of mettle* and *a good boy* are examples of the language of tapsters. The word *Corinthian*, although ultimately a foreign loan from Greek possibly through Latin, was not borrowed into English to mean 'one of the boys, a good fellow' OED "Corinthian B" *sb*. records the word in the sense 'A native or inhabitant of Corinth' from the early sixteenth century. Towards the end of that century the sense 'a shameless or a "brazen-faced" fellow' is found, because of Corinth's reputation as a rich city noted for its luxury and licentiousness; indeed the name *Corinth* developed the sense 'brothel' in English. Is *Corinthian* a word used by tapsters and others like them, or is it a word common among educated people and wrongly attributed by the Prince to the lower echelons of society? *Iack, lad* and *boy* are words which can be used jocularly or scornfully and are to that extent common in an informal context, but the expressions *proud Iack, a lad of mettle* and *a good boy* are not, as far as we can tell, specifically informal—or at least are not found elsewhere in this register. These examples illustrate the problems of tracing informal English. Some authors may describe certain words or expressions as informal, though it is difficult to confirm such claims because the words are also found in a less marked register and it maybe difficult to judge from the context how to interpret the word. In quotation (2) is Prince Hal a reliable informant when it comes to reporting the language of tapsters or is he merely reporting what he thinks the language of tapsters is? It is precisely this difficulty in deciding whether a given word is used with particular connotations which makes the study of informal English so fascinating.

How then does one determine which words constitute Shakespeare's informal vocabulary? Informal English is often seen as a negative feature, because it is not part of polite language, for it includes the more colourful words in the language. Because it is set in contrast with formal English, it may be easier to think what formal English is. This is the language used in careful writing and speech, when one is trying to create an impression of education, standing and respectability. It is usually associated with the standard written form of a language, that form one would teach to non-native speakers of the language. Perhaps it is possible to think of formal English as the core of a language which may be represented as an inner circle, with everything outside that circle being potentially informal. Outside that circle at its figurative top could be placed fashionable varieties, that usage employed by speakers trying to impress others with their *savoir faire*, although usually they manage to overdo it. An example of this language is satirised by Mercutio in quotation (4). But when Cloten, Cymbeline's rather stupid step-son, says *with admirable rich words* (Cym 2.3.17), this is serious, for Shakespeare wants us to understand that this is a dull fellow trying to persuade others that he knows how to speak in a courtly way. At the bottom of the circle might lie the colloquialisms and abbreviated forms characteristic of speech, which are most frequently identified with those who take little care about their enunciation. These forms at the top and bottom are in principle open to all speakers of the language, for they can be assimilated with effort as exemplified by Prince Hal. To each side of the inner core might lie those varieties which are used by native speakers of English from outside England, the speakers of English dialects, and the English of foreigners who often mangle the language. Such forms are less frequently adopted by other speakers because they are part of a wider system, and I do not include any of these "lateral" forms within the context of informal English, which I regard as something available to all speakers of the language. Sociolinguistics has taught us that we all use informal English from time to time, whereas we do not suddenly break into Scots or Dorset dialect forms, if only because most of us could not do so with conviction.

4. The different types of Shakespeare's informal English

I have chosen *Romeo and Juliet* 2.3.136–160 as a specimen on which to base the analysis of Shakespeare's informal English. It is reproduced from F with some readings from Quarto 1 [Q1] and the Fourth Folio [F4] in square brackets. Mercutio who has been indulging in witticisms at the Nurse's expense has just departed and has left her in an indignant state:

> (5) *Nur.* I pray you sir, what sawcie Merchant was this that was so full of his roperie? [Q1 *roperipe*; F4 *Roguery*]
>
> *Rom.* A Gentleman Nurse, that loues to heare himselfe talke, and will speake more in a minute [Q1 *houre*], then he will stand to in a Month.
>
> *Nur.* And a speake [Q1 *stand to*] any thing against me, Ile take him downe, & a were lustier then he is, and twentie such Iacks: and if I cannot, Ile finde those that shall: scuruie knaue, I am none of his flurt-gils, I am none of his skaines mates, and thou must stand by too and suffer euery knaue [Q1 *Iacke*] to vse me at his pleasure.
>
> *Pet.* I saw no man vse you at his pleasure: if I had, my weapon [Q1 *toole*] should quickly haue beene out, I warrant you, I dare draw assoone as another man, if I see occasion [Q1 *time and place*] in a good quarrell, and the law on my side.
>
> *Nur.* Now afore God, I am so vext, that euery part [Q1 *member*] about me quiuers, skuruy knaue [Q1 *Iacke*]: pray you sir a word: and as I told you, my young Lady bid me enquire you out, what she bid me say, I will keepe to my selfe: but first let me tell ye, if ye should leade her in a fooles paradise, as they say, it were a very grosse kind of behauiour, as they say: for the Gentlewoman is yong: & therefore, if you should deale double with her, truely it were an ill thing to be offered to any Gentlewoman, and very weake dealing.

In the opening of the Nurse's speech there are three expressions which might be considered informal: *I pray you, sawcie Merchant* and *roperie*. The word *Merchant* is typically informal in that it has lost almost all its standard meaning. OED "Merchant A" *sb.* defines *merchant* as 'one whose occupation is the purchase and sale of marketable commodities for profit; originally applied *gen.* to any trader in goods not manufactured or produced by himself'. But when *merchant* is used informally, this semantic information is reduced to 'one . . . himself', i.e. a man. The rest of the meaning has been discarded so that the outer form or surface of the word is retained to add colour, but its inner semantic core is abandoned. It is not in itself decisive of informality that the merchant is characterised as *sawcie*, since a real merchant could easily be "rude". It is characteristic of informal language that *merchant* can be replaced by other words which are also drained of their semantic meaning so that it would make little apparent difference to the Nurse's message if she had referred to him here as *scuruie knaue* (a phrase she uses later of Mercutio) rather than *sawcie Merchant*. There are a large number of words in Shakespeare's works whose meaning is no more than 'man, young man', especially those used in a jocular or abusive way; they include *kern, knaue, lob, lozel, lubber, milksop, noddy, patch, punk, quat* as well as those which are Christian names such as *Jack*. But, as we shall see, the word *merchant* (which is recorded by OED *sb.* 3 as 'A fellow, "chap"' from 1549 to 1610) may have more resonance than at first seems apparent. Other concepts for different types of men and for parts of the body such as the head exist in variant informal forms: *block, noddle, mole, pash, pate, poll, sconce*, to mention just a few.

The word *roperie* illustrates another category of informal word. Many words or phrases differ between F and Q and this variation may signal that one edition (usually Q) was trying to make the word more accessible. This might be the case here, although *roperipe* could be a simple typographical variant. However, the word does not fit into the context, because *roperipe* as an adjective means 'Ripe for the gallows' (OED "Roperipe"), but the syntax demands a noun, and as a noun it means 'one who is ripe for the gallows' which is not semantically appropriate. The change from *roperie* to *roperipe* may indicate that some had difficulty understanding *roperie*—a suggestion which is strengthened by its change to *Roguery* in F4. It is possible to take *roperie* as a malapropism for *roguery*, or to assume it was a misprint for *roperipe*, although neither explanation is acceptable, and *roperie* is retained in Q2, F2 and. F3. OED glosses "Ropery" as '1. A place where ropes are made; a rope-walk. 2. Trickery, knavery, roguery.' Neither sense is common, with 1 recorded from 1363 and 2 first recorded in this passage. It is claimed by some editors that *rope* was slang for penis, but evidence that this was so in the sixteenth century is absent. Nevertheless, it is likely that both *roperie* and *roperipe* were informal words with a sexual overtone probably implying 'lewd talk'.

At first sight it seems as though *merchant* and *roperie* are introduced merely as informal words of little semantic content, suggesting "chap, fellow" for the first and "underhand behaviour, bawdy talk" for the second. But we need to take account of the form *skaines mates* a few lines later. OED "Skaines mate" indicates that its 'origin and exact meaning [are] uncertain' and has this example as its sole quotation. Some editors translate 'cut-throat companions' by linking it to *skene* 'knife'; but others relate it to a dialect form *skain* 'rascal'. Green (1998:1079) defines "skainsmate", of which this is his only example, as 'a prostitute. [ety. unknown. . . . The context seems to indicate a prostitute. ?dial *skain*, a dagger; thus fig. a penis or *skein* of thread or wool, and thus relates to the 'sewing' imagery of intercourse (cf. NEEDLE WOMAN)].' Although Green's comment is helpful, it may not go far enough. At one level Shakespeare has taken ordinary words, *merchant, roperie* and *skain*, and deprived them of their main semantic content. But at another level he has added to their meaning by linking words together so that *merchant, roperie* and *skains mate*, all connected with merchants and merchandise consisting of rope or wool, are given a sexual meaning. They are informal, but they also have a witty resonance which links them together in a quite unexpected way. In addition to its semantic link with *merchant* and *roperie*, *skains mates* is associated with *flurt-gill*, based on the female name *Gill/Jill*. The name *Jill* was a common name for a woman (as in the nursery rhyme *Jack* and *Jill*), often used deprecatingly, and the verbal noun *flirting* is recorded from 1593. The compound *flirt-gill is* attested here for the first time in the *Oxford English Dictionary*, though some examples also occur in the early seventeenth century. It may be a Shakespearian compound, though both elements were common enough and the form *Gill-flirt* is found from 1632 in the *Oxford English Dictionary*.

Two of the three words in the Nurse's opening speech, *merchant* and *roperie*, are not only linked but also clearly informal, though more evocative than the concept "informal" might suggest. They are supported by *sawcie*, which is also informal. Numerous other adjectives of this type occur throughout the plays, and we have noted *scuruie* in the Nurse's second speech. Others include *bully, cogging, cony-catching, cozening, lousy, ramping; testy* as well as some which maybe Shakespearian creations.

The third possible informal expression in the opening of this first speech is *I pray you*. This phrase also presents problems of interpretation, since it may be the formal main clause which has a subordinate object clause dependent on it. But F has a question mark at the end of this first sentence and that question mark is often reproduced in modern editions (Levenson 2000:237). Most take this to be a robust direct question, with *I pray you* as a discourse marker emphasising the question which follows, rather than a main clause introducing a tentative indirect question. The expression *I pray you* appears elsewhere as *pray you* or *prithee*, and it fulfils much the same function as modern *please*, though these expressions are less formal. There are a number of verbs which resemble *pray* in this discourse function, including *quoth, say, speak, tell* and *think* as well as slightly different verbs like *see*. *Say* as a discourse marker occurs in different forms, such as the preterite and past participle. Several interesting examples of *say* in Shakespeare's works may be misinterpreted by editors. When in *As You Like It* Orlando leads in the exhausted Adam, who can barely walk, Adam prepares to die and says his farewell to Orlando: *Heere lie I downe, And measure out my graue.* (AY 2.6.2). Orlando then replies with a lengthy harangue, in which he says he will bring food shortly and that Adam must not die in the meantime. In the middle of this speech, he says:

(6)   but if thou diest
        Before I come, thou art a mocker of my labor.
        Wel said, thou look'st cheerely.
        And Ile be with thee quickly:

                                                                (AY 2.6.11–14)

Although Adam says nothing in response to Orlando's care of him, Orlando exclaims *Wel said.* Some editors assume that Adam has mumbled something, and Hattaway (2000:115) comments "This either means 'Well done', or indicates that Adam makes some inarticulate response." *Well said* is hardly an appropriate response to some inarticulate mumbling, and this expression must be a discourse marker equivalent to modern *Come on* or even *Snap out of it.* The other alternative, *Well done,* suggested by Hattaway and offered by other editors, does not seem appropriate, since it operates less as a discourse marker than as a compliment in Modern English.

An equally contentious example occurs at the start of the play where Orlando and Adam come on stage together. Hattaway's comment "The play begins in the middle of a conversation between Orlando and Adam." (2000:73) is characteristic of editors' comments on this play's opening, though none actually explain why they believe these two are in mid-conversation. The opening sentence is:

(7) As I remember *Adam,* it was vpon this fashion bequeathed
     me by will, but poore a thousand Crownes, and as thou saist,
     charged my brother on his blessing to breed mee well: and
     there begins my sadnesse:

                                                                (AY 1.1.1–4)

Presumably, editors accept *as thou saist* to mean that Adam was speaking to Orlando about the will before they entered. But Adam is an old servant who is hardly likely to remind Orlando of the terms of his father's will and, in the play, he gives no indication of being informed on such matters. He does not speak until Orlando has finished his lengthy diatribe and then only to say that Orlando's brother is approaching. There is no indication in this opening of a conversation in any meaningful way. It is better to take *as thou saist,* as a discourse marker meaning no more than 'assuredly, indeed'. A more forceful marker is not appropriate to Orlando's character, for he is portrayed as gentle and cultivated. But he does feel strongly about the position he is in and so this marker is intended not to tell us that Adam has reminded him of the terms of the will, but of the injustice that he, Orlando, suffers under.

Examples of "say" and other verbs are provided by other plays. When the Venetians are taunting Shylock that his daughter has run away, he exclaims: *I say my daughter is my flesh and bloud.* (MV 3.1.34). Here F has no comma after *I say*, and this punctuation is followed in modern editions; but it is an expression which could readily be replaced by *Truly, In sooth* etc. and may be best accepted as a discourse marker. When Portia and Nerissa return home after the trial scene and are standing before the house, they hear music which Nerissa says is Portia's own. To this Portia responds: *Nothing is good I see without respect,* (MV 5.1.99). Once again F has no commas, but here most editors do insert them making *I see* a discourse marker. The marriage of Antony to Octavia is greeted with surprise by some, for when told by Enobarbus of this marriage Menas responds: *Pray'ye sir.* (AC 2.6.113), which is rather like modern *You don't say.* Modern editors often add a question mark, but it could just as easily be a statement expressing surprise or disbelief.

Discourse markers, a significant feature of conversation, help to emphasise certain statements, inject more emotion into a conversation, indicate some hesitation on the part of the speaker, or act as a hedge in the dialogue. Although they are found most often at the beginning of a sentence, they can occupy any position depending on the function they fulfil. Two which occur at the beginning of a sentence are *why* and *what,* and they can cause difficulty in interpretation since there is uncertainty as to whether they are discourse markers or interrogative adverbs. Some are clearly discourse markers, though almost drained of any meaning. When Petruccio's servants greet the recently returned Grumio, each utters a greeting in turn, and these consist of *Welcome home* or *How now* or *What* (TS 4.1.95–99), where *What* is no different as a greeting from *Welcome home* and *How now.* All three are informal. But *why* and *what* have more significant uses in other contexts. *What* expresses surprise, impatience or even exultation, whereas *why* may either introduce a new topic or else express reluctance or anxiety. These interjections are found on the lips of members of all classes. Antony can say to Cleopatra: *What Gyrle, though gray Do somthing mingle with our yonger brown, yet ha we A Braine* (AC 4.9.19–21), and young Rutland cries out in anguish to Clifford: *I neuer did thee harme: why wilt thou slay me?* (3H6 1.3.39). Other words resemble discourse markers but are not as frequently attested as one might expect with discourse markers. When Hamlet acknowledges that Polonius has just announced the arrival of the players, he says: *Buzze, buzze.* (Ham 2.2.395), which has a wider range of implications than would be conveyed by a simple discourse marker. But this is appropriate for someone of Hamlet's rank, since he is revealing his wit as well as his linguistic dexterity.

In the foregoing discussion some differences between Q1 and F in quotation (5) are highlighted. These are important not only because they may reveal what words were informal, but also because they may indicate that words dying out of the language survived longest at an informal level. Examples take several forms. The first is when several examples of a word in Q often, though not regularly, appear as a different word in the F, or even occasionally *vice versa*. Thus *afeard* in Q is often replaced in F by *afraid*, as when Costard, a Clown, says in Q *a Conquerour, and a feard to speake?* (LL 5.2.573–574), where F has *afraid*. Similarly, *albeit* is often replaced in F by *although*. Probably words like *afeard* and *albeit* were obsolescent except in the informal language of less educated people. Likewise Q's *alate* may be less formal than F's *of late*, as many forms with initial (a-) representing a reduced preposition were gradually lost from the language.

The second type is where a form in either Q or F is unique in Shakespeare and is omitted or replaced in the other text. This may occur either because a form is otherwise obsolete or because the word is new not only in Shakespeare, but also in English. Queen Margaret, married by proxy in France to Henry VI, addresses her husband and sovereign in rather inflated language, although she refers to her *ruder termes, such as my wit affoords* (2H6 1.1 [Add.Pass. A7]). In a passage found only in F she addresses Henry as *mine Alder liefest Soueraigne* ([Add.Pass. A5]). The word *alderliefest*, formed from the Old English genitive plural *ealra* 'of all' and *leofost* 'dearest', was archaic by the end of the fifteenth century. It is possible that this was regarded as old-fashioned and hence no longer appropriate in courtly circles; to that extent it might be regarded as informal. A similar example is the form *anchor* 'an anchorite, hermit', found in Q2 of *Hamlet* (Add.Pass. E2), where it is used in the play within a play, where the language is often old-fashioned and distanced from the rest of the main play's language.

A different example of this second type is the word *answerer* with the meaning 'one who answers a charge or appeal' which occurs in the *Lear* quarto, known today as *The History of King Lear*. Regan taunts Gloucester after his arrest for helping Lear to escape, and one might expect words from the informal register in such utterances by Regan, because she is being aggressively rude as part of her attack on the old man. She says *Be simple answerer, for we know the truth.* (HL sc.14.42), where F has *simple answer'd* (3.7.42), which makes less sense. This word *answerer* may be an informal variant of *defendant*. It occurs only here in Shakespeare, though it is found occasionally in English from the sixteenth century onwards. In consideration of this example, several other words in (-er) as an agent noun appear to be less formal, even those added to a Latinate stem to form a hybrid. Examples which occur only once in Shakespeare include *opener, pauser, perfumer* and *picker*. *Pauser*, a noun in the expression *the pawser, Reason.* (Mac 2.3.111 'someone who hesitates to evaluate something fully'), and *perfumer* in the sense of 'one who fumigates a room' are *hapax legomena* in English according to the *Oxford English Dictionary*, but *opener* in the sense of 'one who reveals something' was found in the language from the middle of the sixteenth century. *Picker* was common in the informal phrase *pickers and stealers* 'thieves, robbers', but Hamlet extends the meaning to 'hands, i.e. which do the stealing' (Ham 3.2.323). There are many similar examples, which suggest that *answerer* might also be informal.

A third type is where Q and F have different words, both of which are used by Shakespeare elsewhere, so that it is difficult to decide which is Shakespeare's original form or even whether both are his. When Slender is complaining about being ill-treated by Falstaff's companions, he refers to them as *your cony-catching Rascalls,* (MW 1.1.117) in F, where Q has *your cogging companions.* The verb *cog* and its participle *cogging* 'cheating, deceptive' occurs several times in Shakespeare, usually dismissively, as when Emilia exclaims *Some cogging, cozening Slaue,* (Oth 4.2.136). It also occurs in one other example in *Merry Wives.* The verb *cony-catch* and its past participle form *cony-catched* occur elsewhere in Shakespeare, though not so frequently, but this example of *cony-catching* is the only time the present participial adjective occurs. The sense of this verb is the same as *cog,* meaning 'to cheat, deceive'. Both words were common at this time and either makes excellent sense in the passage, so it is difficult to choose between these two informal words as to which maybe genuine Shakespeare. It probably does not matter, for both have to be accepted as examples of Shakespearian informal language. Later, Mr Page says to Mr Ford in F *Looke where my ranting Host of the Garter comes:* (MW 2.1.179), where Q uses *ramping* instead of *ranting.* The participial adjective *ramping* is found once elsewhere in Shakespeare in the sense 'unrestrained, extravagant'. Constance, in berating the Duke of Austria, says *What a foole art thou, A ramping foole,* (KJ 3.1.47–48). This word belongs to the language of insults. The verb *rant* occurs in Shakespeare, when Hamlet jumps into Ophelia's grave and shouts at Laertes *and thou't mouth, Ile rant as well as thou.* (Ham. 5.1.280–281), where the sense is 'talk loudly and boastingly'. This verb was more common and probably in *Merry Wives* it replaced *ramping,* which was less familiar. Both belong to a specialised vocabulary of insults, with *rant* being less hurtful than *ramp,* and it is often preferred by editors who think of the Host as loud-mouthed rather than unrestrained, though the difference is not great. In such cases both words belong to the informal register and the variation suggests that they were becoming generalised words of abuse which were losing their primary meanings and thus could be freely exchanged.

In quotation (5) we may note that Q1 has *Iacke* where F has *knaue.* The names, *Jack, John* and *Jill/Gill,* are used frequently as terms of contempt. *Jack* occurs as a generic name for a man as well as the figure that strikes the bell. Examples include: *Since euerie Iacke became a Gentleman, There's many a gentle*

person made a Iacke. (R3 1.3.72–73), *While I stand fooling heere, his iacke o'th'*
Clocke (R2 5.5.60), *scuruy-Iack-dog-Priest:* (MW 2.3.57), *I am withered like an*
olde Apple Iohn. (1H4 3.3.4), *poore-Iohn:* (Tem 2.2.27 'type of fish'), and *Iohn*
a-dreames, (Ham 2.2.570). One might also mention Mrs Quickly's corruption
of *genitive to Ginyes case;* (MW 4.1.56 'Jenny's case'), since it is not difficult to
imagine this as a typical schoolboy corruption picked up by Shakespeare at
grammar school. Abbreviations of names are also common and belong to the
informal language *Nan* 'Anne', *Ned* and *Yedward* 'Edward', *Hal* 'Henry', *Nick*
'Nicholas', *Nob* 'Robert' and others. There is also *Dame Partlet the Hen,* (1H4
3.3.94 'Dame Pertilote', Falstaff to Mrs Quickly).

The use by the Nurse in quotation (5) of *a* for 'he' is a colloquialism,
reflecting informal pronunciation through the dropping of syllables or pho-
nemes. Such forms occur in the speech of all people, and this finds expression
in Shakespeare's plays in characters of all ranks. Sociolinguistics has revealed
that we all drop initial /h/ in words when we are in an informal mode. Most
people will say /i:/ rather than /hi:/ in an utterance like "What's he up to",
although we always write the (h) in representations of our own speech. We
might not, however, include the (h) in any representation in writing of the
speech of lower-class characters. In Shakespeare's plays this form is represented by the form (a), in the language of people of high or low status. The
Princess of France in *Love's Labour's Lost* can say *Who ere a was, a shew'd a*
mounting minde: (4.1.4). Presumably, dropping one's *h*'s carried little or no
stigma at the time. This presents a problem for the modern editor of the plays,
who may represent this form by ('a), as though the speaker had dropped the
/h/, which creates an uncomfortable feeling today that the speaker was being
less than polite. It is more probable that at that time people accepted that
there were two forms of this word, an emphatic and an unemphatic (or informal) form, and that either could be used in writing, though one does find (a)
attributed more frequently to less elevated characters. Other words which fall
into this category include *cos,* a shortened form of *cousin* used more frequently
by high-status characters, and many oaths to be considered below.

A more interesting question is the status of aphetic forms of words.
Most survive today only in their longer forms, such as *hospital* and *appren-*
tice, which also occur as *spital* and *prentice.* In modern editions they may
appear with an apostrophe: *'spital* and *'prentice,* as though editors think them
non-standard. Certainly today where such forms occur, such as *'fraid* (as in
the common phrase *'fraid so*), they are colloquial and, previously, writers like
Swift were vehemently opposed to this type of shortening (Blake 1986). But
it is more difficult to be certain what attitudes to such aphetic forms were in
Shakespeare's time. Some types of shortening were regarded as rhetorically
elegant, but it is doubtful whether this applied to forms like *'spital.* Some
examples are found only in the speech of less elevated characters, as when

Grumio, Petruccio's servant, uses *lege* for *allege* in *Nay 'tis no matter sir, what he leges in Latine* (TS 1.2.28). On the balance of probability such forms may be considered informal. After all, the omission or addition of a morpheme at the front of a word often occurs in the speech of those characters who use malapropisms. Dogberry uses *opinioned* for *pinioned* when he says of the malefactors *Come, let them be opinion'd.* (MA 4.2.65), which as with many malapropisms suggests a confusion of words. Both verbs *pinion* and *opinion* were introduced into English in the middle of the sixteenth century. Similarly the Second Murderer uses *passionate* as a variant of *compassionate* when, as he and his companion are about to murder Clarence in the Tower, he says: *I hope this passionate humor of mine, will change,* (R3 1.4.114–115). That is the reading of F, though Q and some modern editors replace *this passionate humor of mine* with *my holy humor.* OED 'Passionate" *a.* 5 records the sense 'Moved with sorrow; grieved, sad, sorrowful' from 1586, but this example from *Richard the Third* is its first for the allied sense 'inclined to pity, compassionate'. But *compassionate* was a relatively recent borrowing. Are we to understand a type of gallows humour here? Would contemporaries have understood *passionate,* because the different reading in Q suggests they might not? Is *passionate* in this sense an informal usage?

In quotation (5) the Nurse refers to a *very grosse kind of behauior,* and intensives like *gross* are usually part of informal language which may have a short existence as vogue words. *Gross* in its meaning 'glaring, flagrant, monstrous' is recorded only from 1581 (OED "Gross" *a.* 4a), and should probably be understood as still informal in this passage. The combination of *very* with *gross* is characteristically informal, and Mercutio makes use of this exaggeration in quotation (4). The use of Latinate adjectives was often regarded as a sign of excess, though to what extent all such cases should be considered ironic or humorous is difficult to determine. When Armado uses *immaculate* in his *My Loue is most immaculate white and red.* (LL 1.2.87), this was a way of satirising the excesses of courtly love language, especially as in this case Moth responds *Most immaculate thoughts Master* (LL 1.2.88, often emended to *maculate* by modern editors). A word like *excellent* was over-used at this time as both adverbial and adjective, but how many of the examples are to be treated as ironic is more difficult to determine (Blake 2000). When Sir Andrew Aguecheek exclaims of Feste's song *Excellent good, ifaith.* (TN 2.3.44), he is trying to imitate fashionable language; when Poins responds to Hal's question as to whether he should tell him something with *Yes: and let it be an excellent good thing.* (2H4 2.2.28), he is aping elegant language, as suggested by his use of *sweet Hony* (1H4 1.2.158); and when the Clown in *The Winter's Tale* says *thou talkest of an admirable conceited fellow,* (WT 4.4.203–204), he uses *admirable* to indicate that he knows elegant language, though educated people would take this as a sign of his ignorance. Other types of word may also be satirised. The noun *humour* appears to have been misused as a fashionable word to judge by the way it is adopted by some of the lower-class characters. It is used by Pistol in *These be good Humors indeede.* (2H4 2.4.159) and by Bottom *my chiefe humour is for a tyrant.* (MN 1.2.24). But it is particularly associated with Nym. He uses it as both noun and the first element of a compound *I thanke thee for that humour.* (MW 1.3.57), *here take the humor-Letter;* (MW 1.3.71–72). The same type of humour is found in the malapropisms and other misuses of words, associated especially with Mrs Quickly and others, who use such forms as *allicholy* for *melancholy, Canaries* (possibly for *quandary* although that word is not used by Shakespeare) and *adultery* to mean something like 'mayhem'. Possibly to be regarded as similar are idiomatic, semi-proverbial phrases like *fooles paradise* in quotation (5) which the *Oxford English Dictionary* shows was common at this time with the general sense 'seduce and abandon' (Cf. Dent 1981: F523). There are a number of idiomatic expressions which may be considered informal, though they also occur in more formal contexts. These include such phrases as *Ile goe wih thee cheeke by iowle.* (MN 3.2.339 'closely'), *I haue tane you napping* (TS 4.2.46 'caught you unawares in the act'), *the new made Duke that rules the rost,* (2H6 1.1.106, usually taken to mean 'that sits at the head of the table, i.e. to be top dog', though the modern equivalent is *rule the roost*), *he is now at a cold sent.* (TN. 2.5.119 'gone astray') and many others. Some of these phrases are semiproverbial and are found in Tilley's collection (Tilley 1950).

The spelling and metre in F and Q suggest that some words were pronounced with one or two syllables and that in polysyllabic words a medial vowel was suppressed in speech. Learned words are abbreviated in informal language. In Q Mrs Quickly uses *atomy* as a variant of *anatomy* in her expletive *Thou atomy, thou.* (2H4 5.4.29, F has *Anatomy*), implying someone who is all bones, but with a further suggestion of *atom* 'something diminutive'. Similar abbreviated forms are found earlier in the language. In The Miller's Tale in *The Canterbury Tales* some manuscripts have *astromye* for *astronomy,* and this may represent an informal usage (Blake 1979). In other cases in Shakespeare two forms of a word exist side by side relatively commonly, such as *parlous* and *perilous,* and these forms can interchange between F and Q, though whether the form *parlous* was becoming old-fashioned and informal is less certain. *Perilous* became the standard form, just as *perfect* had replaced *parfait,* but when exactly the change occurred and how speakers regarded the relation between the two forms is more difficult to determine. Sometimes the reduction in the number of syllables pronounced was expressed in writing through omission or an apostrophe: the word *listening* regularly omits medial (e) in F no matter who the speaker is, as in Falstaff's *it is worth the listning too* (1H4 2.5.215). Presumably the pronunciation with two syllables was common at this time and should not be considered informal. But a word like *even* can be spelt in full or abbreviated to *ev'n: Euen so by Loue*, (TG 1.1.47), and *And ev'n that Powre* (TG 2.6.4). Is this variation significant or not? And if it is, should the shortened form be regarded as informal? The same can go for the omission or inclusion of non-lexical words like articles and prepositions. Are the verbs *arrive* and *arrive at* distinguished in their level of formality? There may be variation with the presence or absence of an article both between Q and F: *as good deede* (Q) and *as good a deed* (F, 1H4 2.1.29); and between the occurrence of the same phrase in different contexts: *What no man at doore* (TS 4.1.106) and *his Father is come from Pisa, and is here at the doore* (TS 5.1.25–26). In *The Taming of the Shrew* the first context is distinctly colloquial, as Petruccio rails at his servants, whereas in the second he is speaking in a more formal manner. These may be no more than compositors' preferences, though such preferences may not be without significance for informal English. There are also words which are shortened at the end: *Proball* (Oth 2.3.329 'such as approves itself'), a *hapax legomenon*, is probably a shortened form of *probable*, which Honigmann (1997:201) compares with Dekker's *admiral* for *admirable*. We might remember in this connection that other words like *mechanic* and *practic* from French were varied with the Latinate *mechanical* and *practical* so that speakers of the language were familiar with variant endings, though whether the forms carried any implication of formality/informality has yet to be shown.

In quotation (5) the Nurse's *afore God* is an oath which fulfils a similar function to discourse markers. By their nature they are informal and used by all classes of people, especially in situations of anger and frustration, though they are especially associated with the everyday conversation of characters of lower status. They share features with other types of informal language, since the original words in an oath may be corrupted or abbreviated to prevent them from being blasphemous, as remains true today where *Gee* is a clipped form of *Jesus*. Consequently some oaths have lost their power to offend and are little more than discourse markers. The corruption of names of the deity are common enough. *Marry* may well be a variant of *Mary*, the mother of Jesus. *God* is turned into *cock* in such phrases as *By Cocke* (Ham 4.5.61 in a song sung by Ophelia), *Cockes passion*, (TS 4.1.105, spoken by Grumio), and *By cocke and pie*, (MW 1.1.283, spoken by Mr Page), the last being possibly a corruption of *God* and the service book of the Catholic Church. Some commentators think it may be literally a cock and pie, though given the frequency of the corruption of *God* to *Cock*, most listeners would think there was more to this oath than a simple culinary meaning. *Jesus* is corrupted to *Gis* in Ophelia's song, where it appears as *By gis*, (Ham 4.5.58). The name of the deity is often reduced to the possessive singular inflection, represented by initial (s) or (z) in such forms as *sblood* 'God's Blood', *swounds* 'God's wounds', which occur frequently in the quartos, but which after the blasphemy laws of James I were often replaced in F by anodyne expressions like *heavens* or *mercy*.

There are several phrasal verbs in quotation (5): *stand to, take down, stand by, be out* and *enquire out*. In Modern English phrasal verbs such as *to sit in* start life as colloquialisms, though many end up being accepted into the standard language. The same may apply to Elizabethan English, and some individual forms which were established by Shakespeare's time had probably been accepted into formal language. However, others like *stand to* and *take down* have a secondary, sexual sense and presumably remained informal. A phrasal verb like *stand by* has two non-sexual meanings, namely 'to support, assist' and 'to stand aside as an unconcerned spectator', both of which could be invoked here. The status of these phrasal verbs is unclear, but their frequent use in this type of conversation suggests that the majority were informal.

Insults are another source of informal language, though there are none in quotation (5). They fall into certain patterns, of which the most common is the pronoun *thou*, which expresses contempt or anger, followed by one or more adjectives which may not in themselves be informal but are made so by their occurrence in this context, and finally one or more nouns, many of which may well be rare and belong to the vocabulary of insults. Thus Macbeth addresses the Messenger who brings news of the English advance against Dunsinane as *thou cream-fac'd Loone:* (Mac 5.3.11). As it happens neither *cream-fac'd* nor *Loone*, 'fellow, wretch', is found elsewhere in Shakespeare. Though *Loone* is colloquial and probably always derogatory (OED "Loon" 1), *cream-fac'd* 'pale, wan' is a form that one could imagine occurring in neutral or rhetorical contexts, for *pale-faced* and *white-faced* do not have such unfavourable connotations. Macbeth also addresses the Messenger as *Thou Lilly-liuer'd Boy.* (Mac 5.3.17), though *boy* is not so derogatory as *loon*. Another form of insult is employed by Macbeth in the same scene, for he calls the Messenger a number of names, consisting either of a simple or compound noun: *Patch* and *Whay-face* (Mac 5.3.17, 19), the latter taking up the sense of cowardice found in *cream-fac'd* and *Lilly-liuer'd*, but the former being a derogatory noun used several times as an insult in Shakespeare.

Words with sexual implications in quotation (5) are varied in Q1: *toole* for *weapon*, and *member* for *part*, though they have the same overtones (Williams 1997:205, 229, 310, 334). The problem is knowing where to draw the line in seeing a submerged sexual sense. *Double-dealing*, recorded in the *Oxford English Dictionary* from 1529 as a noun and 1587 as an adjective, lies behind the expression *deal double*, the first quotation under OED "Double B" *adv.* 3. The verb *deal* has the sense 'to have sexual intercourse' (OED "Deal" *v.* 11b) from 1340 to 1662, which may be implied by the use of the phrase *deal double* rather than the less explicit *double-dealing*. If the noun *dealing* had assumed a sexual significance from the verb, it could colour our understanding of *weak*. Some editors accept that Shakespeare wrote *wicked* instead of *weak;* but if *dealing* has a sexual implication, then *weak* may be right, for only 'to deal double' might in the Nurse's view be no more than 'weak dealing'. If so, this raises the question how to understand *ill thing*, which may have the sense 'wicked matter', but could also be implying 'penis'. After all, *thing* is used by Shakespeare to suggest someone or something contemptible, *O thou Thing*, (WT 2.1.84). The problem of how much of this passage contains sexual innuendo and how many of its words should be included in the category of informal English may never be resolved.

At the more elevated level of English there are words which may have been current among certain types of people and which Shakespeare used ironically to suggest characters who were social climbers with pretensions. When the Hostess addresses her husband Pistol as *'Prythee honey sweet Husband, let me bring thee to Staines.* (H5 2.3.1–2), she is trying, with the phrase *honey sweet*, to ape the language of her betters. Poins reverses the expression in addressing Prince Hal as *my good sweet Hony Lord*, (1H4 1.2.158), another example of a speaker overreaching himself. However, when Helen in *Troilus and Cressida* addresses Pandarus as *My Lord Pandarus, hony sweete Lord.* (TC 3.1.64), it is to suggest that Pandarus uses this type of expression too often in his conversation, which indeed he does later in the scene addressing Helen as *hony sweete Queene:* (TC 3.1.138). It may be difficult to decide in many cases whether this type of language should be classified as informal, for it is making fun of the inflated language of gentility.

Other words occur in contexts which are insulting or potentially so. For example, *alias* never occurs in a legal, but only in a derogatory context; however, whenever it occurs, its meaning is 'otherwise known as'. Lavatch in *All's Well That Ends Well* can say *The blacke prince sir, alias the prince of darkenesse, alias the diuell.* (AW 4.5.42–43), and Menenius in *Coriolanus* can say *a brace of vnmeriting proud, violent, testie Magistrates (alias Fooles)* (Cor 2.1.42–44). Latinate words are used by characters who try to impress, though there is nothing in the words to indicate they are informal. In such cases, it may be the general attitude to excessive borrowing which was under attack. For example, Pistol, Polonius and various clowns use *perpend* in the sense 'pay heed to, consider'. Thus Pistol says *perpend my words O Signieur Dewe*, (H5 4.4.8) to the French soldier he has captured; Polonius says to the king and queen: *Thus it remaines, and the remainder thus. Perpend,* (Ham 2.2.105–106); and Touchstone when addressing Corin in *As You Like It* says: *learne of the wise and perpend:* (3.2.64–65). All are situations where the speaker is trying to impress the addressee, and we may assume that *perpend* was associated with pomposity.

These examples raise the question of the status of foreign words. I suggested earlier in reference to *Corinthian* that foreign words were not borrowed as part of the informal vocabulary, but some do end up as part of that vocabulary. There are several ways in which this could happen. Because foreign words and morphemes are often considered affected and ridiculous by speakers of a language, the corruption of a word by adding a foreign morpheme to it may lead to its isolation from the rest of the context. In Modern English the addition of final (-a) is designed to add humour by suggesting words are Italianate, as in the old advertisement *Drinka pinta milka day*. This is found in Shakespeare in older songs, but whether the morpheme was introduced for the same reason is less certain. In Q2 the Gravedigger in *Hamlet* sings *O me thought there a was nothing a meet*. (5.1.64). *Moustache* is a French loan in English, but when it is given the form *mustachio*, which is either Spanish or Italian, it is humorous and is used only by characters who are extravagant in their language. Gadshill uses it as part of a derogatory expression (*these mad Mustachio-purple-hu'd-Malt-wormes* 1H4 2.1.74–75) and Armado as part of his attempt to enrich his language: *with his royall finger thus dallie with my excrement, with my mustachio:* (LL 5.1.98–99). The malapropisms noted earlier involve foreign, usually Latinate, words and fulfil much the same function. Some words are given an apparently English form, but retain their foreign look, as with Sir Toby's *he's a Rogue, and a passy measures panyn:* (TN 5.1.198), where *passy measures* is a corruption of Italian *passamezzo*. In other cases a foreign word is introduced into English by a member of the upper class to create an affectionate, but quizzical, tone or simply to create confusion. Lady Hotspur addresses her husband *Come, come, you Paraquito,* (1H4 2.4.83), whereas Hamlet answers Ophelia's request for an interpretation of the dumb-show prologue to the play within a play with: *Marry this is Miching Malicho, that meanes Mischeefe.* (Ham 3.2.131–132), which may well be designed to confuse her. The origin of *Malicho* (the quartos spell it *Mallico*) is uncertain, though it is usually understood as a form of Spanish *malhecho*, the form adopted in some editions. Otherwise, foreign words are mostly used by braggarts like Pistol and Armado who want to boast or by pedants like Holofernes who wish to impress others with their learning and sophistication. The former use words from modern European languages, as Sly does with *Paucas pallabris,* (TS Ind.1 5, a corruption of Spanish) and Sir Toby does with *Cubiculo:* (TN 3.2.50), but the latter words from the classical languages. However, the influence of foreign languages goes deeper than that, for some morphemes may have become anglicised, as is true of the Dutch diminutive *-kin*, which is used to create a suggestion of affectionate familiarity. This is found in Fabian's *This is a deere Manakin to you* (TN 3.2.51) and by Edgar as Mad Tom in *for one blast of thy minikin mouth,* (HL sc.13.39).

Reduplicating forms are traditionally regarded as informal, though some do appear in more formal writings and to that extent are like phrasal verbs which are also gradually accepted into the standard language. Thus *hurly burly* is used by the witches in the sense 'battle, tumult': *When the Hurley-burley's done,* (Mac 1.1.3), and in this sense it was used by historians and others at the time. Henry IV uses it to Worcester, one of the rebels, as an adjective in: *Of hurly-burly Innouation:* (1H4 5.1.78), referring to 'warlike insurrection', though doubtless using *hurly-burly* deliberately (because of its informal nature) to get across his displeasure and sense of outrage. Other forms of this type are simply informal: *hugger mugger* 'secretly' (Ham 4.5.82), *kickie wickie* (AW 2.3.277), otherwise unknown but assumed to be a humorous term for 'mistress' and later Folios have *kicksie wicksie,* and *Pell, mell,* 'in a confused melee' (LL 4.3.344). One might include in this group *linsie wolsy* ('nonsense, hodge podge of words' AW 4.1.11). The reduplication may be expressed as two words, as in Evan's *pribbles and prabbles,* 'useless chat' (MW 1.1.50). Other pairs like this include *flout 'em, and cout 'em:* (Tem 3.2.123, in a song), *snip, and nip,* (TS 4.3.90) *slish and slash,* (TS 4.3.90), *he scotcht him, and notcht him* (Cor 4.5.191–192), to say nothing of *the Prouerbes, and the No-verbes.* (MW 3.1.96), and *Cesar, Keiser and Pheazar* (MW 1.3.9). Many of these forms are said by lower-class characters, but by no means all of them. Some of these words on their own are part of ordinary vocabulary, and it is only when they are paired in this way that they become informal. Others are invented words for the occasion, like *No-verbes* and *Pheazar.*

The authenticity of a word like *prenzie,* in the phrases *The prenzie, Angelo?* (MM 3.1.92) and *In prenzie gardes;* (MM 3.1.95), is questioned by OED "Prenzie" and by some editors (Bawcutt 1991:234), though no satisfactory emendation is found (Wells & Taylor 1988:802 emend to *precise*). Its meaning appears to be something like 'prim, precise' and its context suggests a derogatory word, even possibly an insult, for in the first example it is used by Claudio who has been condemned to death by Angelo and in the second by his sister Isabella, who uses it in association with *the cunning Liuerie of hell* and presumably picked it up from him. It is not unexpected that such informal words may not appear elsewhere and we may accept the word as genuine, even though we do not know its precise meaning. Other words are of uncertain origin, although they occur more frequently. Old Capulet dismisses Tybalt, who shows signs of disobedience with *you are a Princox, goe,* (RJ 1.5.85). This word, meaning 'disobedient fellow', is a *hapax legomenon* in Shakespeare, but is found occasionally in English, spelt either in *-cox* or *-cock,* from 1540 (OED "Princock, -cox").

While it is impossible to cover all aspects of Shakespeare's informal English in this article, I have tried to show the interest that exists in compiling a dictionary of this sort and to illustrate some of the difficulties that lie in wait for those trying to tackle this area of lexicography.

Notes

* This article is based on a shorter paper delivered at a conference of the Dictionary Society of North America held at the University of Michigan, Ann Arbor, on 6-10 May 2001. I am indebted to the participants, especially Professor Eric Stanley, for their comments and suggestions made after my talk.

1. The *Sonnets* are quoted from Booth 1977, the plays from the First Folio (Hinman and Blayney 1996) unless a quarto text is specified (Allen and Muir 1981, where available, or other facsimiles). However, line references are to Wells and Taylor 1988.

2. The following abbreviations of Shakespeare's works are used: *Antony and Cleopatra* AC; *As You Like It* AY; *All's Well That Ends Well* AW; *Coriolanus* Cor; *Cymbeline* Cym; *Hamlet* Ham; *Henry IV Parts I and II* 1H4/2H4; *Henry V* H5; *Henry VI Parts II and III* 2H6/3H6; *The History of King Lear* (Q) HL; *The Tragedy of King Lear* (F) KL; *Love's Labour's Lost* LL; *Much Ado About Nothing* MA; *Macbeth* Mac; *Measure for Measure* MM; *A Midsummer Night's Dream* MN; *The Merry Wives of Windsor* MW; *Othello* Oth; *Richard II and III* R2/R3; *Romeo and Juliet* RJ; *Troilus and Cressida* TC; *The Tempest* Tem; *Twelfth Night* TN; *The Taming of the Shrew* TS; *The Winter's Tale* WT.

Works Cited

Allen, Michael J. B., and Kenneth Muir. 1981. *Shakespeare's Plays in Quarto. A Facsimile Edition*. Berkeley, Los Angeles, London: University of California Press.

Bawcutt, Nigel W. 1991. *Measure for Measure*. The Oxford Shakespeare. Oxford. Oxford University Press.

Blake, Norman F. 1979. "Astromye" in "The Miller's Tale". *Notes and Queries* 224: 110–111.

———. 1981. *Non-standard Language in English Literature*. London: Deutsch.

———. 1986. Jonathon Swift, and the English language. *Englisch Amerikanische Studien* 8: 105–119.

———. 1989. Standardizing Shakespeare's non-standard language. In: Joseph B. Trahern Jr. (ed.). *Standardizing English: Essays in the History of Language Change in Honor of John Hurt Fisher*. Tennessee Studies in Literature 31. Knoxville: University of Tennessee Press, 57–81.

———. 1992. *Why* and *what* in Shakespeare. In: Toshiyuki Takamiya and Richard Beadle (eds.). *Chaucer to Shakespeare: Essays in Honour of Shinsuke Ando*. Cambridge: Brewer, 179–193.

———. 2000. *Excellent* in Shakespeare. In: Dieter Kastovsky and Arthur Mellinger (eds.). *The History of English in a Social Context: A Contribution to Historical Sociolinguistics*. (Trends in Linguistic Studies and Monographs 129). Berlin and New York: Mouton de Gruyter, 1–23.

Booth, Stephen. 1977. *Shakespeare's Sonnets Edited with Analytic Commentary*. New Haven: Yale University Press.

Dent, R.W. 1981. *Shakespeare's Proverbial Language: An Index*. Berkeley, Los Angeles, London: University of California Press.

Edelman, Charles. 2000. *Shakespeare's Military Language; A Dictionary*. London, New Brunswick, NJ: Athlone.

Gaskell, Phillip. 1978. *From Writer to Reader: Studies in Editorial Method*, Oxford. Clarendon Press.

Green, Jonathon. 1998. *Cassell's Dictionary of Slang*. London: Cassell.

Hattaway, Michael. 2000. *As You Like It*. The New Cambridge Shakespeare. Cambridge: Cambridge University Press.

Hinman, Charlton, and Peter W. M. Blayney. 1996. *The First Folio of Shakespeare*. The Norton Facsimile. 2nd edn. New York and London: W. W. Norton.

Honigmann, Ernst A. J. 1997. *Othello*. The Arden Shakespeare 3rd series. Walton-on-Thames: Thomas Nelson.

Levenson, Jill L. 2000. *Romeo and Juliet* (The Oxford Shakespeare). Oxford: Oxford University Press.

Rubinstein, Frankie. 1984. *A Dictionary of Shakespeare's Sexual Puns and their Significance*. London, Basingstoke: Macmillan.

Schäfer, Jürgen. 1980. *Documentation in the O.E.D.: Shakespeare and Nashe as Test Cases*. Oxford: Clarendon Press.

Sokol, B. J. and Mary Sokol. 2000. *Shakespeare's Legal Language: A Dictionary*. London, New Brunswick, NJ: Athlone.

Spevack, Marvin. 1993. *A Shakespeare Thesaurus*. Hildesheim, Zürich, New York: Georg Olms.

Tilley, Morris P. 1950. *A Dictionary of Proverbs in England in the Sixteenth and Seventeenth Centuries*. Ann Arbor: University of Michigan Press.

Wills, Stanley, and Gary Taylor (gen. eds.). 1988. *William Shakespeare, The Complete Works, Compact Edition*. Oxford: Clarendon Press.

Williams, Gordon. 1997. *A Glossary of Shakespeare's Sexual Language*. London and Atlantic Highlands, NJ: Athlone.

TANYA POLLARD

"A Thing Like Death":
Sleeping Potions and Poisons in
Romeo and Juliet *and* Antony and Cleopatra

Romeo and Juliet and *Antony and Cleopatra* abound in references to potions, both soporific and poisonous. These ambivalent drugs suspend the plays uneasily between competing plot trajectories, calling attention to other rifts and tensions. As Shakespeare's only double tragedies and, along with *Othello,* his only ventures into the Italianate "tragedy of love," the plays represent a hybrid genre intrinsically divided between the domain of tragedy (death) and that of comedy (erotic desire).[1] Both plays, accordingly, toy with genres, veering sharply between almost slapstick comedy and unsettling tragic intensity.[2] Although critics have noticed the generic ambivalence that characterizes these plays, its significance has not received much discussion, perhaps in part due to lack of attention to the curious potions that correspond to the plays' many oppositions. In the context of early modern pharmacy, the narcotic soporific drink, with its ambiguous position between medicine and poison, reflects and comments on the plays' uncertain generic status. If the promise of ease, pleasure, and reawakening links sleeping potions with the realm of comedy, their implicit threat of death evokes the specter of tragedy as well. While the nature of potions is uncertain for much of these plays, their final casting as poisons upholds the plays' generic status as tragedy, and yet it suggests that the poison of tragedy may be, in its own paradoxical way, medicinal.

Renaissance Drama, Volume 32 (2003): pp. 95–121. Copyright © 2003 Northwestern University Press.

The juxtaposition of narcotic potions and generic oscillation in the two plays also raises larger questions about the significance of these potions and their relationships to the plays in which they appear. As Derrida has observed, the disturbingly uncertain nature of drugs has offered a vocabulary for the ambiguous status of language and literature at least since Plato's time.[3] In his notorious attack on poetry in *The Republic,* Plato refers to literature as a *pharmakon,* a dangerous blend of poison and remedy. Aristotle turned a similar vocabulary toward a different end, arguing that plays could have a medicinal value by bringing about a *katharsis,* or purgation, of the emotions they elicit. In early modern England, writers echoed and varied this debate by drawing on the language of pharmacy to describe the effects of theater on spectators. Disapproving moralists referred to plays as "charmed drinkes, & amorous potions,"[4] "vigorous venome," and "Soule-devouring poyson."[5] Supporters, meanwhile, described playwrights as "good Phisitions" and mulled over the various effects of theatrical "potions."[6] In the context of these literary attacks and defenses, what does it mean for Shakespeare to juxtapose narcotic and poisonous drugs and align them with generic oscillations? And further, why, after experimenting with this juxtaposition in an early play, repeat it late in his career? Shakespeare's treatment of ambiguous potions and their relationship to the world of the play in *Romeo and Juliet* and *Antony and Cleopatra* offers insights into their meaning in his theatrical vocabulary.

* * *

The device of the sleeping potion in *Romeo and Juliet* occupies a crucial intersection between the play's twin poles of desire and death and, similarly, between its warring genres of comedy and tragedy.[7] While many critics see Mercutio's death as the dividing point between the play's comic beginning and tragic ending, early foreshadowing and ongoing elements of farce suggest that the play's generic fortunes stay intertwined much longer. The sleeping potion and, by association, the imaginative realm of sleep and dreams temporarily suspend the play's identity, holding out the possibility of a return to comedy by offering the lovers the means to escape a tragic ending. The foreclosure of this possibility, and accordingly the play's resolution into a tragedy, does not become final until the intermediate mode of the sleeping potion is replaced by Romeo's actual poison.

From the outset, the romantic love that is the focus of the play is directly associated with poison. In an attempt to divert Romeo from his unrequited yearning for Rosaline, Benvolio counsels,

> Tut, man, one fire burns out another's burning;
> One pain is lessn'd by another's anguish;
> Turn giddy, and be holp by backward turning.

> One desperate grief cures with another's languish;
> Take thou some new infection to thy eye,
> And the rank poison of the old will die.

(1.2.45–50)[8]

Even before Juliet has entered the play, her imminent appearance in Romeo's life is identified with the effect of a poison, albeit a curative one. Despite the comic case and apparently pragmatic intentions of Benvolio's advice, the solution he offers has a distinctly negative ring. His easy symmetries and correspondingly neat rhymes suggest that his cure will only replace one "anguish" and "desperate grief" with another: Juliet, this model implies, will ultimately cause as much pain as does Rosaline.

The dark undertones of the poisonous love cure proposed by Benvolio are echoed in Friar Lawrence's meditations on the powers and perils of medicinal herbs. Musing over the "baleful weeds and precious-juiced flowers" he collects (2.3.4), the Friar considers the double-edged potential of his plants:

> Within the infant rind of this weak flower
> Poison hath residence, and medicine power:
> For this, being smelt, with that part cheers each part;
> Being tasted, stays all senses with the heart
> Two such opposed kings encamp them still
> In man as well as herbs: grace and rude will;
> And where the worser is predominant
> Full soon the canker death eats up that plant.

(2.3.19–26)

In explicating how herbal concoctions contain the potential for both poison and medicine, the Friar can be seen as unwittingly describing the play itself, or the erotic passion that the play dramatizes. The flower's "infant rind" evokes the extreme youth associated with the lovers; Shakespeare pointedly makes Juliet even younger than the already young girl of his source, and both of the protagonists are portrayed as distinctly adolescent, still tended and controlled by their parents.[9] The Friar's emphasis on the tension between the two "opposed kings," similarly, calls to mind the feud that lies at the core of the play. His reduction of the conflict, however, to an opposition between grace and "rude will," or lust, offers too simple an understanding of passion, one at odds with the portrait offered by the play itself. By differentiating between the scent, which cures, and the taste, which kills, the Friar suggests that the primary distinction between cordial and poison is one of degree: love may be broached, but not consumed. Although his identification of desire with the triumph of "the canker death" accurately foreshadows the play's ending, his moralistic condemnation of passion runs counter to the play, both in the jubilant celebrations of love endorsed by its comic moments and in the dignity ultimately bestowed on the lovers in the tragic close.

Beyond its relevance within the world of the play, the Friar's meditation on the proximity of medicine and poison would have resonated with broader contemporary concerns. In Shakespeare's time, as now, the line between medicine and poison was a fine one, largely defined by degree: as the physician Paracelsus (1493–1541) famously asserted, "Poison is in everything, and no thing is without poison. The dosage makes it either a poison or a remedy."[10] This ambiguous potential was particularly unsettling in the rapidly changing and controversy-ridden state of contemporary medical opinion, in which consensus regarding the correct contents, preparation, and dosage of remedies was hard to come by.[11] New diseases and medicines from the New World and new translations of classical medical writings threatened the already tenuous stability of medical knowledge. Most significantly, the widespread impact of Paracelsus and the rapidly growing use of chemical medicine in the sixteenth century posed a severe challenge to the medical establishment.[12] Drawing on highly toxic chemicals such as mercury and arsenic, as well as many of the magically inflected remedies of the folk tradition, Paracelsus advocated a homeopathic doctrine of treating like with like, or poisons with poisons, directly contradicting the accepted Galenic model of curing through contraries, using herbal purgatives and expulsives to cleanse the body of its excessive humors. The emergence of increasingly potent drugs into the medical marketplace, combined with shrill accusations of pharmaceutical poisonings from each side, heightened consumers' fears about the reliability of medicines of any sort.

The Friar's speech on poison and medicine draws on contemporary fears of uncertain medicines, implicitly highlighting the precariousness of Romeo's position. Framed between Romeo's unseen entrance and his interruption to announce his love for Juliet and his request to be wed, the speech implicitly associates the lovers' fate with the equivocal effects of medicinal herbs. Romeo echoes this vocabulary in his plea for the Friar's support of his marriage: "Both our remedies," he tells the Friar, "Within thy help and holy physic lie" (2.3.47–48). Unfortunately, as the Friar's musings have just shown, the "remedies" of his "holy physic" are distinctly risky. Not only are his professional judgment and authority shown to be questionable, casting doubt on his fitness to diagnose and cure the problems of the play, but his ingredients are in themselves profoundly ambivalent, as capable of killing as of curing.

The overlay of pharmacy, desire, and death in the Friar's speech is echoed in the following act, when he and his holy physic are called upon for another remedy: this time to the lovers' enforced separation after Romeo's banishment

for Tybalt's death. In its presentation of one lover's apparent death and the
other's readiness to die in response, this curious middle act provides an odd,
almost farcical, foreshadowing of the play's ending; it also offers a comic alternative to such an ending. After Romeo's duel with Tybalt, Juliet's query
for news of her love elicts a characteristically confused and frantic exclama-
tion from her nurse: "he's dead, he's dead, he's dead! / We are undone, lady,
we are undone. / Alack the day, he's gone, he's kill'd, he's dead" (3.2.37–39).
Despite the conventional understanding that the play becomes a tragedy after
Mercutio's death, the nurse's breathless and repetitive hysteria, framed by the
audience's comfortable knowledge that Romeo is alive, makes this scene a
comic parody of a death announcement.[13] Following immediately upon the
poetry of Juliet's erotic epithalamium, the nurse's misinformation introduces
anxiety but fails to undermine the elated freedom of the lovers' comic world.

The woefully underinformed Juliet, however, responds to Romeo's hypo-
thetical death by taking it as a figurative poison:

> Hath Romeo slain himself? Say thou but "Ay"
> And that bare vowel "I" shall poison more
> Than the death-darting eye of cockatrice.
>
>   (3.2.45–47)

As long as Romeo's death remains in the realm of language—and uncertain
language at that—Juliet's poisons remain limited to language as well. The
wounding power of the letter "I" goes deep, however, evoking the play's
broader concerns with the vulnerability of the eye—and, correspondingly,
the "I," or subject—to the darts of love. The letter's poisons prove powerful;
in response to the nurse's confirming chorus of "I's",[14] Juliet immediately
leaps to proclamations of suicide: "Vile earth to earth resign, end motion
here, / And thou and Romeo press one heavy bier" (3.2.59–60). Even when
it becomes clear that Romeo is still alive, news of his banishment and her
wedding to Paris is enough to inspire doom: "I'll to the Friar to know his
remedy. / If all else fail, myself have power to die" (3.5.241–242). The Friar's
remedy is presented as an alternative, and perhaps an uneasy twin, to death.
Once again, both the lovers' remedies lie within the Friar's help and holy
physic; Juliet's figurative poisons hover uneasily between the threat of liter-
alization and the promise of being replaced with medicinal cures.

Juliet echoes the association between remedy and death when she con-
fronts the Friar himself. "If in thy wisdom thou canst give no help, / Do
thou but call my resolution wise, / And with this knife I'll help it present-
ly" (4.1.52–54). "I long to die," she repeats shortly, "If what thou speak'st
speak not of remedy" (4.1.66–67). In introducing the sleeping potion, Friar

Lawrence, like Juliet, links it with death. If she has the strength of will to kill herself, he suggests,

> Then is it likely thou wilt undertake
> A thing like death to chide away this shame,
> That cop'st with death himself to scape from it.
> And, if thou dar'st, I'll give thee remedy.
>
> (4.1.73–76)

As a "thing like death," the potion—or the comatose state it will induce—is intended to divert Juliet from "death himself," functioning as an apotropaic remedy.[15] But the likeness is so persuasive that the distinction becomes uncomfortably blurred. Even Juliet questions the drug's reliability, wondering, "What if it be a poison, which the Friar / Subtly hath minister'd to have me dead . . . ?" (4.3.24–25). This threat becomes a certainty to her audience the following morning: unable to wake her, the nurse cries hysterically: "Lady! Lady! Lady! / Alas, alas! Help, help! My lady's dead!"; and, "She's dead, deceas'd! She's dead! Alack the day!" (4.5.13–14, 23).

While the nurse's grief is sincere—and the audience, in fact, cannot be sure that she is mistaken in believing Juliet dead—the echoes of farce in her frenzied interjections remind us that the idea of the contrived false death as a plot device is typically a motif of comedy, or tragicomedy.[16] Typically, the eventual discovery that the death is not real provides renewed grounds for festive celebration; Juliet's temporary belief in Romeo's death, shortly followed by both the discovery that he was alive and the consummation of the lovers' marriage, partly fits this model. With the advent of the sleeping potion, however, the generic rules change: the nurse's wails are simultaneously wrongheaded and prophetic, and our laughter is uneasy. While false deaths in comedy tend to be constructed of rumor only, Juliet's is built of the more binding force of chemical intervention, a more dangerous realm for experimentation. The nurse's mistaken assumption will become true: Juliet's ambiguous potion ultimately, if indirectly, proves fatal.

Juliet's sleep has an uneasy dramatic status: as a likeness or imitation of death, it looks ahead to the tragedy of the play's ending, yet as an apotropaic substitute for actual death, it suggests the prototypically comic possibility of young lovers' triumph over adversity. In the first half of the play, sleep is associated with the carefree world of comedy. The Friar explicitly identifies it with the comforts of youth: "But where unbruised youth with unstuff'd brain / Doth couch his limbs, there golden sleep doth reign" (2.3.33–34). Similarly, Romeo associates sleep with serenity and ease. "Sleep dwell upon thine eyes, peace in thy breast," he calls to the departing Juliet, "Would I were sleep and peace so sweet to rest" (2.2.186–187).

Juliet's artificial sleep, the pivot of the play's action, becomes the occasion for her own private theater. "My dismal scene I needs must act alone," she comments before drinking the Friar's potion (4.3.19). On the threshold of sleep, she is assailed by waking dreams, or nightmares, of its consequences:

> Alack, alack! Is it not like that I
> So early waking, what with loathsome smells
> And shrieks like mandrakes torn out of the earth,
> That living mortals, hearing them, run mad. . . ?
>
> (4.3.45–48)

Juliet's terror of the uncertain state which she will be entering leads her aptly to thoughts of mandrakes. A source of much fascination in the Renaissance, the mandrake, like Friar Lawrence's herbs, was understood to be both poisonous and medicinal.[17] As a medicine, it was attributed soporific and aphrodisiac powers, linking it with Juliet's sleeping potion as well as with the love that necessitates it.[18] As the name suggests, mandrakes were also considered quasi-human: popular lore held that the plant sprung from the seed of a hanged man, and that when the root was dug up, it would emit screams that would kill or madden anyone within hearing distance.[19] Simultaneously animate and inanimate, fertile and fatal, medicine and poison, the mandrake that haunts Juliet's imagination on the verge of her sleep suggests the suspended play of oppositions that her artificial sleep embodies.

Just as Romeo's false death is succeeded by Juliet's false death, Juliet's nightmarish intimations are followed by Romeo's dream of his own death. "If I may trust the flattering truth of sleep," Romeo rather inauspiciously opens the final act,

> My dreams presage some joyful news at hand.
> My bosom's lord sits lightly in his throne
> And all this day an unaccustom'd spirit
> Lifts me above the ground with cheerful thoughts.
> I dreamt my lady came and found me dead—
> Strange dream that gives a dead man leave to think!—
> And breath'd such life with kisses in my lips
> That I reviv'd and was an emperor.
> Ah me, how sweet is love itself possess'd
> When but love's shadows are so rich in joy.
>
> (5.1.1–11)

Romeo's naive faith in "the flattering truth of sleep" continues his belief, expressed earlier to Mercutio, in a dream as a negative omen.[20] This second

dream marks a curious half-truth; as Marjorie Garber points out, it is true
that he will die and that Juliet will kiss him, although unfortunately he will
not revive nor become an emperor.[21] Romeo's dream, like those Mercutio
attributes to Queen Mab, seems to represent a wish rather than a true pre-
diction. Just as Juliet's sleep is arranged to evade the catastrophe of having
to marry Paris, so Romeo's sleep offers an escape from the doom he has
envisioned, replacing the tragic ending of death with the comic ending of
an erotic consummation.

Both of the lovers' sleeps, however, are only temporary; far from fulfilling the positive transformation they promise, they eventually bring about that
which they sought to avert. Juliet's artificial death leads to its actuality. News
of her death reaches Romeo through an unwittingly accurate euphemism:
"Her body sleeps in Capels' monument" (5.1.18). In response, Romeo vows
to enter the same figurative sleep, cast in erotic terms: "Well, Juliet, I will lie
with thee tonight. / Let's see for means" (5.1.34–35). While the false report
of Romeo's death led to figurative and false poisons, and eventually to Juliet's
false death, Juliet's more persuasive counterfeit of death leads to real poisons
and Romeo's real death, which will itself be reflected back in her own actual
death. Dangerous potions here become the middle term in a mimetic tri-
angle: pretense inspires the accessories that bring greater authenticity to the
next imitation.

The poisons Juliet invokes upon believing Romeo dead, as well as the
pseudopoisons of her sleeping potion, become literal when Romeo believes
her dead. Romeo's encounter with the apothecary parallels Juliet's visit to
Friar Lawrence, but at an even higher pitch of desperation. Unlike the Friar,
who volunteers his drugs, the apothecary sells his poisons under pressure and
against his will, and whereas Juliet sought a temporary solution for temporal
problems—exile, imposed marriage—Romeo seeks a final remedy for an apparently permanent ending:

> Let me have
> A dram of poison, such soon-speeding gear
> As will disperse itself through all the veins,
> That the life-weary taker may fall dead,
> And that the trunk may be discharg'd of breath
> As violently as hasty powder fir'd
> Doth hurry from the fatal cannon's womb.
>
> (5.1.59–65)

Romeo's odd assimilation of poison to gunpowder conveys an eroticized
urgency, likening death to an explosive sexual consummation. The figure
closely recalls the Friar's early concern over the intensity of the lovers'

infatuation: "These violent delights have violent ends / And in their triumph die, like fire and powder, / Which as they kiss consume" (2.6.9–11). In evoking this earlier reference, Romeo's words appropriate the scale and force of a cannon for his own humbler means of death; they also serve to identify his suicidal frenzy with the passion that spawned it.

Romeo explicitly links death with marriage in his suicide, which he casts as a reunion with Juliet. "Here's to my love," he cries before drinking his poison; "O true apothecary, / Thy drugs are quick. Thus with a kiss I die" (5.3.119–120). As M. M. Mahood notes, these final lines embody their own paradox; the apothecary's drugs are "quick" in the sense both of speedy and of life-giving, in that they return him to Juliet.[22] Moments later a horrified Juliet echoes him both in action and in words:

> What's here? A cup clos'd in my true love's hand?
> Poison, I see, hath been his timeless end.
> O churl. Drunk all, and left no friendly drop
> To help me after? I will kiss thy lips.
> Haply some poison yet doth hang on them
> To make me die with a restorative.
>
> (5.3.161–166)[23]

Like Romeo's "quick" drugs, Juliet's hope to "die with a restorative" highlights the paradoxical status of poisons and pseudopoisons throughout the play. The Friar's mock poison is intended as a kind of love potion. Ultimately, though, it robs her of her love by bringing about his suicide. Similarly, the apothecary's real poison purports to offer Romeo a reunion with his wife in death but prevents him from a reunion while still living.

After an uneasy rivalry between tragedy and farce for the soul of the play, tragedy suddenly, and rather surprisingly, wins, recalling the warning with which the Chorus opened the play. Yet despite, or perhaps because of, this generic resolution, these ultimately poisonous potions confer on the lovers what seemed out of their reach when alive: their star-crossed and convention-laden love acquires dignity, pathos, and immortality, even acknowledgment from their embattled parents. Poison is Romeo's "timeless end" not only because (as editors tend to gloss the term) it is untimely, cutting him off unexpectedly in youth, but also because the ending it gives him places him outside and above time, into the space of legend.

* * *

Although *Romeo and Juliet* may offer the most famous dramatization of the confusion of narcotic with poison and of artificially induced sleep with death, the device recurs throughout contemporaneous plays. Barabas, in Marlowe's

Jew of Malta, recounts employing such a potion to escape notice, and punishment: "I drank poppy and cold mandrake juice; /And being asleep, belike they thought me dead" (5.1.81–82). Similarly, the queen in Shakespeare's *Cymbeline* is foiled in her attempt to poison Imogen when it turns out that her doctor substituted a sleeping potion for a poison. In Edward Sharpham's *The Fleire*, the Knight's attempt to poison Sparke and Ruffel is later revealed as unsuccessful when they awaken; in John Day's *Law Tricks*, the Counts Lurdo and Horatio are surprised when Lurdo's wife reappears to confront them after apparently having been poisoned by them; and Don John in Dekker's *Match Me in London* is similarly confronted with Don Valasco's survival of his poisoning. Throughout these generically unstable plays, as in *Romeo and Juliet*, the sleeping potion becomes a pivot on which the play's ambiguity turns: it suspends the plot, holding out the simultaneous possibilities of death and rebirth. The recurrence of the motif suggests that narcotics held a special appeal and metatheatrical significance for the drama: the sleep they induce parallels the suspension of time and identity produced by plays themselves.

Playwrights' interest in the ambivalent pleasures of sleeping potions was informed by radical shifts in early modern pharmacy. Epidemics of plague and syphilis, combined with escalating interest in the chemical medicine of Paracelsus and other Continental scientists, led to a surge in the use of powerful, though often toxic, remedies. Medical accounts of the seductive overlay of pleasure and danger associated with soporific drugs, in particular, offered a compelling vocabulary for a theatrical establishment fascinated by this juxtaposition, especially in light of similar characterizations of the theater itself. Describing the increased use of opium during the plague, for example, Dr. Eleazer Dunk wrote in 1606 that the drug "was very acceptable to patients for a while, for it stayed the violent flowing of the humors, it procured present sleepe, and mitigated paine."[24] Yet its ultimate effect, he claimed, was death: "a great number had their lives cut off; some died sleeping, being stupied with that poisoned medicine."[25] Dunk's dismay toward the growing popularity of an often fatal drug was echoed throughout the medical community, which drew on opium's dangers to emphasize a line of continuity between sleep and death. *Bulleins Bulwarke of Defence* (1579) claims of poppy that "it causeth deepe deadly sleapes."[26] Similarly, in 1580 the physician Timothy Bright warned that opium must be taken in very small doses, "least it cast the patient into such a sleepe, as hee needeth the trumpet of the Archangell to awake him."[27] Philip Barrough echoed, in 1596, that with these drugs, "you may cause him to sleepe so, that you can awake him no more."[28] And lastly, in 1599 André Du Laurens wrote,

> in the vse of all these stupefactiue medicines taken inwardly; wee must take heed to deale with very good aduise, for feare that in

stead of desiring to procure rest vnto the sillie melancholie wretch, wee cast him into an endless sleepe.[29]

The recurring medical pronouncements on this topic both testify to anxieties about the use (and overuse) of narcotic drugs and emphasize the perceived fragility of the boundary between ordinary sleep and the endless deep of death. Once the patient falls asleep, they suggest, the force of inertia, if given any assistance, will keep him that way. Shakespeare, whose son-in-law John Hall was a prominent physician, could hardly help but be aware of these concerns.[30] In the context of these portraits of sleeping drugs, Juliet's decline from slumber into death seems an inevitable response to Friar Lawrence's would-be remedy.

As the emphasis on the link between sleep and death suggests, fears about artificial sleeping drugs drew on concerns not only about pharmacy, but about sleep itself, widely seen as a near relation to death.[31] Medical accounts of sleep refer to its capacity for enervation as well as restoration; Du Laurens describes it as "the withdrawing of the spirits and naturall heate, from the outward parts, to the inward, and from all the circumference vnto the center."[32] Paré expands on this definition, depicting sleep as

> the rest of the whole body, and the cessation of the Animall facultie from sense and motion. Sleepe is caused, when the substance of the brain is possessed, and after some sort overcome and dulled by a certaine vaporous, sweete and delightsome humidity; or when the spirits almost exhaust by performance of some labour, cannot any longer sustaine the weight of the body.[33]

Paré's description, like that of Du Laurens, portrays sleep as a temporary death, a cessation from sense and motion. The mind slips into suspension—possessed, overcome, and dulled, losing any possibility of control—while simultaneously the spirits lack the strength to sustain the body. In fact, the medical disorder of excessive sleep is explicitly linked with the idea of death; Barroughs lists a lengthy catalog of sleep disorders that, somewhat monotonously, all come to be equated with death.[34] Like soporific drugs, sleep is understood as containing both medicinal and poisonous potential.

The representation of sleep in the theater shares these doctors' emphasis on the proximity of sleep and death and the fragility of the boundary between them. David Bevington notes that both characters and audiences have difficulties at times distinguishing between the two states.[35] In *A Midsummer Night's Dream*, Helena wonders, upon seeing Lysander spread out on the ground, "Dead, or asleep?" (2.2.101); later, in a mock-tragic mirror image of this scene, which arguably parodies *Romeo and Juliet*, Thisbe interrogates

Pyramus's body, "Asleep, my love? / What, dead, my dove?" (5.1.324–325). This confusion, which can be seen in countless other dramatic examples,[36] highlights a metatheatrical resonance: in the suspended reality of the stage, all deaths are feigned, as are all sleeps, living out Lady Macbeth's maxim that "The sleeping and the dead / Are but as pictures"(2.2.50–51). Shakespeare's recurring trope of the play as a dream, staged while the audience sleeps, suggests that images of sleepers onstage can be understood to reflect the uncertain status of the play's spectators as well.[37]

In the light of medical accounts of sleep and sleeping drinks, the comparison is a dangerous one. In the theater as well, sleep is not only similar to death but susceptible to it. Just as Juliet's deep sleep unwittingly catalyzes both her own death and Romeo's, sleeping in plays often proves fatal. Recounting his "foul murder" to his son, the ghost of King Hamlet repeatedly dwells on his oblivion to the murderer: "sleeping in my orchard, / A serpent stung me"; "Sleeping within my orchard, / My custom always of the afternoon, / Upon my secure hour thy uncle stole"; "Thus was I, sleeping, by a brother's hand / Of life, of crown, of queen once dispatch'd" (1.5.35–36; 59–61; 74–75).[38] Lady Macbeth facilitates the murder of the sleeping Duncan by making the guards sleep soundly: "I have drugg'd their possets / That death and nature do contend about them, / Whether they live or die" (2.2.6–8).[39] Even in the safer contexts of comedy or romance, sleeping is risky: in *The Taming of the Shrew*, Christopher Sly is tricked into a new identity after succumbing to drunken oblivion; the sleeping lovers in *A Midsummer Night's Dream* are medicined with troublemaking love potions; and Caliban schemes to murder Prospero while he sleeps. If sleep can be a figure for the world of the play, theatergoers are, by analogy, depicted as being at risk when they surrender themselves to it. The vulnerability associated with the passivity of sleep may be implicitly identified with the position of the spectator.

Renaissance antitheatricalists drew precisely this comparison, identifying the suspended quality of theatrical performances with sleep and its concordant threatening associations of pleasure, sin, and death. "Stage-haunters are for the most part lulled asleepe in the *Dalilaes* lappe of these sinfull pleasures," William Prynne writes, "yea they are quite dead in sinnes and trespasses."[40] The biblical reference offers a resonant image of both the seductive temptation and the catastrophic results of surrender to sleep. Accordingly, just as medical writers insist on the necessity of moderating both sleep and intake of soporific drugs, Prynne suggests that exposure to the theater must be limited in order to avoid dangerous consequences:

> the recreation must *not be overlong, not time-consuming;* it must be onely *as a baite to a traviler, a whetting to a Mower or Carpenter, or as an houres sleepe* in the day time to a wearied man; we must *not*

spend whole weekes; whole dayes, halfe dayes or nights on recreations as now too many doe, *abundance of idlenesse in this kinde, being one of Sodomes hainous sinnes.*[41]

Prynne distinguishes between the potentially reviving capacity of a brief rest and the danger of excessively long leisure. For other moralizing critics, however, exposure to the theater operates on a continuum, defying safe containment in small quantities. Stephen Gosson invokes a model of incremental gradations to illustrate the contagious force of the theater, which, he writes, takes the audience "from pyping to playing, from play to pleasure, from pleasure to slouth, from slouth to sleepe, from sleepe to sinne, from sinne to death, from death to the Divel."[42]

If the stage lulls its spectators into the deathlike state of excessive sleep, the theater itself can be seen as a sleep-inducing drug. Prynne explicitly links theatrical idleness with toxic potions. "Such prevalency is there in these bewitching Stage-plays," he writes, "to draw men on to *sloth, to idlenesse, the very bane, the poyson, and destruction of mens peerelesse soules*" (506). Stage plays, according to his model, parallel the function of drugs in drawing spectators to sloth, a poisonous state. The transformation effected in spectators by plays claims the potency of a permanent, and fatal, chemical reaction and suggests that the ambiguous status of the sleeping potion onstage could ultimately reflect the impact, as well as the form, of the play that features it.

* * *

In the world of the theater, the ambivalent interweaving of sleep, potions, poisons, and plays is perhaps most fully dramatized in *Antony and Cleopatra.* Just as it revisits the structural pattern of *Romeo and Juliet,* the play explores a similar confusion between sleeping potions and poisons.[43] Throughout the play, Cleopatra and Egypt are associated with pleasurable narcotics, both figurative and literal. Rooted in Rome and the apparent genre of history, Antony wavers between grasping at comedy—in which the languorous hedonism of Cleopatra's world brings pleasure and ultimately marriage—and tumbling into tragedy, where sinister charms mesmerize him into a sleepy incapacitation and ultimately death. By the end of the play, Egypt's ambiguous sleepy drugs, like Friar Lawrence's potion, prove officially poisonous, killing the protagonists and defining the play as a tragedy. As in *Romeo and Juliet,* however, the evolution of soporifics into poisons ultimately serves to rescue the lovers rather than to destroy them. Antony's death gives rise to Cleopatra's imaginative production of a more heroic Antony, and her own suicide elevates her theatrical power, which often provoked skepticism and suspicion while she lived, to the realm of myth. Although the raucous comedy of Cleopatra's Egypt evolves steadily into tragedy, the play closes on a note of triumph.

Despite the play's parallels with *Romeo and Juliet*, however, there are important changes. The lovers' roles are redistributed: as the entranced consumer of dreams, spectacles, sleeping potions, and poisons, Antony plays both Romeo and Juliet, whereas Cleopatra, like Friar Lawrence and the apothecary, is more source than recipient of the play's intoxicating potions. She occupies, moreover, the center of the play's explicit meditations on dramatic spectacles. Accordingly, the play is significantly more self-conscious than *Romeo and Juliet* in its examination of drugs and their relationship with the theater, and its closing celebration of the lovers is both more problematic and more telling.

In the play's opening act, Cleopatra echoes Juliet by seeking refuge from her lover's absence in sleep-inducing potions. "Give me to drink mandragora," she orders Charmian, "That I might sleep out this great gap of time / My Antony is away" (1.5.4–6). Cleopatra's choice of sleeping potion links her with Juliet, identifying Cleopatra's daydreams with the nightmare vision of Juliet's mandrake-surrounded tomb. Yet mandragora, with its ambiguous conflation of sleeping potion, aphrodisiac, and poison, is here presented as a remedy to the unsettling emptiness created by Antony's departure, becoming a replacement or double for Antony himself. The sleep it offers suggests both an erotically pleasurable idleness and a deathlike retreat, which suspends time during Antony's absence.

Despite her call for mandragora, however, Cleopatra medicines herself with daydreams rather than drugs. Distracting herself from her distress, she luxuriates in pleasurable fantasies:

>   O Charmian,
> Where think'st thou he is now? Stands he, or sits he?
> Or does he walk? or is he on his horse?
> O happy horse to bear the weight of Antony!
> Do bravely, horse, for wot'st thou whom thou mov'st
> The demi-Atlas of this earth, the arm
> And burgonet of men. He's speaking now,
> Or murmuring, "Where's my serpent of old Nile?"
> For so he calls me. Now I feed myself
> With most delicious poison.
>
>   (1.5.18–27)[44]

Cleopatra represents the absent Antony in her own internal theater, filling the empty horizon with a catalog of his imagined places, postures, and thoughts. Neatly inverting her own lack, she scripts him as looking for an absent Cleopatra. With its erotic charge and comforting reversal of roles, the private theater of her daydreams serves a pharmaceutical function, constructing the sleepy oblivion she craves. Her remedy, though, has ambiguous effects: she describes her reveries as "most delicious poison," linking her escapist pleasures with corrosive perils. Cleopatra is simultaneously patient and pharmacist, consumer and producer of the drugs she craves. Her request for the sleepy aphrodisiac poison of the mandrake is answered in her erotic fantasies.

Although in this scene Cleopatra is drugged by her own sleepy reveries, throughout the play it is primarily Antony and his Roman soldiers who consume the pleasurable but poisonous soporifics associated with Egypt and its queen. Just as she herself confines fantasy with narcotic drugs, so the Romans are seduced by a combination of Cleopatra's dramatic spectacles and her wine-seeped feasts, underlining the parallel between theatricality and sleepy potions.[45] Enobarbus's tales of Egyptian extravagance are laced with references to drunken somnolence. "We did sleep day out of countenance," he vaunts to Maecenas and Agrippa, just before describing Cleopatra's performance at Cydnus, "and made the night light with drinking" (2.2.177–178). Scenes of drinking seem inevitably to conjure up Egypt, theatricality, and oblivion: after negotiations with Pompey, Caesar, and Lepidus, Enobarbus asks Antony, "Shall we dance now the Egyptian Bacchanals / And celebrate our drink?" (2.7.101–102). "Come, let's all take hands," Antony responds, "Till that the conquering wine hath steeped our sense / In soft and delicate Lethe" (2.7.104–106).

Although Enobarbus describes Egypt's alcoholic and theatrical revels in festive terms, Antony's allusion to Lethe, the river of forgetfulness, points to darker aspects of the surrender of consciousness that they represent. Somnolence, and the potions that produce it, threatens not only to suspend the self but to dissolve it.[46] Antony's dependence on the sleepy calm brought on by drink becomes more desperate as the play progresses. Wine allays tensions with Cleopatra: amid their post-Actium reconciliation, Antony calls, "Some wine within there, and our viands!" (3.11.73). Later, after forgiving Cleopatra's conference with Caesar's deputy Thidias, he calls for "one other gaudy night . . . Fill our bowls once more" (3.13.183–184). Just as Juliet's sleeping potion held out the promise of reuniting her with Romeo, the sleepy potions of wine offer to bring Antony back to Cleopatra and the comedic goal of marital bliss. While Juliet and Romeo each drink only a single draft of their respective potions, however, Antony's self-medication is ongoing and apparently insatiable. Rather than killing at once, his soporifics draw him into a self-perpetuating addiction that slowly and gradually destroys him.

From a Roman perspective, Antony's constant consumption of sleep-inducing drink signals his broader surrender to the dangerously seductive charm of Egypt. "Let witchcraft join with beauty, lust with both," Pompey exults to Menocrates,

> Tie up the libertine, in a field of feasts,
> Keep his brain fuming; Epicurean cooks
> Sharpen with cloyless sauce his appetite,
> That sleep and feeding may prorogue his honour,
> Even till a Lethe'd dullness—
>
> (2.1.22–27)

Antony's surrender to sleep, according to Pompey, suggests he is victim to a form of witchcraft: he is lured into oblivion, a "Lethe'd dullness," by an inexorable assault on his appetites. Antony becomes an object rather than a subject, tied up, fumed, and, most important, prorogued: suspended, deferred, kept in abeyance.[47]

Cleopatra and her performances are at the center of this luxurious but unsettling languor: in response to her faltering attempts to delay his departure for Rome, Antony chides, "But that your royalty / Holds idleness your subject, I should take you / For idleness itself" (1.3.91–93). The paradoxical structure of his assertion captures an essential aspect of Cleopatra's nature: she seems simultaneously to embody somnolence and to control it, both to be implicated in an Egyptian passivity and to manipulate it, actively, for her own gains. The soporific drug for which she calls is both a potion at her disposal and an emblem of her own effect on others.

As Antony's response to this scene of Cleopatra's suggests, his consumption of Egypt's soporific food and drink is paralleled with his spectatorship of Cleopatra's performances. Cleopatra's primary power lies in her ability to draw all eyes to her: describing her spectacular arrival at Cydnus, Enobarbus claims that the city's rush to view her on the barge left behind only air, "which, but for vacancy / Had gone to gaze on Cleopatra too, / And made a gap in nature" (2.2.216–218). Antony is hardly immune to her magnetic pull: in a disconcerting reversal of roles, she turns down his dinner invitation to insist that he come to her, where he "for his ordinary, pays his heart, / For what his eyes eat only" (2.2.225–226). Visual consumption is equated with, and substituted for, oral and is in both cases costly.

This pattern, of gazing on Cleopatra and subsequently losing himself, is repeated at Actium. Upon seeing Cleopatra withdraw from the battle, Antony "(like a doting mallard) / Leaving the fight in heighth, flies after her" (3.10.20–21). His will is no longer his own: "My heart was to thy rudder tied by the strings," he tells Cleopatra (3.11.57). The scene depicts the culmination of a process that began at Cydnus, the dissolution of his autonomous self. "I never saw an action of such shame," Scarus tells Enobarbus; "Experience, manhood, honour, ne'er before / Did violate so itself" (3.10.23–24). Antony's surrender to Cleopatra's spectacles parallels, and extends, his surrender to the oblivion of drink and sleep, implicitly suggesting that spectators of the play (who also, of course, gaze on Cleopatra) share, at least temporarily, the loss of self the play dramatizes.[48]

This surrender, the play insists, is dangerous. Despite his enchantment with Cleopatra, Antony himself links her narcotic pleasures with the threat of poison. Early in the play, he worries that "Much is breeding, / Which like the courser's hair, hath yet but life / And not a serpent's poison" (1.2.190–192). While he holds back from attributing poison to the magically animated hair, his choice of image and cautionary "yet" imply that it is only a matter of time. Shortly after this, he echoes Pompey's skeptical account of his Egyptian subjection by apologizing to Caesar that "poisoned hours had bound me up / From mine own knowledge" (2.2.90). Even Cleopatra echoes the association, identifying herself as Antony's "serpent of old Nile" (1.5.25). These foreshadowings of the poison that will later bring about the play's tragic end offer a physical correlative for the corrosion of Antony's will; they remind the audience from early on that the bawdy jests and playful banter of Cleopatra's court are not without troubling side effects.

The idea of Cleopatra's seductive appeal as a type of poison was explicitly encoded in Shakespeare's sources. North's translation of Plutarch's *Life of Marc Antonie* describes Antony's falling off from martial greatness as a kind of poisoning: Antony was "so rauished & enchaunted with the sweete poyson of her love, that he had no other thought but of her, & how he might quickly returne againe . . ."[49] Later he writes similarly that Caesar claimed "that *Antonius* was not Maister of him selfe, but that *Cleopatra* had brought him beside him selfe, by her charmes and amorous poysons."[50] North's "sweet poyson" and "amorous poysons" stem in both cases from Plutarch's *"pharmakoi,"* evoking, like Cleopatra's mandrake, an ambiguous array of meanings: poison, remedy, drug, and aphrodisiac.[51] The embedded presence of North's language and its attendant ambiguities can be seen in the play's recurring imagery of poison, and particularly in its emphasis on the literal poison with which Cleopatra kills herself.

As in *Romeo and Juliet,* the play's closing suggests that its near poisons, or figurative poisons, metamorphose into literal and fatal poisons, that Lethe becomes lethal. The play's oscillations between farce and fear settle formally into tragedy as its ambiguous potions become firmly defined. Shakespeare presents the long, slow drama of the lovers' deaths as beginning after the final lost battle, with Antony's rage at his perceived betrayal by Cleopatra. "The shirt of Nessus is upon me," he laments; "teach me, / Alcides, thou mine ancestor, thy rage" (4.12.43–45). Antony's reference to the shirt of Nessus is the last, and least heroic, of the allusions that throughout the play link him with Hercules.[52] Referring to the poisoned shirt with which Hercules' wife Deianeira brought about his death, the allusion suggests that Antony's death is already under way, brought about by Cleopatra's poisonous treachery.[53]

Antony's claim that he is dying of Cleopatra's poisons proves quickly, if indirectly, to be true. Alarmed by his accusations and threats, Cleopatra imitates Juliet in feigning death. Like Juliet, Cleopatra does not conceive of the idea independently; in response to her plea, "Help me, my women!" (4.13.1), Charmian suggests that she lock herself in her monument and send word to Antony that she is dead. Unlike Juliet, however, Cleopatra seems to be aware that her ruse will hurt her lover, even that it may bring about his death. Diomedes announces to the dying Antony that his mistress "had a prophesying fear / Of what hath come to pass," and that she has sent him, "fearing since how it [her ruse] might work" (4.14.120–121, 125).[54] Cleopatra, in fact, seems more certain than fearful; when Diomedes returns from bearing the message, she immediately inquires, "How now? is he dead?" (4.15.6). Just as Juliet's imitation of death mimetically re-created itself in Romeo's actual death, Cleopatra's staging immediately brings about Antony's suicide. While Juliet's death was undertaken with reassurances that Romeo would be warned, however, Cleopatra's relies for its efficacy precisely on Antony believing it true. Cleopatra's theatrical imagination, the metaphorical mandragora that she fed herself in act 1, ultimately acts as a poison that brings about Antony's death.

Fittingly, Cleopatra's performance of death leads Antony to a death envisioned as a long-awaited slumber. "Unarm, Eros," he responds, "the long day's task is done, / And we must sleep" (4.14.35–36). Death offers Antony a purer version of the escapist oblivion he has courted in Egypt; like the drunken revels, it imitates and intensifies, it also seems to promise a return to Cleopatra, and erotic union. "I will be / A bridegroom in my death," he pronounces, "and run into't / As to a lovers bed" (4.14.99–101). Like Romeo, he fuses together tragedy and comedy by identifying the defeat of death with the triumph of marriage.

Just as Antony's temporary disappearance to Rome became the occasion for Cleopatra's dreamlike reveries and calls for mandragora, his permanent disappearance to death brings on a literal dream, leading her to call again for both sleep and poison. "I dreamt there was an Emperor Antony," Cleopatra tells Dolabella. "O such another sleep, that I might see / But such another man!" (5.2.76–78). Cleopatra's resurrection of an "Emperor Antony" can be seen as the belated fulfillment of Romeo's dream "that I reviv'd, and was an emperor" (4.1.9). Although the narcotic enchantment of her theatrical spectacles worked to undo the literal Antony, the same soporific imagination offers recompense by reconstituting his image in fantasy.

Having brought about Antony's death and resurrection through the force of her theatrical imagination, Cleopatra sets about attending to her own. The play seems to begin anew, as she stages a reproduction of the spectacle that started her romance: "I am again for Cydnus," she tells her women, "To meet Mark Antony" (5.2.227–228). In an ironic juxtaposition of genres, the asp that literalizes the play's figurative poisons is conveyed by an emblem of comedy: a clown. "What poor an instrument," Cleopatra comments, "May do a noble deed!" (5.2.235–236). As the carrier of the poisons that will fulfill Cleopatra's tragic final scene, the clown's presence implicitly suggests that the play's earlier scenes, with their bawdiness and farce, were a necessary vehicle for what would follow: her playfully ambiguous mandragora has evolved into literal poisons with final and permanent effects.

Like Antony, and Romeo and Juliet before him, Cleopatra paradoxically looks to dying as revivification and reunion: "I have / Immortal longings in me," she pronounces; "Husband, I come, / Now to that name, my courage prove my title!" (5.2.279–280, 286–287). Watching Iras die after a farewell kiss, Cleopatra again conflates poison with pain-alleviating, and even seductive, pleasures:

> Have I the aspic in my lips? Dost fall?
> If thou and nature can so gently part,
> The stroke of death is as a lover's pinch,
> Which hurts, and is desir'd.
>
> (5.2.292–295)

Cleopatra's attribution of erotic pleasure to death draws on the play's frequent punning on dying as orgasm. In fact, the speed of Iras's death evokes sexual jealousy: "If she first meet the curled Antony," Cleopatra worries, "He'll make demand of her, and spend that kiss / Which is my heaven to have" (5.2.300–302). Death, as she conceives it, will return her to Antony and erotic fulfillment. By staging her suicide as a marriage, Cleopatra confounds generic rules: although the play ends as a tragedy, it also stages the traditionally comic celebration of a wedding and new life.

Shakespeare's detailed description of Cleopatra's death represents an imaginative interpolation from his source. Plutarch refers to the idea of the asp conveyed in a basket of figs as only one of a number of possible manners of Cleopatra's death.[55] In contrast to Shakespeare's dramatization of the conveyance and biting of the asp, Plutarch insists that we will never know exactly how she died. He emphasizes, however, her ingenuity and preparations in researching her means of death. In a particularly intriguing passage, Plutarch relates that, since early in the troubles with Rome, Cleopatra had been experimenting with the effects of various poisons on condemned prisoners in order to find the most painless form of death:

So when she had dayly made diuers and sundrie proofes, she found
none of all them she had proued so fit, as the biting of an Aspicke,
the which only causeth a hauines of the head, without swounding
or complaining, and bringeth a great desire also to sleepe, with
a little swet in the face, and so by litle and litle taketh away the
sences and vitall powers, no liuing creature perceiuing that the
pacients feele any paine. For they are so sorie when any bodie
waketh them, and taketh them up: as those that being taken out
of a sound sleepe, are very heauy and desirous to sleepe.[56]

Cleopatra's means of suicide, then, was chosen particularly for its resemblance
to a sleeping potion; her death can be seen as a carefully choreographed
extension of her earlier soporific pleasures.

Shakespeare essentially omits this striking anecdote from his play, limiting its mention to an afterthought by Caesar that "her physician tells me /
She hath pursued conclusions infinite / Of easy ways to die" (5.2.352–354).
Its residual echoes, however, can be seen not only in the play's recurring references to narcotics but in Shakespeare's association of Cleopatra's death with
the peace and pleasure of sleep. "O for such another sleep," she muses after her dream of Mark Antony, "that I might see / But such another man!"
(5.2.77–78). And the play suggests that her desire for sleep is granted. "Peace,
peace," she bids Charmian, as she hovers on the brink of dying, "Dost thou
not see my baby at my breast, / That sucks the nurse asleep?" (5.2.307–309).
Poison, ultimately, is her sleeping potion: upon viewing her dead body, Caesar
eulogizes that "she looks like sleep, / As she would catch another Antony / In
her strong toil of grace" (5.2.344–346). In her death, Cleopatra captures that
aspect of sleep which differentiates it from death and gives it the pleasure
of comedy: its promise of waking. The images of renewal—the baby at her
breast, another Cydnus, the catching of another Antony—suggest that her
play is suspended rather than over.

* * *

Antony and Cleopatra, like Romeo and Juliet before them, find a monument
in death: "She shall be buried by her Antony," Caesar specifies; "No grave
upon the earth shall clip in it / A pair so famous" (5.2.356–358). As their
monuments suggest, both plays end on a note of awe. Despite the ambiguous
interferences of comedy and farce, with their ongoing threat of ridicule, the
deaths with which the plays close confer a measure of dignity on not only
the lovers but the plays themselves. The intermediate, uncertain generic
mode of the sleeping potion settles into the poison of tragedy, but even this
poison turns out to be ambiguous in function. While it takes away the lovers'

lives, it also gives them back their marriage, leaving doubt as to the ultimate nature of the ending.

Despite the uncannily similar patterns these plays follow, the differences between them are significant. Youthful and star-crossed, Romeo and Juliet prove almost accidental consumers of the ambiguous and disturbing potions that pervade their play. Their uncertain drugs guide their oscillations between comedy and tragedy, but the parallelism the play establishes between types of plays and types of potions offers only tentative implications as to its significance. Cleopatra, on the other hand, is the font of her play's poisons. Her dreamlike imagination and dramatic performances are explicitly identified with the potions that pervade the play, and she exerts an intoxicating, narcotic effect on all of her audiences, including Antony and, ultimately, herself. Antony, accordingly, offers a model for the spectator as consumer of dangerous remedies: mesmerized, ensnared, undone, even annihilated, but—in the end—triumphantly reborn in the imagination. By identifying the play's ambivalent potions with dramatic spectacles, Shakespeare suggests that the dangerous seduction of enchanting potions is akin to that of the theater itself; he presents a complex and sophisticated model of theatrical agency as seeping into audiences and transforming them with a chemical force. Going beyond a simple revisitation of the earlier play, *Antony and Cleopatra* exploits and advances the juxtapositions set up in *Romeo and Juliet,* transforming its insights about the ambivalence of narcotic potions into a broader reflection on the suspended reality of the theater.

NOTES

For reading and commenting on versions of this essay, I would like to thank David Quint, Jennifer Lewin, Raphael Falco, Katharine Craik, Will Stenhouse, and members of the inter-disciplinary works-in-progress group at Macalester College. I would also like to thank the Wellcome Institute for Medical History, the Warburg Institute, and the Folger Shakespeare Library for support with research.

1. I use the term "double tragedy" to refer to tragedies with two protagonists of equal stature, both named in the title. The term could also, however, describe the many other forms of generic and thematic doubleness encompassed in these particular plays. On the rise of love tragedy in this period, and its intrinsic generic complications, see especially Martha Tuck Rozett, "The Comic Structures of Tragic Endings: The Suicide Scenes in *Romeo and Juliet* and *Antony and Cleopatra,*" *Shakespeare Quarterly* 36:1 (1985): 152–164; and Charles Forker, "The Love-Death Nexus in English Renaissance Tragedy," in *Skull Beneath the Skin: The Achievement of John Webster* (Carbondale and Edwardsville: Southern Illinois University Press, 1986), 235–253. As Rozett observes, the genre was new in the 1590s, and *Romeo and Juliet* seems to have been the first English play in which love was the subject of tragedy (152).

2. On the mixing of genres in *Romeo and Juliet,* see especially Susan Snyder, *The Comic Matrix of Shakespeare's Tragedies* (Princeton, N.J.: Princeton University

Press, 1979), 56–70. On *Antony and Cleopatra*, see Janet Adelman, *The Common Liar: An Essay on Antony and Cleopatra* (New Haven, Conn.: Yale University Press, 1973), esp. 1–52; J. L. Simmons, "The Comic Pattern and Vision in *Antony and Cleopatra*," *English Literary History* 36 (1969): 493–510; and Barbara C. Vincent, "Shakespeare's *Antony and Cleopatra* and the Rise of Comedy," *English Literary Renaissance* 12:1 (1982): 53–86. Rozett treats the two plays together in "Comic Structures of Tragic Endings."

    3. Jacques Derrida offers a provocative account of the complexities of the term *pharmakon* and its relationship to writing in "Plato's Pharmacy," in *Dissemination*, trans. Barbara Johnson (Chicago: University of Chicago Press, 1981), 63–171. "There is no such thing as a harmless remedy," he asserts, reflecting on Plato's uneasiness with the word's irreducible ambiguity; "The *pharmakon* can never be simply beneficial" (99).

    4. Anthony Munday, *A second and third blast of retrait from plaies and Theaters* (London, 1580), 101.

    5. William Prynne, *Histriomastix: The Player's Scourge* (London, 1633), 467, 38.

    6. Thomas Lodge, *A Defence of Poetry, Music and Stage-Plays* (London, 1579), 5.

    7. On genre, see Snyder, *Comic Matrix*. Much has been written on the play's yoking of love and death; see, for example, Marilyn Williamson, "Romeo and Death," *Shakespeare Studies* 14 (1981): 129–137; and Lloyd Davis, "'Death-marked love': Desire and Presence in *Romeo and Juliet*," *Shakespeare Survey* 49 (1996): 57–67.

    8. All references to *Romeo and Juliet* are from the Arden edition, edited by Brian Gibbons (London: Methuen, 1980).

    9. Snyder comments on the play's emphasis on extreme youth; see "Ideology and the Feud in *Romeo and Juliet*," *Shakespeare Survey* 46 (1998): 87–88.

    10. Paracelsus, *Selected Writings*, vol. 1, ed. Jolande Jacobi, trans. Norbert Guterman (New York: Pantheon, 1958), 107.

    11. See, for example, Andrew Wear, "Epistemology and Learned Medicine in Early Modern England," in *Knowledge and the Scholarly Medical Traditions*, ed. Don Bates (Cambridge: Cambridge University Press, 1995), 151–173.

    12. On Paracelsus, see especially Walter Pagel, *Paracelsus: An Introduction to Philosophical Medicine in the Era of the Renaissance* (Basel: Karger, 1958), Charles Webster, *From Paracelsus to Newton: Magic and the Making of Modern Science* (Cambridge: Cambridge University Press, 1982); and Henry Pachter, *Paracelsus: An Introduction to Philosophical Medicine in the Era of Guterman* (New York: Pantheon, 1958). On the impact of Paracelsus in England, see Allen Debus, *The English Parascelsans* (London: Oldbourne, 1965); and Paul Kocher, "Paracelsan Medicine in England," *Journal of the History of Medicine* 2 (1947): 451–480. Jonathan Gil Harris offers a suggestive analysis of the relationship between Paracelsan conceptions of pharmacy and early modern political models in *Foreign Bodies and The Body Politic* (Cambridge: Cambridge University Press, 1998).

    13. The ambivalent comedy of the nurse's response is echoed by the musicians' banter after Juliet's apparent death; both scenes are replayed, more darkly, with Balthasar's false report of Juliet's death to Romeo at the beginning of act 5.

    14. "I saw the wound, I saw it with mine eyes . . . I swounded at the sight" (3.2.52–56).

15. The Friar similarly tells the families, at the end of the play, that his sleeping potion achieved his intended aim in giving her "the form of death" (5.3.246).

16 Snyder points out that the reputed deaths of Hero in *Much Ado About Nothing*, Helena in *All's Well That Ends Well*, Claudio in *Measure for Measure*, and Hermoine in *A Winter's Tale* all succeed in their goal to avert or resolve a conflict by effecting a transformation in other characters (Snyder, *Comic Matrix*, 67). The generic ambivalence in each of these plays could be seen to identify them with tragicomedy, where the same motif is prevalent; see, for example, *Philaster, King and No King*, and *Match Me in London*. On characteristics and motifs of tragicomedy, see, for example, Gordon McMullen and Jonathan Hope, *The Politics of Tragicomedy: Shakespeare and After* (London and New York: Routledge, 1992), and Marvin T. Herrick, *Tragicomedy: Its Origins and Development in Italy, France, and England* (Urbana: University of Illinois Press, 1955).

17. On the range of associations with mandragora, see C. J. S. Thompson, *The Mystic Mandrake* (London: Rider and Co., 1934). Other noted literary references to mandrake in the period include John Donne's poems "Song" ("Go, and catch a falling star") and "Twicknam Gardens," as well as Webster's *The Duchess of Malfi*, in which Ferdinand describes his discovery of his sister's marriage as having "digg'd up a mandrake" (2.5.1).

18. On its soporific powers, Ambroise Paré writes, "Mandrage taken in great quantity, either the root or fruit causeth great sleepinesse, sadnesse, resolution, and languishing of the body, so that after many scritches and gripings, the patient falls asleep in the same posture as hee was in, just as if hee were in a Lethargie" (*The Workes of that famous Chirurgion Ambroise Parey*, trans. Thomas Johnson [London, 1634], 806) William Bullein remarks that it is "properly geuen to helpe conception, some say, as it appeereth by the Wyues of the holy Patryarche *Iacob*, The one was fruictful, the other did desire help, by the meanes of Mandracke, brought out of the fyeldes, by the handes of *Ruben Leas* sonne" (*Bulleins Bulwarke of Defence against All Sicknesse, Soarenesse, and Woundes that doe dayly assuaulte mankinde* [London, 1579], 41v–42).

19. Bullein writes, "Many . . . doe affyrme, that this herbe commeth of the seede of some conuicted dead men," and goes on to describe "the terrible shriek and cry of thys Mandrack. In which cry, it Doth not only dye it selfe, but the feare thereof kylleth the Dogge or Beast, whych pulled it out of the earth. And this hearbe is called also *Anthropomorphos* because it beareth the Image of a man" (*Bulleins Bulwarke*, 41v).

20. In response to Mercutio's claim "That dreamers often lie," he rebuts, "In bed asleep, where they do dream things true" (1.4.51–52).

21. See Marjorie Garber, "Dream Language in *Romeo and Juliet*," in *Dream in Shakespeare: From Metaphor to Metamorphosis* (New Haven and London: Yale University Press, 1974), 44–47. Garber suggests, however, that Romeo's dream is not false, as the resurrection it envisions is metaphorically borne out in the monuments that enshrine the lovers' memory.

22. M. M. Mahood, *Shakespeare's Wordplay* (London: Methuen, 1957), 72.

23. This passage must have hung in the mind of Anthony Munday when he was composing the ending of *The Death of Robert Earl of Huntington* (London, 1601): "See how he seekes to suck, if he could drawe, / Poyson from dead Matildaes ashie lips" (3005–3006).

24. Eleazer Dunk, *The Copy of a Letter written by E. D. [Eleazer Dunk] Doctour of Physicke to a Gentleman* (London, 1606), 31.

25. Ibid.

26. Bullein, *Bulleins Bulwarke*, 25v.

27. Timothy Bright, *A Treatise: Wherein is declared the sufficiencie of English Medicines, for cure of all diseases, cured with Medicine* (London, 1590), 15–16.

28. Philip Barrough, *The Method of Phisick, Containing the Causes, Signes, and Cures of Inward Diseases in Mans Body from the Head to the Foote* (London, 1596), 24.

29. André Du Laurens, *A Discourse of the Preservation of the Sight: of Melancholike diseases; of Rheumes, and of Old age*, trans. Richard Surphlet (London, 1599), 115.

30. Although Shakespeare's writings are not as saturated with medical imagery and references as are some of his contemporaries' plays, such as those of Jonson and Webster, doctors and apothecaries appear in a number of his plays, including *Cymbeline, King Lear, Macbeth*, and *All's Well That Ends Well*. Interestingly, in contrast to most contemporary literary portrayals of doctors as sinister and malicious, Shakespeare's doctors tend to be competent and kindly, and his observations about current medical treatments are for the most part very accurate. For more background on Shakespeare's medical knowledge and representations of doctors, see Robert Simpson, *Shakespeare and Medicine* (Edinburgh: E. & S. Livingston, 1959); and Herbert Silvette, *The Doctor on the Stage: Medicine and Medical Men in Seventeenth-Century England*, ed. Francelia Butler (Knoxville: University of Tennessee Press, 1967).

31. For an overview of medical perspectives on sleep in this period, see Karl H. Dannenfeldt, "Sleep: Theory and Practice in the Late Renaissance," *Journal of the History of Medicine and Allied Sciences* 41 (1986): 415–441.

32. Du Laurens, *Discourse*, 95.

33. Paré, *Workes*, 35.

34. He describes, for example, *"the Lethargie," "Carus or Subeth," "Congelation or taking,"* and *"dead sleepe*, or, *Coma"* (Barrough, *Method of Physick*, 24, 29, 30).

35. See David Bevington, "Asleep Onstage," in *From Page to Performance: Essays in Early English Drama*, ed. John A. Alford (East Lansing: Michigan State University Press, 1995), 51–83.

36. To point to merely a few other instances in Shakespeare, in *The Taming of the Shrew* a Lord asks of Christopher Sky, "What's here? One dead, or drunk" (Ind. 1.30); in *Henry IV, Part Two*, Hal mistakes his sleeping father for dead (4.5.21–47); and in *Cymbeline*, Lucius, like many others, wonders of Imogen, "Or dead or sleeping . . . ?" (4.2.356).

37. Puck in *A Midsummer Night's Dream*, for instance, encourages the audience to think "That you have but slumb'red here / While these visions did appear / And this weak and idle theme, / No more yielding but a dream" (5.1.425–428). The framing device for *The Taming of the Shrew* and Prospero's comments on sleep and theater at the end of *The Tempest* suggest the same model.

38. George Walton Williams comments on the play's uneasiness toward sleep in "Sleep in *Hamlet*," *Renaissance Papers 1964*, ed. S. K. Heninger, Peter G. Phialas, and George Walton Williams (Durham, N.C.: Southeastern Renaissance Conference, 1965), 17–20.

39. Other examples abound; in *Richard III*, the young princes are killed while sleeping in the tower (4.3.1–22).

40. Prynne, *Histriomastix*, 956.

41. Ibid., 946–947, emphasis in original.

42. Stephen Gosson, *The Schoole of Abuse* (London: Shakespeare Society, 1841), 14.

43. *Antony and Cleopatra* can be seen as reenacting essential aspects of *Romeo and Juliet* with older and more seasoned lovers. In both plays, lovers from opposing camps cross a political divide for the sake of a grand passion, yet the scheme undertaken to circumvent obstacles to their union—the female lover staging her own apparent death—leads to her lover's suicide and ultimately her own.

44. All references to *Antony and Cleopatra* are from M. R. Ridley's Arden edition (London: Methuen, 1954).

45. Cleopatra's theatricality has been discussed by a number of critics. For a sampling of arguments about their uses and effects, see Adelman, *Common Liar;* Jonathin Dollimore, "Shakespeare, Cultural Materialism, Feminism, and Marxist Humanism," *New Literary History* 21 (1990): 471–493; Heather James, "The Politics of Display and the Anamorphic Subjects of *Antony and Cleopatra*," in *Shakespeare's Late Tragedies,* ed. Susanne Wofford (Upper Saddle River, N.J.: Simon and Schuster, 1996), 208–234; Phyllis Rackin, "Shakespeare's Boy Cleopatra, the Decorum of Nature and the Golden World of Poetry," *PMLA* 87 (1972): 201–212; and Jyotsna Singh, "Renaissance Anti-Theatricality, Anti-Feminism, and Shakespeare's *Antony and Cleopatra*," *Renaissance Drama*, n.s., 20.

46. On imagery of dissolution and deliquescence, see especially Adelman, *Common Liar.*

47. The verb "prorogue" offers an interesting link with *Romeo and Juliet*, where it is used twice, both times in connection with the lovers' trials; at 2.2.78 Juliet declares dying preferable to postponing death for a life without Romeo, and at 4.1.48 the friar refers to the apparent impossibility of postponing Juliet's marriage to Paris. Shakespeare's only other use of the word comes after *Antony and Cleopatra*, in *Pericles.*

48. It should be noted that the audience does not, in fact, witness these two particular spectacles; both of them, like so much of the play, are reported secondhand. Perhaps Cleopatra's most effective performances, like a basilisk or Gorgon, can only be withstood through an oblique view.

49. Plutarch, "The Life of Marcus Antonius," *The Lives of the Noble Grecians and Romanes,* trans. Thomas North (London, 1579), 987.

50. Ibid., 998.

51. Plutarch, "Antony," *Plutarch's Lives,* ed. Bernadotte Perrin (London: William Heinemann, 1920), 37.4, 60.1.

52. On Antony's explicit links to Hercules throughout the play, see especially Eugene M. Waith, *The Herculean Hero in Marlowe, Chapman, Shakespeare, and Dryden* (New York: Columbia University Press, 1962).

53. According to myth, the shirt was given to Deianeira by the centaur Nessus, who was shot by Hercules with a poisoned arrow. Believing the shirt to be a love charm, Deianeira gave it to Hercules, unwittingly causing his death. The allusion represents the tragic culmination of Antony's Herculean unmanning, comically depicted earlier in the scene in which Cleopatra trades clothing with Antony ("I drunk him to his bed; / Then put my tires and mantles on him, whilst / I wore his sword Philippan" [2.5.21–23]), which alludes to Hercules's bondage to Omphale.

54. Arguing that Cleopatra's theatrical feigning is malicious, Laura Levine cites this scene as the basis for broader claims about the theater's dramatization of its own dangers: "Such a moment seem to cast theatre itself as something so potent and so dangerous it has the capacity to make its spectator go home and kill himself. It casts theatre, in other words, in terms much more bleak than the terms of the attacks." See *Men in Women's Clothing: Anti-Theatricality and Effeminization, 1579–1642* (Cambridge: Cambridge University Press, 1994), 2.

55. "Others say againe, she kept it in a boxe, and that she did pricke and thrust it with a spindell of golde, so that the Aspicke being angerd withal, lept out with great furie, and bitte her in the arme. Howbeit fewe can tell the troth. For they report also, that she had hidden poyson in a hollow raser which she caried in the heare of her head: and yet was there no marke seene of her bodie, or any signe discerned that she was poysoned, neither also did they finde this serpent in her tombe" (Plutarch, "Marcus Antonius," 1010).

56. Ibid, 1004. Interestingly, Cleopatra's experiments with poisons make an implicit reappearance in *Cymbeline,* when the physician Cornelius describes how the queen (probably played by the same boy actor who played Cleopatra) had practiced poisoning animals in preparing her attempted murder of Imogen (5.4.249–258).

DAVID SALTER

Shakespeare and Catholicism: The Franciscan Connection

In the early months of 1598, Thomas Speght, a relatively obscure English schoolmaster and antiquary, published a new edition of the *Works* of Geoffrey Chaucer: the first to appear in almost forty years.[1] With a few exceptions, Speght simply reproduced what he found in the earlier printed versions of Chaucer's *Works,* but his edition is notable for the fact that it is the first to employ (albeit in a rudimentary form), the beginnings of a critical, scholarly apparatus, designed to help overcome the difficulties that sixteenth-century readers were increasingly coming to experience when confronted by the obscurity of Chaucer's language, and more generally by the historical remoteness of his time.[2] Among the explanatory material that Speght included in his edition is a short biographical sketch of Chaucer, in which he outlined what he believed to be the principal facts of the poet's life.[3] While its relevance to the subject of Shakespeare's religious affiliations may not be immediately apparent, one particular incident from Speght's *Life of Chaucer* casts an unexpected light on the ways in which Catholicism was discussed and understood in the closing years of the sixteenth century. For this episode—a supposed encounter between Chaucer and a Franciscan friar—not only reflects the pervasive hostility to the Catholic Church that was the dominant discourse in England during Shakespeare's time, but it also highlights the important rhetorical role that the Franciscan Order had

Cahiers Élisabéthains: Late Medieval and Renaissance Studies, Volume 66 (Autumn 2004): pp. 9–22. Copyright © 2004 David Salter.

unwittingly come to play in anti-Catholic polemic. By considering the ways in which Shakespeare responds to this contemporary anti-Franciscan rhetoric we can shed some new light on the increasingly contested question of his own religious sensibilities and sympathies.

In the first instance, then, I shall approach the question of Shakespeare's relationship to Catholicism indirectly, through a consideration of this anecdote from Speght's biography of Chaucer. And I hope that this initial discussion, however tangential it might at first appear, will both clear the ground for, and provide a point of entry into, a more informed exploration of the tradition of anti-Franciscan writing—a tradition to which Shakespeare responded in such an original and singular way. I shall then, in the third and final part of this essay, turn to the plays themselves, examining the prominent Franciscans who figure in three of Shakespeare's best-known works: *Romeo and Juliet*, *Much Ado about Nothing* (which was written just a few months after the appearance of Speght's edition of Chaucer), and *Measure for Measure*.

***

The relevant section of Speght's biography deals with Chaucer's education. After spuriously identifying the poet as an alumnus of the universities of both Oxford and Cambridge, he goes on to discuss what might now be called Chaucer's postgraduate studies:

> About the latter end of King Richard the seconds daies he [Chaucer] florished in Fraunce, and got himselfe great comendation there by his diligent exercise in learning. After his returne home, he frequented the Court at London, and the Colledges of the Lawyers, which there interprete the lawes of the lande, and among them he had a familiar frend called John Gower [. . .] It seemeth that both these learned men [Chaucer and Gower] were of the inner Temple: for not many yeeres since, Master Buckley did see a Record in the same house, where Geoffrey Chaucer was fined two shillings for beating a Franciscane fryer in Fleetstreete.[4]

Although it is rather appealing to think of Chaucer as an impetuous young student, brought before the college authorities for brawling in the street, unfortunately—like virtually every other claim made by Speght in his short biography—it has no basis in fact.[5] Even if we simply consider the short extract just quoted, it is inaccurate in almost every detail. We now know that contrary to Speght's contention, Chaucer attended neither the University of Oxford nor Cambridge.[6] While Chaucer is known to have visited France on a number of occasions, he never lived there for a prolonged period of time.[7] And during the latter years of the reign of Richard II, far from being a student prone to youthful pranks—as Speght suggests—Chaucer was in fact well into middle age, and a highly respected public servant who had connections with some of the most powerful and influential figures in the land.[8] What is more, the claim that Chaucer was a student at the Inner Temple seems to be based on an anachronistic misreading of the history of that institution.[9] For although the Inns of Court—that is, Lincoln's Inn, Gray's Inn, the Inner Temple, and the Middle Temple—did indeed provide young students with a formal training in the law during Speght's lifetime (thereby assuming a function analogous to that of the two universities), recent studies have suggested that they had not developed this role at the end of the fourteenth century. At that time they simply acted as residences for practising lawyers from the provinces, who needed accommodation near Westminster during the law terms.[10] So, not only was Chaucer entirely the wrong age to be engaged in youthful high jinx at the time that Speght alleges, it would also seem that during his lifetime the Inner Temple did not even function as an educational institution, making it extremely unlikely, to say the least, that Chaucer was ever in attendance there as a student.[11]

But, if the incident reported by Speght could not possibly have occurred (or at least not in the way that he suggests), how can it advance our knowledge of Shakespeare's relationship to Catholicism, the subject of this essay? What new light might it cast upon the question of Shakespeare's religious convictions? Although not immediately apparent, the answer to these questions lies with the unfortunate Franciscan friar whom Chaucer is alleged to have beaten up on Fleet Street. For whatever the source of Speght's story, it is no coincidence that the victim of Chaucer's supposed attack—and, presumably, the source of his antipathy—was a member of that religious Order which later-sixteenth-century English Protestants had come to regard as the embodiment of everything that was wrong with the Church of Rome.[12] It is worth noting in this regard that throughout the second half of the sixteenth century, as Chaucer's reputation as the founding father of English poetry was repeatedly asserted, so too were his supposed sympathies for many of the causes that the Protestant reformers espoused.[13] So taking just one example among many, writing in the 1570 edition of his *Ecclesiastical History*, John Foxe, the great propagandist of the English Reformation, felt able to appropriate Chaucer on behalf of the Protestant cause by claiming that the poet "saw in Religion as much almost as we do now".[14] Ironically, Chaucer's reputation as a fierce critic of the Catholic Church, and as a figure whose works brought his readers—again to quote Foxe—"to the true knowledge of religion",[15] was based in part on two violently anti-Catholic satires that were falsely attributed to him during the sixteenth century: *Jack Upland* and *The Plowman's Tale*, of which the first is a virulent attack on none other than the Franciscan Order.[16] Viewed in this context, then, it would seem that for

Chaucer's sixteenth-century Protestant readers, beating up a Franciscan friar was no mere random or casual act of violence, but a calculated and highly charged political statement, to be seen as a natural continuation or extension of the poet's writing. For Speght's anecdote would appear to suggest that such was Chaucer's hostility to the Catholic Church, that he could not confine his criticism of it simply to the realm of satire. Rather, his antagonism was so virulent that he expressed it in the form of a violent physical assault on that most representative of Catholic figures—a Franciscan friar. While the pen maybe mightier than the sword, Speght's thinking seems to run, it is no substitute for the fist.

At the time that Shakespeare was working as a playwright in London, then, the Franciscan Order fulfilled a distinct and well-recognised role in Protestant discourse. How the Order came to assume this function is a question to which I shall turn shortly, but what is worth noting at the moment is that for sixteenth-century English Protestants, writing about Franciscans had become an established shorthand way of attacking, satirising, and generally pillorying the Catholic Church. And as noted earlier, this is of particular relevance to a discussion of Shakespeare because three of his plays—*Romeo and Juliet, Much Ado about Nothing,* and *Measure for Measure*—feature prominent Franciscan characters. Gauging the extent to which, and the manner in which, Shakespeare's sympathies are genuinely engaged by his Franciscan figures, will thus provide us with one means of assessing his relationship more generally towards the religious controversies of his time.

Until recently, the question of Shakespeare's religious affiliations provoked relatively little interest from critics—at least compared to other areas of his life and work—although there is a long-standing (if somewhat marginal) critical tradition that has identified him as a Catholic. Perhaps the principal reason why this issue was relegated to the critical sidelines was because Shakespearean drama was generally seen as a predominantly secular form.[17] Indeed, the whole history of the English theatre in the sixteenth century has traditionally been viewed as a kind of evolutionary narrative, in which—with the exception of a brief period in the middle of the century dominated by religious plays—succeeding generations of playwrights were thought to have progressively freed themselves from the influence of religion and the Church. Thus, the so-called "primitive" religious drama of the early 1500s is said to have given way to ever more secular and sophisticated forms, culminating at the end of the century with the entirely secular theatre of Shakespeare and his contemporaries.[18] And this Whiggish interpretation of sixteenth-century literary history is one that has cast Shakespeare—however implicitly—in a Protestant mould, in that it has aligned him with the forces of progress and reform, and in opposition to what came to be seen as the irrational and superstitious tendencies manifest in the earlier drama associated with Catholic ritual and practice. What is more, Shakespeare's identification as the national poet has further consolidated his association with the national religion. And the fact that Shakespearean drama tends to steer clear of religious controversy—unlike the militantly Protestant writings of such figures as Spenser and Milton—only bolstered the view that his was the kind of restrained and understated Protestantism that is now so closely identified with the Anglican Church.[19]

However, while mainstream critical opinion labelled Shakespeare a Protestant, albeit one of a secular bent, a succession of opposing voices going all the way back to Shakespeare's own lifetime, identified him as a Catholic.[20] Among the best-known exponents of this view were Thomas Carlyle, who famously described Shakespeare in his 1840 lecture on "The Hero as Poet" as the noblest product of the Catholicism of the Middle Ages, and Cardinal John Henry Newman, who in 1873 declared that Shakespeare was "at heart a Catholic". This is a view that has been enthusiastically taken up in recent years, based in part on newly interpreted biographical evidence suggesting that Shakespeare's family remained loyal to the old faith in the later sixteenth-century, despite suffering persecution.[21] Moreover, Shakespeare's personal allegiance to the old faith may have been further consolidated if we are to accept the increasingly popular theory that he entered the service of the Catholic Houghton family in Lancashire during the 1580s.[22] And in addition to the biographical evidence pointing to a Catholic affiliation—or at the very least association—on Shakespeare's part, a number of recent studies have argued that his Catholic sympathies are reflected in the plays themselves.[23]

While offering some support to this Catholic interpretation of Shakespeare and his work, the approach I shall be adopting here is somewhat different from those that I have outlined above. For, whatever the methods they employ and the conclusions they ultimately reach, debate on Shakespeare and religion—not surprisingly or unreasonably—has focused on the figure of Shakespeare himself. Where my approach differs, a difference that I hope is reflected in the title of my essay, is that I shall be examining Shakespeare's treatment of Franciscans not only as a means of gauging his own religious sympathies and convictions, but also to throw light upon the use that Shakespeare (and a number of his contemporaries) made of the Franciscan Order. In this way we will gain a better understanding of its broader cultural significance in post-Reformation England. In so doing, I shall consider what it was about the Order that appealed so greatly to Shakespeare. For if, as I shall argue, he stands outside the Protestant tradition of anti-Franciscan writing—a tradition evident in Speght's *Life of Chaucer*—why did he choose to present such highly controversial figures in his plays? What artistic opportunities did the Franciscan Order offer him? Was his use of Franciscans ideologically motivated? What areas of human experience did their presence in the plays allow him to explore?

In the pages that follow, I shall consider each of Shakespeare's three "Franciscan" plays in the order in which they were produced, starting with *Romeo and Juliet* (which is believed to have been written in 1594), moving onto *Much Ado about Nothing* (composed approximately four years later in 1598), and concluding with a discussion of *Measure for Measure* (which is thought to have been completed either in late 1603 or early 1604). But, in order to understand the nature of Shakespeare's engagement with the Franciscan movement, it is first necessary to look briefly at the set of literary and artistic conventions that were associated with the Order in the Renaissance, and that shaped the ways in which it was represented and understood. For, although I shall argue that Shakespeare's Franciscans constitute a radical departure from the way in which the Order was conventionally depicted, the novelty and originality of his Franciscan protagonists can only fully be appreciated when they are set alongside the stereotypical figures that represent the norm.

Perhaps the best way to describe the complex amalgam of conventions and protocols that governed literary depictions of the Franciscans is to explain how they came into force. For the turbulent history of the Order lies behind and feeds into the literary representations of its members.

***

The famous fresco of *The Dream of Innocent III* in the basilica of the Upper Church of San Francesco in Assisi (a work that is often attributed to Giotto) provides a useful point of entry into the cultural history of the Franciscan Order (see p. 13). Although the veracity of Innocent's dream has often been called into question, an event of great historical significance nonetheless lies behind the image.[24] In 1210, Francis of Assisi—accompanied by his first twelve followers—travelled to Rome to seek approval and official sanction from Pope Innocent III for the religious Order that he was hoping to establish. Adopting the name *fratres minores,* or lesser brothers, Francis required members of his Order to observe literally and in every degree the life of preaching and absolute poverty, which—according to the Gospels—was followed by Christ and his disciples. Innocent was said to have been impressed by Francis's piety and sincerity, but he feared that the Rule he was proposing was too austere. However, the fresco depicts the divinely inspired dream Innocent is said to have experienced that night, which convinced him to grant his approval to the Order. Hence, in the fresco, on the right of the composition Innocent can be seen lying asleep in bed, while on the left the artist has represented his dream. In the latter a church (which the legend identifies as the papal basilica), is in a state of near ruin, and only the presence of Francis—who can be seen physically supporting the building with his shoulder—prevents its complete collapse.[25]

The Dream of Innocent III brings together a number of important factors that were to prove crucial in determining how the Order was subsequently perceived and understood, by both its supporters and its detractors. Clearly, the basilica's unstable edifice is a particularly apt metaphor for the allegedly ruinous spiritual state of the Church, and Francis—and by implication the Order he founded—is seen to play a crucial role in restoring its integrity and stability. However, from the point of view of the present discussion, what is of even greater significance is that the image reveals just how intimately the history of the Order was bound up with that of the Papacy. From its very inception—and often to the dismay of Francis himself—the Order functioned as the instrument of papal policy.[26] The popes of the early thirteenth century saw that the Church was in desperate need of reform (or, to adopt the symbolic language of Innocent's dream, perilously close to collapse), and Francis and his followers provided them with the ideal means of tackling the crisis that they faced.[27]

Paradoxically, however, the power and prestige that the Papacy conferred on St Francis and his followers acted as a source of conflict within the wider Church. The bishops and priests in whose diocese and parishes the Franciscans were sent often resented the intrusion into their jurisdiction, and the competition that these interlopers provided. And because the Order was founded on such high and exacting ideals, any suggestion of moral compromise on the part of the friars laid them open to accusations of hypocrisy. For although they were supposed to lead lives of mendicancy and itinerancy, it was claimed that in reality the friars were far from sparing in their pursuit of material comforts.[28]

Such charges gave rise to a critical discourse which ossified into particular tropes highlighting a popular view of Franciscan corruption, typically including traits such as hypocrisy, greed, carnality, and lechery. While it had its origins in clerical controversy, such a disparaging construction of the Franciscan friar swiftly found its way into popular literary forms such as comic tales and satires.[29] What it is important to note, however, is that this was a Catholic literary tradition, arising out of a particular conflict between two competing models of Church governance. On the one hand, there was the traditional understanding of ecclesiastical organisation based on bishops holding—through apostolic succession—autonomy within their own dioceses, free from interference from Rome. On the other hand, there was a more centralised and centralising conception of the Church, with the Pope claiming the right to intervene in all ecclesiastical affairs. Because the Franciscan Order was perceived as a tool of this centralising papal tendency, it became a natural target of wider resentment within the Church as a whole. Therefore, one obvious way to attack papal policy was by attacking the Franciscans.

It is important to realise that Catholic writing critical of the Franciscan Order was not simply a response to the fact that the Order failed to live up to the ideals it espoused—it often reflected fundamental differences in the ecclesiology of the Catholic Church. So in the Catholic tradition, Franciscans could be attacked for not being Catholic enough, in that they were seen to exist outside existing structures, hierarchies, and identities. According to their critics, they were neither priests nor monks, and so both literally and figuratively they had no fixed abode within the Church.[30] In this context, far from Innocent III's original vision, the Order was perceived in many quarters not as the mainstay of the Church, but as the most obvious threat to its stability.

It is not surprising that in the wake of the Reformation this tradition of anti-Franciscan writing appealed to and was appropriated by English Protestant writers, although the transition from a Catholic to a Protestant milieu reveals both continuities and differences. On one level, the reformers were able simply to repeat the criticisms of Franciscans that they found in Catholic works, albeit applying them to radically different ends. The corruptions and abuses that Catholic critics accused the Franciscans of committing could now profitably be turned against the Roman Church as a whole. As a result, Protestant polemic was able to take advantage of this ready-made mode of attack.

Although the Order was suppressed in England in the early years of the Reformation, Franciscan friars continued to maintain a visible presence in Protestant literature, with attacks on Franciscans forming a commonplace of anti-Catholic polemic from Bale to Milton and beyond. Among the better-known instances of such writing is Marlowe's *Doctor Faustus*. When initially confronted by Mephistophiles, the devil's appearance is too awful for Faustus to bear, so he dismisses the spirit with the command: "Go and return an old Franciscan friar / That holy shape becomes a devil best" (3, 26–27).[31] And this disparagingly comic attack on the Order of St Francis is of a piece with the strongly anti-Catholic tone of the play as a whole, particularly given the jokes Faustus plays upon the Pope in Rome, who is, of course, surrounded by a retinue of friars.

In John Webster's *The White Devil,* once again we find the Franciscan habit used as a cloak to disguise evil intentions. In the last act of the play, two followers of the aptly named Francesco, Duke of Florence, disguise themselves as Capuchin friars (the Capuchins being a branch of the Franciscan Order established in 1525, in an attempt to restore the movement to the austerity and simplicity that it originally espoused). Under the mask of holiness that their borrowed habits confer, the two disguised Franciscans bring

the drama to a suitably bloody conclusion by assassinating a whole host of
their master's enemies, in ever more cruel and sadistic fashion.[32] In Webster's
drama, then, not only are Franciscans identified with violence and hypocrisy,
but there is also the strong implication that these traits—particularly when
undertaken with characteristic Italian chic—are somehow typical of Catholicism in general.

But the appropriation of this mode of satire for distinctly Protestant
ends is perhaps even more pronounced in George Whetstone's Elizabethan
rendering of a tale from Boccaccio's *Decameron*, in which the translation from
Italian to English also involves a cultural transposition from a Catholic to a
Protestant ethos. In Boccaccio's version of the story, which is set in Venice, a
lecherous Franciscan, Frate Alberto, persuades a gullible woman that she is
the lucky recipient of the Angel Gabriel's amorous attentions. However, the
friar tells the woman that because mere mortals are unable to enjoy sexual
intimacy with angels, Gabriel wishes to come to her in human form—and not
surprisingly the form that the Angel chooses to adopt is that of Frate Alberto
himself. Only after a considerable length of time is the friar exposed through
the vanity of the woman, who boasts to her friend of her special status as the
Angel Gabriel's lover.[33] But while Boccaccio's tale focuses on the cupidity of
friars and the gullibility of women, Whetstone's translation, which appeared
in 1582, goes much further. First he moves the action from Venice to rural
Umbria, with the specific intention of providing the birthplace of St Francis
as the setting of the tale. (Whetstone indicates at the very beginning of his
narrative that its setting is: "a little Village among the Appenine Mountaynes
not far from the place, where Sainct Frances lyeth intomed".)[34] The reason
for this geographical shift is that in the English Protestant version of the
tale, the young woman is told that it is the spirit of St Francis himself, rather
than the Angel Gabriel, that intends to visit her, again through the medium
of the friar's body. And in making these changes, Whetstone considerably
widens the scope of his attack. For in addition to the corruption of friars and
the stupidity of women, his satirical target also includes the Catholic culture
of rural Italy, with its roots firmly set in superstition and ignorance—the very
bonds which Protestant writers believed held Catholics in thrall. (Whetstone
thus notes that in the mountainous region of central Italy where the tale is
set, Franciscans are revered "rather for their habyt, than their honestie: *for
the poor ignorant people,* reverenced Sainct Frances, as a seconde Christe, for
whose sake, they hold his Disciples, not inferior to Saincts".)[35] Moreover,
the replacement of the Angel Gabriel by St Francis himself as the woman's
putative suitor, adds a further level of anti-Franciscan satire to the tale. At no
point does the woman query the saint's intentions: his lechery is simply taken
for granted.

***

This brief account of the origins and development of the tradition of anti-Franciscan writing enables us to consider Shakespeare's friars in their proper historical and cultural context, allowing us better to assess any religious or extra-literary significance they might possess. And perhaps what is most immediately apparent when examining *Romeo and Juliet* from the perspective of this literary tradition is just how deliberately and emphatically Shakespeare identifies the character of Friar Lawrence as a Franciscan. Two of Lawrence's own utterances—"Holy Saint Francis" (II.1.65), and "Saint Francis be my speed!" (V.3.121)—clearly point to his Franciscan affiliation, while he is called "Holy Franciscan friar" (V.2.1) by his fellow mendicant, Friar John.[36] Moreover, Friar Lawrence swears by his "holy Order" (III.3.113), and elsewhere in the play his priestly office and membership of a religious brotherhood are repeatedly emphasised. So Lawrence is no mere generic priest or friar; rather, he is quite explicitly identified as a Franciscan. Bearing in mind what we have observed in the work of Marlowe, Webster, and Whetstone, such an identification might lead us to expect the portrait of friar Lawrence to be somehow derogatory or satirical. And the earlier versions of the story—both English and Continental—certainly offered Shakespeare a great deal of scope to present the role in such a way. However, far from exploiting the character of Friar Lawrence for partisan Protestant ends, Shakespeare portrays his Franciscan in a far more positive light, investing him with a great deal of moral and dramatic authority.

Shakespeare's principal source for *Romeo and Juliet* was Arthur Brooke's *The Tragicall Historye of Romeus and Juliet* (published in 1562), which was itself a translation—through an intermediary French version—of Matteo Bandello's Italian novella: *"La sfortunata morte di dui infelicissimi amanti . . ."* ("The unfortunate death of two most wretched lovers . . ."). Bandello's account of the story (which was first published in 1554) was in turn based on an even earlier Italian source: a novella by Luigi da Porto, which was the first version of the tale to be set in Verona, to call the warring families Montecchi and Capelletti (Shakespeare's Montagues and Capulets), to give the lovers the names of Romeo and Giulietta, to identify the friar as a Franciscan, and to name him Lorenzo (Lawrence).[37]

Significantly, both of these Italian versions of the tale reveal a residual distrust of Frate Lorenzo, whose motives are never above suspicion. Nowhere is this more apparent than in the famous scene in the Capelletti crypt, when Giulietta awakes from her death-like sleep to find herself unexpectedly lying next to a man. This is, of course, the body of her dying lover, Romeo, but Giulietta at first suspects that it is Frate Lorenzo who is lying by her side, presumably because this is the kind of base and lecherous conduct that one expects from a Franciscan in the world of Italian novelle.[38] While Giulietta's misgivings in this case prove to be unfounded, both da Porto and Bandello repeatedly draw attention to the self-serving motivation underlying the friar's actions. For instance, we are told that the reason why Lorenzo befriends Romeo in the first place is because he is powerful and influential.[39] In addition, the friar agrees to assist the lovers in their plan to marry, not simply because he believes that their union will bring about the reconciliation of their two households, but more importantly, in the hope that his role in ending the family feud will be fully recognised and rewarded.[40]

As he appears in the work of both da Porto and Bandello, then, Frate Lorenzo is an extremely equivocal figure, and it is his role as a Franciscan friar that seems to lie behind and provoke much—if not all—of his emotional ambivalence. On the one hand, as a member of a religious Order, Lorenzo is not bound by ties of loyalty or patronage to either of the two warring families, which enables him to adopt a neutral position in their dispute, and to retain the trust and confidence of both sides. And it is for this reason that although Romeo and Giulietta come from the two rival households—and so have no prior knowledge of one another—they know Frate Lorenzo equally well, and hold him in equally high esteem. Thus, Lorenzo's narrative function within the tale is made possible by virtue of his membership of the Franciscan Order, which confers on him a freedom of movement and association that no other character enjoys, and a detachment from the family feud that so dominates the world of the story.[41] On the other hand, however, and as we have already seen, the suspicion and distrust that generally characterises the portrayal of Franciscans in Italian novelle can be discerned in the treatment of Frate Lorenzo. As Giulietta reveals in the crypt, while the friar seems to enjoy the confidence of all the protagonists, this trust is only skin deep, and even the good that he does perform is shown to be self-serving in its underlying motivation.

There would therefore appear to be a jarring discrepancy—even conflict—between the generic portrayal of Franciscans in Italian novelle, and the actual narrative function of Frate Lorenzo. For, whereas the friar labours under the cloud of doubt and suspicion that characterises literary representations of his Order, the narrative role he is assigned requires him to be a figure who inspires confidence and trust. And the ambivalence that inevitably results from this mismatch between expectation and function is all the more pronounced in Arthur Brooke's English version of the tale, which—as was noted earlier—was Shakespeare's immediate source.

As one might expect from an English Protestant like Brooke, his portrayal of Fryer Lawrence is deeply coloured by the conventions of anti-Catholic polemic, and nowhere is this disdain for the Church of Rome more apparent than in his prefatory address to the reader:

And to this ende (good Reader) is this tragicall matter written, to describe unto thee a coople of unfortunate lovers, thralling themselves to unhonest desire, neglecting the authoritie and advise of parents and frendes, conferring their principall counsels with dronken gossyppes, *and superstitious friers (the naturally fitte instrumentes of unchastitie)* attemptyng all adventures of peryll, for thattaynyng of their wished lust.[42]

Brooke is particularly explicit in condemning the Catholic sacrament of "auricular confession" administered by Fryer Lawrence, which in Brooke's view is the "kay of whoredome, and treason", and which he sees as crucial in "hastyng [Romeus and Juliet] to most unhappye deathe".

So the impression gained from Brooke's prefatory address would seem to be clear and unambiguous. Far from being the victims either of fate, circumstance, or their tyrannical parents, Romeus and Juliet are themselves responsible for their own demise. By selfishly putting their own sexual gratification before the duty of obedience they owe their families, they bear the full burden of guilt and culpability. Moreover, "the superstitious" Fryer Lawrence—a figure of no higher moral standing than a "dronken gossyppe"—wilfully aids and abets the lovers in their perfidious course of action, using the secret, even occultist, rituals of the Catholic Church to achieve his perverse ends.

But, turning from Brooke's prefatory address to the poem itself, a very different picture both of the lovers and of the friar emerges. As Geoffrey Bullough notes, the tone of moral condemnation so pronounced in the preface disappears entirely in the main narrative, giving way to a sympathetic and sentimental portrait of the young couple, whose loving marriage is presented as wholly admirable.[43] This same transformation occurs in Brooke's treatment of Fryer Lawrence. Rather than the anti-Catholic stereotype depicted in the preface, the friar of the poem is a model of virtuous, restrained, moderation. Prompted by motives of pure, disinterested friendship and a genuine desire for civic harmony, he agrees to assist the lovers, offering them wise and reasonable advice throughout. So it is the capriciousness of fate, and not the recklessness or perversity of the friar and the lovers, that brings about the tragic conclusion. And what is so remarkable about this volte-face on Brooke's part is that he seems to be almost totally oblivious of any inconsistency, and he makes no attempt to harmonise the discrepancy between the preface and the main narrative. Perhaps the closest Brooke comes to acknowledging— albeit implicitly—any disparity in his presentation of Lawrence is when he first introduces the friar. For while emphasising Lawrence's goodness and wisdom, Brooke also notes that these qualities tend not to be shared by most members of the Franciscan Order:

This barefoote fryer gyrt with cord his grayish
                                                    weede,
For he of Frauncis order was, a fryer as I reede,
Not as the most was he, a grosse unlearned foole,
But doctor of divinitie proceded he in schoole.
[...]
Of all he is beloved well, and honord much of all.
And for he did the rest in wisdome farre exceede,
The prince by him his counsell cravde and holpe at
                                                    time of neede.
      (ll. 565–568 & 578–580).

The difficulty Brooke seems to face, here, is in reconciling his own antagonism to the Catholic Church—to which the tradition of anti-Franciscan satire
gives such full expression—with the demands and logic of the narrative,
which requires Fryer Lawrence to be a sympathetic figure, who commands
the respect not just of the two lovers, but of Verona society more generally. By characterizing the typical Franciscan as "a grosse unlearned foole",
thereby implying that Fryer Lawrence is something of an anomaly, Brooke
is—to a certain extent—able to square this particular circle. But there still
remain, the fundamental opposition between the dogmatic demands of religious polemic on the one hand, and the requirements of the narrative on the
other, and when taken as a whole, *The Tragicall Historye of Romeus and Juliet*
leaves this opposition unresolved.

The emotional ambivalence that so characterises Brooke's conception of
the friar is conspicuously absent from the protagonist who appears in Shakespeare's *Romeo and Juliet*. Shakespeare completely discards the polemical
subtext that inflects all of the previous portraits of Friar Lawrence—whether Catholic or Protestant—and presents instead a figure of unquestionable
moral integrity. Indeed, Shakespeare seems to go out of his way completely
to exonerate Lawrence of blame for the tragic events in which he plays a
part. Hence, in the final scene of the play, and after all of the unhappy circumstances have been fully brought to light, the Prince clears Friar Lawrence
of any guilt for the lovers' death, indicating: "We still have known thee for a
holy man" (V.3.270). And as the ultimate and undisputed source of authority
within the play, the Prince's judgement commands the respect not just of the
protagonists on stage, but of the audience as well.

Shakespeare thus appears to have had no interest in exploiting the satirical or polemical possibilities presented by the figure of Friar Lawrence, a
temptation to which all of his predecessors had succumbed. Instead, Shakespeare's Franciscan can be said to function more in an archetypal than a
satirical mode.[44] For rather than being a vehicle for anti-Catholic sentiment,

he is presented as a sage who officiates mage-like over both the sacred and secular rites of the play, overseeing the marriage of the young couple, which he hopes will then bring about the civil union of their warring families. (And significantly, there is absolutely nothing self-serving at work here: Friar Lawrence has no wish for recognition or preferment; it is simply the interests of the lovers, and the wider civic good that motivates his actions.) Moreover, as the only character who bridges different worlds and stands above the fray, Shakespeare's friar enjoys the neutrality and detachment that the narrative demands of his role, and yet his priestly office transcends the limiting and limited parameters fixed by the conventions of both Catholic and Protestant anti-Franciscan writing. In his Shakespearean incarnation, then, Friar Lawrence attains the disinterestedness, the capacity to be—in the words of Northrop Frye—"detached but not withdrawn", that is so conspicuously lacking in all of the previous versions of the role.

***

The archetypal functions performed by Friar Lawrence are even more pronounced in romance than in tragedy. The key figure responsible for bringing about the happy ending in *Much Ado about Nothing* is none other than a Friar Francis, whose name alone seems to carry with it an obvious significance, but with none of the polemical baggage of religious controversy. In *Much Ado*, Shakespeare successfully rewrites the ending of *Romeo and Juliet* in romance terms, with Friar Francis triumphantly achieving the marital and civic harmony that eluded Friar Lawrence.

Despite the difference of genre, there are nonetheless compelling structural and thematic affinities connecting *Romeo and Juliet* and *Much Ado about Nothing*. On the most basic and straightforward level, both plays are set in Italy, and each uses a novella of Matteo Bandello as a principal source.[45] In addition, they both centre on young lovers who for one reason or another experience problems in successfully passing from a single to a married state. Adopting an anthropological approach, here, it could be said that the two plays are concerned with marriage as a rite of passage; that is, with marriage as a ritualised ceremony whose purpose—to quote Joseph Campbell—is "to conduct people across those difficult thresholds of transformation that demand a change in the patterns not only of conscious but also of unconscious life".[46] As we have already seen, in the case of *Romeo and Juliet* it is impossible for the young couple to live together openly as husband and wife, because the warring feud between their two families prevents them from publicly acknowledging their relationship. In *Much Ado about Nothing* on the other hand, Claudio mistakenly believes that Hero, his betrothed, has a lover, and for this reason he violently denounces and then rejects her during the wedding ceremony itself. So while the particular problems confronting Claudio and Hero are very different from those facing Romeo and Juliet, when viewed in anthropological terms, the result in both cases is that the lovers' transition from a single to a married state is blocked.

It is here that the similarity in the role of the two Franciscans becomes apparent, for both friars seek to assist the couples in successfully negotiating the pitfalls that hinder or impede their respective marriages. Not only does Friar Lawrence officiate at the wedding of Romeo and Juliet, but he also offers Juliet what she hopes will be a way of preventing her enforced and bigamous marriage to Paris—a sleeping potion that so paralyses the senses that it seems to kill those who take it. And just as Friar Lawrence urges Juliet to feign death in order to achieve a full-married life with Romeo, so Friar Francis tells Hero that she must "die to live" (IV.1.253).[47] For the one way to bring about the hoped-for marital union—the friar argues—is to let it be known that Hero is dead, since it is only by making Claudio feel remorse for his actions, and so causing him to experience a sense of personal loss for Hero's supposed death, that he will come to a proper understanding of her true worth.

In each of the two plays, then, the heroines experience a form of symbolic death, but it is an ordeal that they both have to undergo in order to have at least the prospect of a new life. And it is the two friars—Lawrence and Francis—who oversee these mysterious, quasi-magical rites. Of course, it is significant that the attempt to resurrect Juliet fails, whereas Hero successfully passes through the ritual of death and rebirth, but this is not a reflection on the relative moral worth of the two Franciscans, rather it is a consequence of the different narrative trajectories of tragedy and romantic-comedy. (To quote Byron's somewhat flippant comments from *Don Juan:* "All tragedies are finished by a death / All comedies are ended by a marriage").[48] Moreover, that the conclusion of *Much Ado about Nothing* is a self-conscious reworking of *Romeo and Juliet* is further suggested by the fact that Friar Francis is an invention of Shakespeare's—there is no precedent for the role in any of the play's sources. Shakespeare can therefore be said almost to have reprised the role of Friar Lawrence when writing *Much Ado about Nothing,* a role that he transposed into comic-romantic terms. Or to quote Geoffrey Bullough, Friar Francis is none other than "Friar Lawrence up to his old tricks again".[49]

The shift from tragedy to romantic-comedy gives Shakespeare the chance to exploit much more fully the narrative opportunities inherent in the role of the friar. Appearing only at the moment of crisis, when his wisdom is most needed, Friar Francis emerges as the key to unlocking the romantic possibilities that seem impossibly remote after Claudio's humiliation of Hero. Without Francis there can be no happy ending, for in devising the plan to resurrect a woman mistakenly thought to be dead, he manages not simply to re-unite the lovers, but to re-establish civil harmony as well. As with Friar

Lawrence, Shakespeare invests an enormous amount of moral and narrative authority in Friar Francis, although his significance is in many ways even greater than that of his predecessor. Because he functions not in the tragic milieu of *Romeo and Juliet,* but in the comic world of romance, his almost mystical presence is all the more acceptable and exploitable on a dramatic level. It is his archetypal role to oversee a number of typical romance movements towards resolution and the establishment of harmony. For instance, he is responsible for the shift at the end of the play from a state of penitence and guilt on Claudio's part to one of forgiveness and reconciliation. Likewise, he assists the couple in their passage from youthful immaturity to the adult world of marital responsibility. On a grander scale, a corollary to these transformations could be seen in any one of a number of the archetypal romance movements to which critics such as Northrop Frye draw attention.[50] For in Frye's terms, Friar Francis can be seen as the agent of those romantic, cyclical patterns that underpin the appearance of new life out of death, or more generally the emergence of hope and renewal—symbolised by marriage—when all seemed bleak and sterile. In this sense, then, Friar Francis does indeed fulfil a sacred function, but it is not one that is confined to the strictures laid down in either Catholic or Protestant discourse. As a figure working in alignment with—and as an instrument of—the natural forces of cyclical renewal, Friar Francis can be said to exude a spirituality that in some respects is more pagan than Christian. As Northrop Frye notes: "when [the resolution of a Shakespearean comedy] is accomplished by a human being [...] that character has about him something of the mysterious aura of divinity, symbolised by magic or sanctity".[51]

***

What is surprising about the two friars we have encountered so far is that they are unusual—if not unprecedented—in going beyond the imaginative possibilities typically or stereotypically assigned to Franciscans in both Catholic and Protestant popular literature. However, in *Measure for Measure,* the last of Shakespeare's three "Franciscan" plays, the business of friars and their presentation becomes much more complicated. This is partly because we are presented not with a friar *per se,* but with the secular figure of Duke Vincentio, the prince of Vienna, who disguises himself as a friar in order secretly to observe how his deputy, Angelo, administers justice in his absence. The Duke's adoption of the friar's habit for the purpose of disguise renders his status somewhat ambiguous, for he undertakes some of the sacred duties of a priest, only to cast off the friar's costume at the end of the play when he reassumes his role as a secular ruler. But, while the precise nature of the Duke's religious identity is never fully clarified, the play does have a genuine Franciscan protagonist whose credentials are beyond dispute.

Isabella is a member of the sisterhood of St Clare—the second of the three Franciscan Orders—although she is still a novice, having yet to make her final vows.

As is the case with *Much Ado about Nothing*, the religious or quasi-religious figures of *Measure for Measure*—the Franciscan nun and the disguised friar—are not to be found in any of the play's sources; they are seemingly Shakespeare's invention.[52] Their presence in the play therefore suggests Shakespeare's continuing interest in the dramatic possibilities presented by Franciscans. But while in some respects *Measure for Measure* does revisit ground already explored in the two earlier plays, the inclusion of the element of disguise radically alters the way in which these by now familiar situations and concerns are worked out.

As suggested above, when disguised as Friar Lodowick, the dramatic function of the Duke is in many ways similar to that of Friar Lawrence and Friar Francis. He seeks to bring about justice and to repair the torn fabric of the characters' social and emotional lives by reuniting lovers and solving family crises. In this way, he also oversees the same romantic movement within the plot evident in *Much Ado about Nothing*, although in the case of *Measure for Measure* there are two couples—Claudio and Juliet, and Angelo and Mariana—who are brought together by the Friar-Duke. And once again, the play hinges on the failure of these couples successfully to negotiate unaided the pitfalls and impediments associated with marriage as a rite of passage. On the one hand, Claudio and Juliet gain sexual knowledge of one another before their marriage has been sanctified and legally sanctioned by a legitimate wedding ceremony, while on the other, Angelo rejects Mariana because she is unable to provide him with a sufficiently large dowry. During the course of the play, then, Friar Lodowick attempts to resolve all of the sources of contention and antagonism—whether legal, social, or emotional—that prevent the two couples from entering into a full-married life. In addition, *Measure for Measure* enacts the same ritualised pattern of symbolic death and rebirth that we have observed in *Much Ado about Nothing*. Claudio faces execution for breaking Vienna's "strict statutes and most biting laws" (I.3.19) against fornication.[53] But at the behest of Friar Lodowick the death sentence is not carried out, a fact that is kept from both the legal authorities and Claudio's family. Claudio is kept in hiding until the very end of the play, when his dramatic reappearance has an air of the miraculous, analogous to the "resurrection" of Hero at the end of *Much Ado*. And once again, it is a friar—or at least a friar in disguise—who oversees this seemingly magical rite.

However, while *Measure for Measure* repeats much that is familiar from the earlier plays, the fact that the Duke is a feigned rather than a real friar complicates and makes problematic his role.[54] In part, because he is a secular ruler policing his realm, the disguise serves an ulterior political purpose.

But, even more problematically, the Duke's role as a friar is conflated—and in conflict—with his role as a lover. As a friar, he is of course licensed to roam freely through the city and to access all areas of people's lives, and in that role he commands the trust of those around him. As we have already noted, friars enjoyed the freedom to mix with all strata of society, or in the Duke's words, "to visit both prince and people" (I.3.45), and it is precisely this privilege that makes the role of a friar so amenable to the Duke's purposes. However, the trust, conferred on the Duke by his adoption of the friar's habit is compromised because he seems to use it for his own personal advantage, both as a ruler and as a suitor to Isabella. The Duke has therefore none of the selfless detachment that is so characteristic of Friar Lawrence and Friar Francis. Indeed, there is more than a hint of emotional manipulation at work here. The Duke's actions expose him to the accusation that in the guise of a friar he is granted—and takes full advantage of—the opportunity to inveigle himself into Isabella's affections while her guard is down. As a nun, Isabella naturally trusts, respects, and confides in the figure of Friar Lodowick, whom she believes to be a fellow Franciscan, and whom she consequently treats as a spiritual guide and mentor. The false pretext under which the Duke is introduced to—and establishes a relationship with—Isabella, perhaps renders her unduly susceptible to his powers of influence and persuasion. In other words, it could be argued that part of what defines *Measure for Measure* as a problem play rests with the Duke's use, and possible abuse, of the friar's habit.

The problems and complications of *Measure for Measure* notwithstanding, I hope that what this study has demonstrated is the originality of Shakespeare's use of Franciscans—an originality that stems from what appears to be a complete lack of interest on his part in exploiting the friars for polemical or satirical ends. For Shakespeare carves roles for his friars that transcend the narrow strictures and limitations that define and confine the Franciscans found in the popular literature of both the medieval and the Renaissance periods.

However, placing these three plays in the broader context of anti-Franciscan writing inevitably raises the moot question of what—if anything—they reveal about Shakespeare's religious sympathies. In a climate where hostility to friars was almost an unconscious Protestant reflex, the fact that Shakespeare presents such sympathetic Franciscans appears to carry a great deal of religious significance. Indeed, it is tempting to view Shakespeare's friars as an implicit declaration of Catholic allegiance—or at the very least sympathy—on his part. But as I have argued, I think it would be wrong to see Shakespeare's Franciscans in too overtly religious or ideological a manner. Friar Lawrence and Friar Francis are not Catholic propaganda, deployed by Shakespeare to counter or rebut the overwhelmingly negative portrayal of the Franciscan Order—and by extension the Church of Rome—to which the Protestant literature of the time gave such prominence. Rather, Shakespeare's friars seem to signal more a retreat from the world of religious controversy than an entry into it. Although Franciscans enjoyed a very visible presence in the literature of the late-sixteenth century, by that time the Order itself had been absent from England for more than half a century. To many of Shakespeare's contemporaries, then, Franciscan friars must have appeared to be figures who belonged more to the distant past or to far off lands than to the quotidian world of the here and now.[55] And this remoteness from contemporary English life would have leant them an air of the exotic and the mysterious, making them ideally suited to artistic exploitation on the stage, particularly in the genre of romantic-comedy. And perhaps, if the playwright's family were indeed recusants, of whatever degree of commitment, then that exoticism may have been coloured with a nostalgic hankering for a period when spirituality seemed a simpler, less contested issue." Moreover, while both Friar Lawrence and Friar Francis are unmistakably sacred figures, the aura of sanctity that surrounds them is as much pagan as it is Christian in nature. For both friars can be seen as repositories of power and wisdom, who act in harmony with cyclical, natural energies to bring about individual rebirth and social renewal. So whatever his religious convictions, it is worth remembering that Shakespeare had the discipline and the detachment of a great artist. And perhaps it is these qualities, as much as any religious sympathies, that enabled him both to see and to exploit the imaginative possibilities suggested by the Order of St Francis.

NOTES

1. *The Workes of our Antient and lerned English Poet, Geffrey Chaucer, newly Printed*, ed. Thomas Speght (London: Adam Islip, 1598). This has been reproduced in facsimile in Derek Brewer, ed. *Geoffrey Chaucer: The Works, with supplementary material from the editions of 1542,1561, 1598 and 1602* (Ilkley: Scolar Press, 1974).

2. For a discussion of Speght's edition of the Works of Chaucer, see Derek Pearsall's "Thomas Speght", in *Editing Chaucer: The Great Tradition*, ed. Paul G. Ruggiers (Norman, Oklahoma: Pilgrim Books, 1984), 71–92. See also Alice S. Miskimin, *The Renaissance Chaucer* (New Haven & London: Yale University Press, 1975), 250–253.

3. Speght's "Life" of Chaucer was reprinted by E. P. Hammond in her *Chaucer: A Bibliographical Manual* (New York: Macmillan, 1908), 19–35.

4. Hammond, *Chaucer: A Bibliographical Manual*, 21–22.

5. To a great extent, Speght's biography draws on the accounts of Chaucer's life written by John Leland and John Bale, although the claim that Chaucer attended both the University of Cambridge and the Inner Temple—along with the story of his violent altercation with the Franciscan friar—are not found in any of the earlier sources. Writing at the end of the nineteenth century, Thomas Lounsbury showed that these early biographical accounts of Chaucer's life have almost no basis in fact. For Lounsbury's discussion of what he called "The Chaucer Legend", see his *Studies*

in Chaucer, His Life and Writing, 3 vols. (London & New York: Osgoof & McIlvaine, 1892), vol. 1, 129–224, especially 155–173.

6. For an account of Chaucer's education, much of which would seem to have been informal in nature, and to have taken place in the various noble households in which he served, see Derek Pearsall, *The Life of Geoffrey Chaucer* (Oxford: Blackwell, 1988), 29–34.

7. See Pearsall, *The Life of Geoffrey Chaucer*, 47 and 51–53.

8. The exact date of Chaucer's birth is not known. However, the scholarly consensus is that he was born some time during the early 1340s, which would make him well over fifty during the latter days of Richard II's reign. For the date of Chaucer's birth, see Pearsall, *The Life of Geoffrey Chaucer*, 9–11.

9. I owe this insight to Joseph A. Hornsby's, "Was Chaucer Educated at the Inns of Court?", *The Chaucer Review*, 22 (1988), 254–268.

10. See Hornsby, "Was Chaucer Educated at the Inns of Court?", 260–264.

11. Speght's claim that Chaucer attended the Inner Temple has been the subject of much critical debate over the years. See Edith Rickert, "Was Chaucer a Student at the Inner Temple?", *The Manly Anniversary Studies in Language and Literature* (Chicago: University of Chicago, 1923), 20–31; John Matthews Manly, *Some New Light on Chaucer* (New York: H. Holt & Co., 1926), 7–18; D. S. Bland, "Chaucer and the Inns of Court: A Re-Examination", *English Studies* 33 (1952),145–155; and Pearsall, *The Life of Geoffrey Chaucer*, 29–30 and 317, footnote 13.

12. That Speght's anecdote implicitly aligns Chaucer with the reformers of the sixteenth century has been noted by Joseph Hornsby, "Was Chaucer Educated at the Inns of Court?", 256–257.

13. Caroline Spurgeon—writing in 1925—noted that Chaucer was appropriated by the reformers of the sixteenth century, who identified him as a figure who shared many of their opinions on the Church of Rome. See Caroline Spurgeon, *Five Hundred Years of Chaucer Criticism and Allusion, 1357–1900*, 3 vols. (Cambridge: Cambridge University Press, 1908–1912), vol. 1, xix–xx. See also Linda Georgianna, "The Protestant Chaucer", in *Chaucer's Religious Tales*, ed. C. David Benson and Elizabeth Robertson (Cambridge: D. S. Brewer, 1990), 55–69, 56.

14. Cited in Derek Brewer, ed., *Geoffrey Chaucer: The Critical Heritage*, 2 vols. (London: Routledge & Kegan Paul, 1978), vol. 1, 108.

15. Brewer, *Geoffrey Chaucer*, vol. 1, 108.

16. *Jack Upland* is attributed to Chaucer in the earliest surviving printed edition of the text, which dates from 1536. John Foxe reprinted the tract in 1570—again attributing it to Chaucer—in the second edition of his *Actes and Monuments*. It was first included in an edition of Chaucer's *Works* by Thomas Speght in his second edition of 1602. For a modern edition of the work, see P. L. Heyworth, ed., *Jack Upland, Friar Daw's Reply, and Upland's Rejoinder* (London: Oxford University Press, 1968).

17. A. C. Bradley's comments on the secular milieu of Shakespeare's theatre are reasonably characteristic of this critical tradition. See A. C. Bradley, *Shakespearean Tragedy* (London: Macmillan, 1904), 15. See also George Santayana, "The Absence of Religion in Shakespeare", in *Interpretations of Poetry and Religion* (New York: Scribner's, 1916), 147–165, and Robert Murrell Stevenson, *Shakespeare's Religious Frontier* (The Hague: Martinus Nijoff, 1958), 20.

18. See, for instance, Charles William Wallace, *The Evolution of the English Drama up to Shakespeare* (Berlin: G. Reimer, 1912), 9–10. Writing in the same

year, C. F. Tucker Brooke claimed that the Elizabethan drama of Peele, Kyd, and Marlowe had "enfranchised" and "emancipated" itself from "ecclesiastical tendencies" and "vassalage to the ancient church". See *The Tudor Drama: A History of English National Drama to the Retirement of Shakespeare* (London: Constable & Co., 1912), 440.

19. R. M. Frye characterises Shakespeare's engagement with contemporary theology and religious practice in precisely this way. See R. M. Frye *Shakespeare and Christian Doctrine* (Princeton: Princeton University Press, 1963).

20. The earliest written record explicitly to connect Shakespeare with Catholicism dates back to 1611, when the Protestant historian, John Speed, identified the author of *Henry IV* (he does not actually name Shakespeare) as an associate of the Jesuit missionary, Robert Persons: "this Papist and his poet, of like conscience for lies, the one ever feigning and the other ever falsifying the truth". Quoted by Peter Milward, *Shakespeare's Religious Background* (Chicago: Loyola University Press, 1975), 51. See also M. Mutschman and K. Wentersdorf, *Shakespeare and Catholicism* (New York: Sheed & Ward, 1952), 348, and Gary Taylor, "The Fortunes of Oldcastle", *Shakespeare Survey* 38 (1985), 85–100, 97.

21. For instance, see Milward, *Shakespeare's Religious Background*, 15–23, and Mutschman and Wentersdorf, *Shakespeare and Catholicism*, 33–104.

22. See E. A. J. Honigmann, *Shakespeare: The "Lost" Years* (2nd edn. Manchester: Manchester University Press, 1998). Honigmann's study has given rise to a great deal of research into the question of Shakespeare and Catholicism, centring in particular on the personal networks linking Shakespeare's family with well-known Catholic households from Warwickshire and Lancashire. Much of this work was presented at the "Lancastrian Shakespeare" conference held at the University of Lancaster in July 1999, subsequently published in a two-volume collection edited by Richard Dutton, Alison Findlay, and Richard Wilson: *Theatre and Religion: Lancastrian Shakespeare* (Manchester: Manchester University Press, 2003); and *Region, Religion, and Patronage: Lancastrian Shakespeare* (Manchester: Manchester University Press, 2003).

23. See, for, instance, Mutschman and Wentersdorf, *Shakespeare and Catholicism*, 209–319; Peter Milward, *The Catholicism of Shakespeare's Plays* (Southampton: Saint Austin Press, 1997); and Velma Bourgeois Richmond, *Shakespeare, Catholicism, and Romance* (New York & London: Continuum, 2000). For a more sceptical view of Shakespeare's Catholicism, see Michael Davies, "On this side Bardolatry: The Canonisation of the Catholic Shakespeare", *Cahiers Elisabéthains* 58 (2000), 31–47, and Stanley Wells, *Shakespeare for all Time* (London: Macmillan, 2002), 23–36.

24. The attribution of the fresco cycle to Giotto is extremely controversial, as is the precise date of its composition (with estimates varying from the 1290s to the 1330s). For a brief overview of this critical debate—often termed the "Assisi problem"—see Adrian S. Hoch, "Master of the Legend of St Francis", in *The Dictionary of Art*, ed. Jane Turner, 34 vols., (London: Macmillan, 1996), vol. 20, 712–714.

25. The Fresco Cycle in the Upper Church of Assisi is based on *The Life of St Francis* (the *Legenda Major*) by St Bonaventure, which was commissioned in 1260 and completed in 1263. For his account of Francis's encounter with Innocent III, see Bonaventure, *The Life of St Francis*, trans. Ewert Cousins (New York: Paulist Press, 1978), ch. 3, 205–206. A similar legend—once again involving Innocent III—came to be told about Francis's contemporary, St Dominic, the founder of the

other principal mendicant Order, the Dominicans. A carved image of Dominic supporting the crumbling edifice of the papal basilica forms part of a narrative cycle of the saint's life decorating his tomb in the church of San Domenico, Bologna.

26. For a discussion of the part played by the Papacy in the history of the Order, see John Moorman, *A History of the Franciscan Order from Its Origins to the Year 1517* (Oxford: Clarendon Press, 1968), *passim;* and C. F. Lawrence, *The Friars: The Impact of the Early Mendicant Movement on Western Society* (London: Longman, 1994),181–201.

27. The extent to which the Papacy co-opted the Franciscan Order for its own reforming ends is further suggested by an image from an altarpiece by Giotto roughly contemporary with the fresco cycle at Assisi, and currently in the Louvre. The main picture portrays the stigmatisation of St Francis, but there are three subsidiary images—or *predelle*—at the bottom of the panel, one of which is *The Dream of Innocent III.* Although on a miniature scale, this image resembles very closely the Assisi fresco, but with one significant addition. St Peter can be seen standing over the sleeping figure of Innocent III, gesturing towards St Francis and the crumbling basilica. So, the image implies, St Peter lends the full weight of his authority to the approval of the Franciscan Order.

28. The literature on the early history of the Order—and the wider conflicts within the Church that its appearance generated—is extensive. A good overview of the subject can be found in Moorman, *A History of the Franciscan Order,* 123–139 and 339–349; Lawrence, *The Friars,* 152–165; and Penn R. Szittya, *The Antifraternal Tradition in Medieval Literature* (Princeton: Princeton University Press, 1986), 1–182.

29. For instance, see Arnold Williams, "Chaucer among the Friars", *Speculum* 28 (1953), 499–513; Jill Mann, *Chaucer and Medieval Estates Satire: The Literature of Social Classes and the General Prologue to the Canterbury Tales* (Cambridge: Cambridge University Press, 1973), 37–54; Szittya, *The Antifraternal Tradition in Medieval Literature,* 183–287; and Lawrence M. Clopper, *"Songs of Rechelesnesse": Langland and the Franciscans* (Ann Arbor: The University of Michigan Press, 1997).

30. See Szittya, *The Antifraternal Tradition in Medieval Literature,* 7–9.

31. Christopher Marlowe, *Dr Faustus,* ed. Roma Gill (2nd edition: London: A. & C. Black, 1989).

32. John Webster, *The White Devil,* ed. Christina Luckyj (London: A. & C. Black, 1996), Act V.

33. Giovanni Boccaccio, *Decameron,* a cura di Vittore Branca (Torino: Einaudi, 1980), IV, 2, 487–504. For a modern English translation, see Giovanni Boccaccio, *The Decameron,* trans. G. H. McWilliam (2nd edition: Harmondsworth: Penguin, 1995), IV, 2, 301–312. For a discussion of the representation of friars in Italian novelle, see Robert J. Clements and Joseph Gibaldi, *Anatomy of the Novella: The European Tale Collection from Boccaccio and Chaucer to Cervantes* (New York: New York University Press, 1977), 183–215.

34. *A Critical Edition of George Whetstone's 1582 An Heptameron of Civil Discourses,* ed. Diana Shklanka (New York & London: Garland, 1987), 120.

35. *An Heptameron of Civil Discourses,* 121 (my italics). The tale has also been reprinted by Pamela Benson in her collection *Italian Tales from the Age of Shakespeare* (London: J. M. Dent, 1996), 255–258. For a discussion of Whetstone's *Heptameron,* see Thomas C. Izard, *George Whetstone: Mid-Elizabethan Gentleman of Letters* (New York: Columbia University Press, 1942), 80–130.

36. All quotations are taken from Jill L. Levenson, ed., *Romeo and Juliet* (Oxford: Oxford University Press, 2000).

37. For a discussion of the sources of *Romeo and Juliet,* see Geoffrey Bullough, *Narrative and Dramatic Sources of Shakespeare,* 8 vols. (London & New York: Routledge & Kegan Paul & Columbia University Press, 1964), vol. 1, 269–283. Brooke's poem is reprinted in the same volume, 284–363. The development of the legend is traced by Olin H. Moore, *The Legend of Romeo and Juliet* (Columbus: Ohio State University Press, 1950). For the versions of the story by da Porto and Bandello, see Luigi da Porto, "Istoria novellamente ritrovata di due nobili amanti con la loro pietosa morte, intervenuta già nella città di Verona nel tempo del signor Bartolomeo dalla Scala", in *Novellieri del Cinquecento,* a cura di Marziano Guglielminetti, 2 vols. (Milano-Napoli: Ricciardi, 1972), vol. 1, 241–288; and Matteo Bandello, "La sfortunata morte di dui infelicissimi amanti che l'uno di veleno e l'altro di dolore morirono, con vari accidenti", in *Novelle di Matteo Bandello,* a cura di Guiseppe Guido Ferrero (Torino: UTET, 1978), 438–480. English translations of the earliest Italian and French versions of the story, including those of da Porto and Bandello, can be found in Nicole Prunster, trans. *Romeo and Juliet before Shakespeare: Four Early Stories of Star Crossed Love* (Toronto: CRRS Publications, 2000).

38. See da Porto, 279, and Bandello, 475.

39. See da Porto, 257, and Bandello, 450.

40. See da Porto, 257, and Bandello, 450.

41. In its mission to the towns and cities of Renaissance Italy, the Franciscan Order was much involved in the resolution of disputes between rival families and factions, a task that required that the friars' detachment, neutrality, and freedom of association be respected. See Lawrence, *The Friars,* 113, and Cynthia L. Polecritti, *Preaching Peace in Renaissance Italy: Bernardino of Siena and His Audience* (Washington D. C.: The Catholic University of America Press, 2000), 97–103. Shakespeare makes use of these characteristics in all three of his "Franciscan" plays.

42. Arthur Brooke, *The Tragicall Historye of Romeus and Juliet,* in Bullough, *Narrative and Dramatic Sources of Shakespeare,* vol. 1, 284 (my italics).

43. See Bullough, *Narrative and Dramatic Sources of Shakespeare,* vol. 1, 277.

44. For an alternative view, which sees Friar Lawrence as a much more morally compromised figure, see Stevenson, *Shakespeare's Religious Frontier,* 31–42, and James C. Bryant, "The Problematic Friar in *Romeo and Juliet*", *English Studies* 55 (1974), 340–350.

45. For a discussion of the sources of *Much Ado about Nothing,* see Charles T. Prouty, *The Sources of Much Ado about Nothing* (New Haven & London: Harvard University Press, 1950), and Geoffrey Bullough, *Narrative and Dramatic Sources of Shakespeare,* vol. 2, 61–81. For Bullough's translation of the novella (Novella XXII from *La Prima Parte de le Novelle del Bandello*), see 112–134.

46. Joseph Campbell, *The Hero with a Thousand Faces* (London: Fontana Press, 1993), 10.

47. All quotations are taken from Sheldon P. Zitner, ed., *Much Ado about Nothing* (Oxford: Oxford University Press, 1993).

48. Cited by R. S. White, *"Let Wonder Seem Familiar": Endings in Shakespeare's Romance Vision* (London: Athlone, 1985), 3.

49. Bullough, *Narrative and Dramatic Sources of Shakespeare,* vol. 2, 77.

50. For instance, see Northrop Frye, *A Natural Perspective: The Development of Shakespearean Comedy and Romance* (New York: Columbia University Press, 1965);

and *The Myth of Deliverance: Reflections on Shakespeare's Problem Comedies* (Toronto: University of Toronto Press, 1983).

51. Frye, *A Natural Perspective*, 125.

52. Fora detailed examination of the sources and analogues of *Measure for Measure*, see Bullough, *Narrative and Dramatic Sources of Shakespeare*, vol. 2, 399–417.

53. All quotations are taken from N. W. Bawcutt, ed., *Measure for Measure* (Oxford: Oxford University Press, 1991).

54. For a detailed discussion of the Duke's adoption of the friar's disguise, and the complications it raises, see Rosalind Miles, *The Problem of Measure for Measure: An Historical Investigation* (London: Vision Press, 1976), 161–196.

55. Rosalind Miles has made this point in relation to *Measure for Measure*. See Miles, *The Problem of Measure for Measure*, 168–169.

56. The strongly nostalgic element to Shakespeare's friars has been noted by, amongst others, Peter Milward in his *Shakespeare's Religious Background*, 78. On the more general associations between nostalgia and Catholicism in Shakespeare, see Gary Taylor, "Forms of Opposition: Shakespeare and Middleton", *English Literary Renaissance* 24 (1994), 283–314, 311; Arthur F. Moretti, "Shakespeare and Catholicism", in Dutton, Findlay, and Wilson, ed. *Theatre and Religion*, 218–241, 228; and Eamon Duffy, "Bare ruined choirs: remembering Catholicism in Shakespeare's England", Dutton, Findlay, and Wilson, ed. *Theatre and Religion*, 40–57.

WILLIAM M. McKIM

Romeo's "Death-markt" Imagination and Its Tragic Consequences

In the long history of *Romeo and Juliet* criticism, writers have paid insufficient attention to the differences between the ways the two protagonists imagine themselves as being in love and the tragic significance of those differences. In many critical accounts, the assumption has been that, as the two confront obstacles to their marital success, they counter what G. K. Hunter calls a "rhetoric of society" with a shared voice, a "radiant poetry" that is expressive of their mutually felt desires and outlook (120). Marianne Novy, a contemporary scholar who writes about gender construction as a societal process and its potentially destructive consequences, nevertheless sees Romeo and Juliet as moving toward a "mutuality in love" during the course of their play and Romeo's love of Juliet as constituting not only "a challenge to the feud" but also to the "associations of masculinity and sexuality with violence" (106) that we hear in the Capulet servant's boasts about "thrusting" Montague's "maids to the wall" (1.1.18) and Mercutio's gibes about pricking love "for pricking" and beating "love down" (1.4.28).

Other longstanding critical assumptions consistent with this perception of Romeo and Juliet possessing a shared point of view about what it means to be in love are, first, that, by acting decisively to the report of Juliet's death in Act Five, Romeo demonstrates that, as M. M. Mahood puts it, he has made a successful "rite of passage" from "dream into reality," and, secondly, that we

Kentucky Philological Review, Volume 20, Numbers 4–5 (March 2005): pp. 38–45. Copyright © 2005 Kentucky Philological Association.

as audience end up seeing their self-inflicted deaths as, paradoxically, a "victory," not only over time and society but over the possibility of inner hostility towards each other (398). Northrop Frye, in this regard, says we come to realize, through their sacrifices, that "nothing perfect or without blemish can stay that way in this world and should be offered up to another world before it deteriorates" (32).

Such widely shared sentiments encourage us to reward the play more as lyric triumph than tragedy and, unfortunately, fail to do justice to its psychological and cultural complexity. Rather than presenting us with an uplifting "marriage of two minds" and mutual self-sacrifice, as these readings imply, Romeo and Juliet illustrate radically different perceptions toward each other and the world, differences that become more evident to us as the play goes on, particularly as we note the disparity between their dying speeches. My contentions in this paper are, first, that, rooted in Romeo's poetic conception of what it means to be in love, his imagination of himself being a lover, is a culturally-induced desire for manly, even heroic, attainment through loving that overrides any anticipation on his part for happiness, personal intimacy, or long-term relationship; second, that Romeo's poetic desire for achievement through loving is reflective of a masculine anxiety about worthiness, i.e. being perceived as worthy by himself and others, that is characteristic of the play's males in general, from those who pick fights in the streets, ridicule love, or use their parental and aristocratic status to exercise power over others; third, that this masculine or worthiness anxiety, which links Romeo to male attitudes in his society, is presented as a formative cause of his and Juliet's untimely deaths; and finally, that his "death-marked" imagination, an imagination directed toward violent encounters and self-enhancement through self-sacrifice, is already formed, even scripted, before the action of the play begins and does not significantly change during the course of the play.[1] By contrast, Juliet's poetic imagination, as reflected in her lyric expressions of what it means to be in love with Romeo, is radically free of this self-regarding concern with her own worthiness or personal attainment but is instead characterized by desires for earthly happiness, sexuality, and day-to-day intimacy.

A misleading image of Romeo that persists in the popular imagination, and that is perpetuated in many stage and screen productions, is that of an extraordinarily genteel youth, free of masculine anxieties and tendencies toward violence that are a product of these anxieties. As a corrective to this stereotype, we might consider Romeo's actions and speeches in the play as mirroring, not counteracting, the competitive atmosphere of his society as a whole. In doing so, we might note that his actions and speeches, like those of other male characters in the play, are characterized by recurrent variations on the trope of "standing": standing up, standing out, and standing in for. For example, at the beginning of the play, Sampson, the Capulet servant, brags that he is "able to stand," as long as his "naked weapon is out" (1.1.28, 34), and with his other standing weapon he will "thrust [Montague's] maids to the wall" (16) just as assuredly he will "back" (35) or stand in for his fellow servant and fellow fighter, Gregory, against the Montague servants.

We see a similar pattern repeated, with Romeo involved, later in the climactic duel scene in Act Three. Tybalt prides himself on standing out in his society as a quarreler, so he stands up against Romeo and issues him a written challenge to duel. Mercutio, who has proclaimed that those, like Tybalt, who try to stand out through dueling are nothing but "fashionmongers" (2.3.33) but who himself has no hesitation about himself trying to stand out as a wit (as Romeo describes him: "A gentleman ... that loves to hear himself talk, and will speak more in a minute than he will stand to in a month" [147–149]), uncharacteristically decides to stand up for Romeo's life and honor, and perhaps even his love for him, against Tybalt.[2] When Romeo realizes that Mercutio has sacrificed himself by standing in for him and his cause of honor, he declares his "reputation stain'd" (3.1.111), his having been made "effeminate" by "Juliet's beauty" (114) , so, capitulating to the pressure to perform his manly duty under the imagined gaze of his friend, "for Mercutio's soul / Is but a little way above our heads" (126–127), staying for revenge, he stands up for Mercutio by killing Tybalt.

Romeo's violent and catastrophic response in this scene we may see as prefiguring his hasty and misguided response, at the end of the play, when he hears the false report of Juliet's death. Imagining himself subjected to the eyewitnessing presence of his dead Juliet, as he previously was to that of Mercutio, "Well, Juliet, I will lie with thee, tonight" (5.1.34), he, like the worthy lover he imagines himself to be, manfully stands up for her, by violently challenging death, her imagined adversary: "Thou detestable maw, thou womb of death / . . .Thus I enforce thy rotten jaws to open, / And in despite I'll cram thee with more food" (5.3.45, 47–48).

The intertwined and interconnected nature of these actions is the consequence of already scripted cultural codes of honor that encourage acts of violence, including self-sacrifice, as proof of manliness, worthiness, and constancy. The Montague-Capulet feud, in light of this recurrent pattern, is shown to be more symptom than cause of a more broadly cultural mindset, the erecting, defending, and promoting of one's house serving as a means of standing tall against rivals, and other aggressive efforts to stand tall and stand above, whether through building, fighting, sarcastic discourse, or sexual conquest, functioning as invitations for put-downs and knockdowns of various sorts.

Seen against these patterns of cultural influence and corresponding behaviors, the characterization of Romeo emerges more as an epitome of his society than a counter to it. As we have seen his masculine anxiety emerge with a vengeance in his compulsion to fight Tybalt for a cause and to castigate Juliet's beauty for making him "effeminate," we see Romeo, throughout the play, set forth in a defensive and competitive context. Lady Capulet proclaims about Romeo at the masked ball that "Verona brags of him" (1.5.64), and his father, Montague, says that he expects him to "spread his sweet leaves to the air" and "dedicate his beauty to the sun" (1.1.145–146), in other words stand out among the rest of Verona's young men as the beautiful person his father imagines him and wants him to be. When we first see Romeo in the play, though he has cultivated an image of himself as suffering recluse, his discourse in the streets is not humble and self-effacing, as we might expect from such a pretense, but is characterized instead by an assertive and showy display of witty images and paradoxes: "Love is a smoke made with the fume of sighs ... What is it else? A madness most discreet / A choking gall and a preserving sweet" (1.1.190, 195–194). When talking about his beloved Rosalind, he is not modest but boasting and eloquent. She is "rich in beauty," she "hath Dian's wit" (202) and "will not stay the siege of loving terms" (209), and "the all-seeing sun / Ne'er saw her match since first the world begun" (1.2.92–93). Although he represents himself poetically as defeated in not being able to satisfy his desires, he is, based on that suffering, all the more worthy of admiration since his constancy is "devout religion," standing out above the fickle weakness of "transparent heretics" (88, 91) who haven't the strength to be so self-sacrificing.

Whether in the spirit of play or seriousness or some of both, we see him, throughout the first two acts, translating emotion into displays of public wit, delivered like thrusts in a duel, so aggressively and skillfully that even Mercutio cannot keep up with him: "Come between us, good Benvolio. My wit faints" (2.4.67). Furthermore, we see this competitive concern with presenting a manly and worthy image of himself persist to the end of the play when, just before he enters Juliet's tomb with the intention of lying next to her in death, he gives his servant a letter, a kind of "suicide note," to be delivered to "my lord and father," presumably in an attempt to justify his seemingly mad actions as noble and dutiful, not simply rebellious and willful, comparable to Hamlet's dying charge to Horatio that his friend present his "cause aright" to the "unsatisfied."

Reflective of this self-regarding and self-promoting bent in Romeo's characterization is the learnedly bookish shaping of his imagination, borrowing not only from the Petrarchan sonnet tradition ("now is he for the numbers Petrarch flowed in," says Mercutio [2.4.38–39]), but also Platonism, and the medieval literature of chivalric romance, all of which tend to represent the suffering of the lover as a means of moral improvement and self-transcendence more than experienced earthly happiness. His turning to poetry as his major occupation, "feigning notable images," according to Sir

Philip Sidney's famous and current definition, that are capable of constructing in words a "golden world" superior to the natural one, coupled with his dream-supported tendency to play out his poetry in real life, as noted by Mercutio in his "Queen Mab" speech, reflects an ambitious and idealizing mind wanting to live not in nature or on the earth, but above it, to live "within the zodiac of his own wit," as Sidney puts it.[3]

This idealizing, and, as I argue, fatal tendency in Romeo's imagination is reflected in the way it constructs larger than life roles for himself and his lady, and the adversaries that threaten them, reaching outward and upward, above the earth, toward myth and myth-making.[4] Coleridge, in writing about Romeo, notes this tendency when he describes him as motivated by a self-directed desire of the noble mind for one's "whole being to be united to something or some being felt necessary for its completeness" (134), So whether Romeo is describing Rosalind or Juliet, it is her youthful "beauty," a Platonic absolute abstracted from the matrix of nature and temporarily incarnated in a living being, not her living person, that he uses as a referent in his poetizing, and that beauty is always characterized, ominously and prophetically, as belonging above the earth, in some remote and exalted sphere: "Beauty too rich for use, for earth too dear" (1.5.47).

"Devout religion" (1.2.88), which seeks some perfection and some status beyond the earth not on it, is the primary context within which his love is imagined. He carries this prescribed association over to his meeting with Juliet at Capulet's ball when he characterizes her body as a shrine and himself a saint, himself implicitly as a religious pilgrim. All the images he uses to describe her, in this as in subsequent scenes, are extraterrestrial and competitive in their implication. Her abstracted beauty always stands above, "a snowy dove trooping with crows / As yonder lady o'er her fellows shows" (1.5.48–49), "a bright angle . . . being o'er my head / As is a winged messenger of heaven / Unto the white-upturned wond'ring eyes / Of mortals that fall back to gaze on him . . ." (2.2.26–30), and a "fair sun," drawing envy from the moon, whom she has the power to kill with her rising (2.2.3–6).

All of these images serve implicitly to exalt the poet-lover in his own imagination and constitute a kind a kind of self-fashioning or self-transformation, as he characterizes himself as empowered, lifted above the earth, by his affection for her and, even more, by her affection for him, as if it were an inspiration from a muse or an act of divine grace. As his lady is made to play a personified role in his imagination, that of ideal Beauty which diminishes by comparison all that is earthly, so is he, by implication, exalted into a mythological role himself, that of Love, the aspiring quester after beauty, given superhuman powers of his own by beauty's powerful influence: "Call me but love and I'll be new baptized. / Henceforth I never will be Romeo" (2.2.49–50) and "With love's light wings did I o'erperch these walls, /

For stony limits cannot hold love out, / And what love dares do that love attempt. / Therefore thy kinsmen are no stop to me" (66–69). "For valour, is not Love a Hercules[?]" (*LLL* 4.3.337), as Berowne, one of Shakespeare's previously created poet-lovers, proclaims. Because such beauty incarnated on earth, poetically and mythically speaking, is constantly threatened and inevitably doomed, a recurrent theme in Shakespeare's sonnets, the myth or waking dream created and lived out by the lover-poet is inevitably tragic and emotionally disturbing. Therefore, it is fitting that Romeo envision himself as a ship-tossed, and finally, shipwrecked sailor, the vessel propelling him on his imperiled quest being steered by an unknown but life-threatening pilot: "But He that hath the steerage of my course / Direct my [sail]!" (1.4.112–113) and "Thou desperate pilot, now at once run on / The dashing rocks thy sea-sick weary bark!" (5.3.117–118).

Where in myth or poetry there is such supreme, standout beauty and aspiring love, there is inevitably an envious threat, Orpheus and Eurydice, Proserpine and Dis, and Milton's Adam and Eve being prime examples. So the perilous sense of being threatened, of a struggle, becomes an essential part of the script that is played out in Romeo's dreams and poetry. Stephen Greenblatt, who made popular the word *self-fashioning* as a major focus of early modern critical studies, stated as a principle that literary self-fashioning is always "achieved in relation to something perceived as alien, strange or hostile," some "threatening other" (3). For Romeo the threatening other is less Juliet's kinsmen, unworthy of his overreaching and self-glorifying imagination, but rather personified cosmic forces: "some consequence yet hanging in the stars" (1.4.107); Fortune, which he fears would make him her "fool," not the hero or worthy knight he aspires to be; or death itself, personified either as a beauty-devouring "beast" or a rival lover. Courage, willingness to sacrifice oneself for love, and fidelity, more than long term pleasure or a growing marital relationship, constitute success in such a myth. Beauty incarnated is doomed on earth, but "come what sorrow can" let "love-devouring death do what he dare" (2.6.3, 7) as Romeo says immediately before his wedding to Juliet, "one short minute in her sight" and his right to "call her mine," is, as he confesses to Friar Laurence, "enough" (5, 8).

Thus, in Romeo's poetic constructions, behind every transcendent imagining of Juliet's beauty, and himself a successful lover, there lurks a doom-directed image of some transcendent adversary that is his enemy, that calls upon his soul to encounter, to take arms or poetic voice against. Tragically, we see this already scripted, yet self-constructed, myth acted out to its prescribed conclusion in Romeo's final speech, characteristically a soliloquy, over Juliet's body in the tomb. By violence against himself, in the "feasting presence" (5.3.86) of light cast by Juliet's still-preserved beauty, an echo of his earlier image, in the balcony scene, of Juliet as the sun with power to kill the envious moon, Romeo plays out his already scripted hero's part: "here / will I set up my everlasting rest, / And shake the yoke of inauspicious stars / From this world-wearied flesh" (109–112).

At this most tragic and error-filled moment in the play, Romeo can respond paradoxically, with triumphant assertions more than expressions of grief, because, as we have seen, his poetic imagination, which has entirely taken over his discourse at this point, measures success in love not as happiness but as achievement and worthiness. In his own eyes, he has achieved much. He has not only proved his constancy in love by dying for his beloved, the litmus test of the poet-lover, but he has saved her beauty from being conquered by himself experiencing the sublimity of that "one short minute" in her sight he spoke of just before his wedding: "Death, that hath suck'd the honey of thy breath, / Hath had no power yet upon they beauty. / Thou art not conquer'd, beauty's engin yet / Is crimson in thy lips and cheeks, / And death's pale flag is not advanced there" (92–96).

Juliet too is given a poetic voice in the play and a poetic imagination, but, unlike Romeo's, they are not fully developed or already scripted before the action of the play begins, nor is her poetry shaped, as Romeo's is, from bookish sources, which prescribe love as a vehicle for worthiness more than happiness. Rather, we see her lyric voice, beginning with the balcony scene (2.2), in the process of formation, so much so that it could be argued that, whereas Romeo's love for Juliet is a construction of his poetry, Juliet's poetry is a construction of her love, or, more specifically, her anticipation of happiness through loving Romeo as a person, not an ideal. Her lyric speeches are always reflective of fresh discovery, not literary or mythic borrowing. For example, just before Romeo leaves her that night of their first meeting, she playfully constructs images that express her desires for physical closeness, not personal achievement. Significantly, they are not cosmic and transcendent, like Romeo's images of her beauty, but domestic and earth-directed. In her imagination Romeo would be, not a star or the sun, but a tamed falcon, and her only imagined heroics would be for a voice powerful enough to "lure his tassel-gentle back again" (2.2.159) when, if necessary, he must depart. Or, in a similar image, Romeo would be a pet bird that a child would have on a string, so she could always be able to pull him closer to her. Her main fear, in this domestic scenario, is not some cosmic adversary but her own unbounded desire for physical intimacy: if he were a bird, she might physically "kill" him, she says playfully, with too "much cherishing" (182).

As Edward Snow, in an influential article points out, this tender and playful physicality is outside the range of Romeo's poetic discourse, because. "his desire is operated by eyesight" (170), almost exclusively.[5] Where Romeo, for example, personifies the sea as a threatening alien force driving him to shipwreck and death, Juliet personalizes it and internalizes it, in an optimistic sense, as an image of her newly discovered capacities for loving: "My bounty is as boundless as the sea, / My love as deep; the more I give to thee, / The more I have, for both are infinite" (133–135).

Later in the play, after the wedding but before its sexual consummation, in Juliet's most mythopoeic and full-throated speech, "Gallop apace, you fiery-footed steeds" (3.2.1 ff.), we see these personalizing, familiarizing, and domesticating tendencies at work. It is a speech, virtually unique in all of Shakespeare's works, in which sexual desire is expressed without ironic undertones of guilt or shame.[6] Romeo, lacking a physical or tactile component to his poetic imagination, does not come close. Like Romeo, Juliet too sees their love as set against night and the surrounding darkness, but, unlike Romeo in his grandiose personifications of sorrow, "love-devouring death," fortune, and the stars, she door not see the night as alien and adversarial, a call to arms, but as a familiar and potentially friendly spirit. "Civil night" (10), she calls her, one she might bargain and negotiate, not fall into combat, with: "Spread thy curtain, love-performing night" (5), so we can have privacy for lovemaking. Most of all, as she says to this imaginary folk spirit, "Give me my Romeo, and, when I die / Take him and cut him out in little stars . . ." (21–22), and then, if you wish, you may use his brightness to compete with and outshine the "garish sun" (25). In Juliet's imaginary world, goddesses and spirits may compete with each other for status and rank, but she doesn't feel a need to, and, in her poetry, she can represent her sexual dying joyfully and gratefully as a spiritually assisted experience and her physical death acceptingly as part of a natural process, not grandiosely as a violent mythic encounter.

As in the balcony scene, we see Juliet, in this speech, using earthly and domestic, not extraterrestrial, images to define what it means to be in love. She is the buyer of a house who has not yet "possess'd it," a sold house that has not yet been "enjoy'd" and "an impatient child" who has received new clothes but has yet to "wear them" (26–31). Juliet's images of herself as wanting to be enjoyed, of discovering within her a capacity to love Romeo that is an bounteous as the sea, is foreign to Romeo's self-centered preoccupation with individual attainments. Once again, as in the balcony scene, we see Juliet portraying herself as a child, not in the sense of being subservient or simpleminded but in her unspoiled capacity to desire and experience physical pleasure without shame. In this same speech, she also presents herself and Romeo as virgin lovers playing in a non-competitive game where, as she cleverly puts it, they will both win by losing. An image like this one stands in contrast to the competitive and defensive bent of most of Romeo's discourse, as does her image, also in this speech, of Romeo's beauty lying "upon the wings of night, / Whiter than new snow upon a raven's back" (19). In this comparison, we may hear the reverse echo of an image Romeo used when he first saw Juliet: "So shows a snowy dove stooping with crows / As yonder lady o'er her fellows shows" (1.5.48–49). In Juliet's imagination of Romeo's beauty, white set against surrounding darkness is not one of competition or threat but aesthetic concord and harmony; by contrast, in Romeo's image of Juliet's beauty, the black crows are being put clown in a competitive beauty contest.

It is tempting, with respect to this play, which has often been characterized as a comedy gone wrong, to see Juliet as representing the comic imagination, directed toward envisioning and pursuing happiness through love, while Romeo illustrates the hubristic, if noble, imagination of the tragic overreacher, whose preoccupation with his own attainments and worthiness points toward self-destruction. If Juliet's words, "I must hear from thee every day in the hour, / For in a minute there are many days" (3.5.44–45) seem anticipatory of the deconstructive Rosalind in *As You Like It*, we might imagine her transforming Romeo's scripted and death-marked imagination, given leisurely time and pastoral location, as the comedy, *As You Like It* provides.

On two brief and muted occasions in *Romeo and Juliet*, we hear Juliet applying Rosalind-like correctives to Romeo's preoccupations and anxieties. The first example is immediately before their wedding, when she refuses Romeo's request to "blazon" with "rich music's tongue" (2.6.26–27) her "joy" at "this dear encounter" (29), in other words, construct some hyperbolic poetry of her own to counter what she senses in Romeo as a potentially destructive anxiety, "if the measure of thy joy / Be heaped like mine" (24–25). Instead of complying with Romeo's request, she responds with an eloquent questioning of any need for grandiose and self-justifying rhetoric: "They are but beggars that can count their worth, / But my true love is grown to such excess / I cannot sum up sum of half my wealth" (32–34). The second example of Juliet serving as gentle critic is immediately after their sexual consummation, when Romeo expresses his willingness to stay with her in bed past the coming of dawn, not for the purpose of continuing their lovemaking, as Juliet initially expresses a desire for, but to remain in danger and so die for her if she "wilt-have it so" (3.5.18). Against what she infers as his potentially destructive need to prove himself to her by dying of love ("Come, death, and welcome. Juliet wills it so" [24]), she speaks up on behalf of a comic, not tragic, scenario: "Hie, hence, be gone, away!" (26), and let's try to live for love.

Whereas Romeo's poetizing persists throughout the play and reaches its grand climax in his dying speech, which triumphantly proclaims a symbolic victory over death, time, fortune, and his stars, Juliet's lyric voice, characteristically, is last heard in the play the night of her lovemaking with the living Romeo. Tragically, she has no triumphal self-fashioning, death speech of her own to match or compete with Romeo's 36-line soliloquy. "Then I'll be brief" (5.3.168) is the sum of her epitaph; "thy lips are warm" (167) is her modest, earthy consolation. "No more to build on there," she might well have said in a different poem at a different time.

Notes

1. "Masculine anxiety" is an established term in Shakespearian criticism, linked largely, but not exclusively, with feminist approaches. Valerie Traub, for example, states that the feminist perspective is "concerned with male anxiety toward woman's eroticism and the maternal body" (4–5), both of which are regarded with suspicion and implicit disgust by patriarchal culture, as represented in Shakespeare's tragedies. Janet Adelman, focusing on the later tragedies from *Macbeth to Coriolanus*, sees masculine identity as something constructed to "ward off vulnerability to the mother" as psychologically constructed (134). Bruce Smith, who ranges in survey fashion across the breadth of the topic of masculinity in Shakespeare, represents masculinity in early modern literature as a perilously slippery construction, not an essence. Mark Breitenberg, citing unequal distribution of power in society as the basis for masculine anxiety being a universal phenomenon, so far as to state that "men anxious about their masculinity will [always] be a necessary and inevitable condition of masculinity" (qtd. In Wells, 213). For the most part, *Romeo and Juliet* has been excluded from or de-emphasized in these discussions, although Coppelia Kahn, by distinguishing between two cultural constructions of what it means to be manly, one the sanctioned public way productive of anxiety about individuality and maternal separation, the other a private commitment to fulfilling the duties of being a husband, sees Romeo as "ultimately choosing against the sanctioned public way" (89). Clearly, I see Ms. Kahn as overstating her case here.

2. Mercutio's symbolic linkage with masculine anxiety is illustrated in Roger Allam's comments about playing the role in John Caird's Royal Shakespeare production, 1983–1984. For Allam's Mercutio, Romeo has been "unmanned by love" (*Players* 118) and is becoming increasingly separated from his former friend. Allam, therefore, sees Mercutio's purpose in the duel scene as piling up "an emotional debt" (119) that will force Romeo to act worthily on his behalf. In addition, we may see Mercutio's example of self-sacrifice for love as pointing toward Romeo's dying for Juliet, a connection reinforced by the way his name seemingly alludes to the god Mercury in his role as *psychopomp*, a messenger who directs souls to the land of the dead (Porter 104). Two productions of the play in 1994, one directed in England by Neil Bartlett, the other in Germany by Karen Bier, emphasize this connection between Mercutio and Romeo's being marked for death, by having the same actor who played Mercutio continually reappear later in the play in such roles as the Apothecary, Friar John, and Romeo's servant, Balthazar (Holland 224, 269).

3. In 1595, projected as a reasonable date for the composition of *Romeo and Juliet* by several modern editors, two editions of Sidney's *Apology for Poetry* were published. Considered as a discourse on poetry's enflaming and shaping power over human minds at least as much as a defense of its capacity for teaching morality, *Apology* functions well as a commentary on the way poetry and poetry-making are represented in both *Romeo and Juliet* and *A Midsummer Night's Dream*. In particular, Sidney's language about the poet's being "lifted up" by the "vigor of his own invention" and, in the process, making things "quite anew, forms such as never were in nature as the Heroes, Demigods, Cyclops, Chimeras, Furies . . ." (14), applies to Romeo's poetizing, especially as characterized by Mercutio in his "Queen Mab" speech, as well as to Theseus's argument in *A Midsummer Night's Dream* linking "the poet's eye, in a fine frenzy rolling" (5.1.12) with madness (See Forrest Robinson's note, 14). Sidney's *Apology* is also useful to apply to *Romeo and Juliet* because it

identifies poetic discourse with other types of making, building on its etymological origins in the word *poiein* (12), that men in Verona, not women, are free to practice in competitive ways.

4. In her introduction to the Oxford edition of *Romeo and Juliet,* Jill Levenson goes so far as to say that "the primary source of the Romeo and Juliet fiction is myth" and *Liebestod,* the name Richard Wagner applied to his opera *Tristan and Isolde,* as the particular myth that "informs" it (2). Denis de Rougemont calls *Romeo and Juliet* "the most magnificent resuscitation of [this] myth that the world was to be given" until Wagner (190). Comparing Shakespeare's play to the *Liebestod* is, of course, suggestive but has proved somewhat misleading. First, the comparison ignores the important distinction between the romantic retelling of a myth, as you have in the Wagner opera, and the social focus on myth making that we are presented with in the play. Why Romeo's suicide is driven by destructive myth making but not Juliet's is a question the comparison does not address. The comparison also implies that the motivation for Romeo's suicide is uncontrollable erotic passion, an interpretation contradicted by the performative nature of his dying soliloquy and, as I argue, his anxious and self-centered desire to present himself as a worthy lover.

5. Snow's insightful analysis of the differences in Romeo and Juliet's discourse is, for the most part, supportive of my conclusions in this paper, though he assumes, as I do not, that they "share an imaginative vision" (168). But his point about their representing two contrasting modes of desire, Romeo "reaching out" after something always at a distance, thereby imagining peak performances or attainments accompanied by a falling off, Juliet "unfolding" from within, from bud to flower over time (178), is essential in helping to define their opposing points of view.

6. The point of view toward sexuality in this speech, as well as Juliet's other lyric expressions in acts two and three, in contrast with Romeo's mythologizing, can be seen as reflective of Rianne Eisler's argument, in *Sacred Pleasure* and other books, that the idea of sexuality being regarded as sacramental, bespeaking "a view of the world in which everything is spiritual . . . and the whole world is imbued with the sacred" (57), has been overthrown and usurped in Western culture by the sacralization of pain and violence and, particularly applicable to *Romeo and Juliet,* the "need for glorification built into myths of struggle in which cosmic forces, good and evil, beauty and darkness, eternity and time, God and the devil, are seen in perpetual conflict" (381).

WORKS CITED

Adelman, Janet. *Suffocating Mothers: Fantasies of Maternal Origins in Shakespeare's Plays, "Hamlet" to "The Tempest."* New York: Routledge, 1991.

Coleridge's Writings on Shakespeare. Terence Hawks, ed. New York: Capricorn Books, 1959.

Eisler, Rianne. *Sacred Pleasure: Sex, Myth, and the Politics of the Body.* San Francisco: Harper Collins, 1995.

Greenblatt, Stephen. *Renaissance Self-fashioning from More to Shakespeare.* Chicago: University of Chicago Press, 1980.

Holland, Peter. *English Shakespeare: Shakespeare on the English Stage in the 1990s.* Cambridge and New York: Cambridge University Press, 1997.

Hunter, G. K. "Shakespeare and the Traditions of Tragedy." In *The Cambridge Companion to Shakespeare.* Stanley Wells, ed. Cambridge and New York: Cambridge University Press, 1986. 123–141.

Kahn, Coppelia. *Man's Estate: Masculine Identity in Shakespeare.* Berkeley: University of California Press, 1981.

Mahood, M. M. "Romeo and Juliet." In *Essays in Shakespearean Criticism.* James L. Calderwood and Harold E. Toliver, eds. Englewood Cliffs, NJ: Prentice Hall, 1970. 391–404.

Northrop Frye on Shakespeare. Robert Sandler, ed. New Haven, CT: Yale University Press, 1986.

Novy, Marianne. *Love's Argument: Gender Relations in Shakespeare.* Chapel Hill, NC: University of North Carolina Press, 1984.

Players of Shakespeare 2: Further Essays in Shakespearean Performance by Players with the Royal Shakespeare Company. Russell Jackson and Robert Smallwood, eds. Cambridge and New York: Cambridge University Press, 1989.

Porter, Joseph. *Shakespeare's Mercutio: His History and Drama.* Chapel Hill, NC: University of North Carolina Press, 1988.

Rougement, Denis de. *Love in the Western World.* rev. ed. Montgomery Belgion, trans. New York: Princeton University Press, 1983.

Shakespeare, William. *The Riverside Shakespeare.* 2nd. ed. G. Blakemore Evans, ed. Boston: Houghton Mifflin, 1997. All quotations are taken from this edition.

———. *Romeo and Juliet,* Jill L. Levenson, ed. Oxford: Oxford University Press, 2000.

Sidney, Sir Philip. *An Apology for Poetry.* Forrest G. Robinson, ed. New York: Macmillan, 1970.

Smith, Bruce R. *Shakespeare and Masculinity.* Oxford Shakespeare Topics. Oxford: Oxford University Press, 2000.

Snow, Edward. "Language and Sexual Difference in *Romeo and Juliet,*" *Shakespeare's Rought Magic.* Peter Erickson and Coppelia Kahn, eds. Newark: University of Delaware Press / London: Associated University Presses, 1985. 168–192.

Traub, Valerie. *Desire and Anxiety: Circulations of Sexuality in Shakespearean Drama.* London: Routledge, 1992.

Wells, Robin Headlam. *Shakespeare and Masculinity.* Cambridge and New York: Cambridge University Press, 2000.

ROBERT N. WATSON AND STEPHEN DICKEY

Wherefore Art Thou Tereu?
Juliet and the Legacy of Rape

1. The Balcony

To take Juliet's "Wherefore art thou Romeo?" as a practical question about location is a notorious and vulgar error. Yet her next question might justifiably be, "Wherefore art thou where thou art?" That is the distinct implication of her next "wherefore"—"How camest thou hither, tell me, and wherefore" (2.2.62)—and if audiences and readers could break free from the high-romantic reputation of the scene, they might start asking it for her.[1] But the seemingly exhaustive commentary on Shakespeare's *Romeo and Juliet* has contrived to ignore a cluster of allusions linking the hero to the most notorious rapists of classical culture: Tereus, Hades, Tarquin, and Paris. Though Romeo's covert activities beneath Juliet's window may not seem especially sinister on their own, there is something lurking out there with him: a cumulative culture of sexual extortion from which Juliet will have to extricate her love story. The persistent silent erasure of these threats, great and small, by editors and critics typifies the reduction of the play's exploration of the spectrum of sexual aggression into an absolute binary of rape and consent—a binary that may serve the ethical demands of our culture, but hardly matches the complicated experience of adolescent courtship to which the play speaks so engagingly.

Romeo's own explanation for his whereabouts hardly exonerates him of peeping: he found the place "By love, that first did prompt me to inquire; / He

Renaissance Quarterly, Volume 58, Number 1 (Spring 2005): pp. 127–156. Copyright © 2005 Northwestern University Press.

91

lent me counsel, and I lent him eyes" (2.2.80–81). Certainly the lewd sexual banter Mercutio persistently applies to the situation invites us to suppose that Romeo is seeking out his beloved's "straight leg, and quivering thigh, / And the demesnes that there adjacent lie" (2.1.19–20) by all available means and to the fullest extent possible. If, as Romeo complains, Rosaline was unwilling to "bide th' encounter of assailing eyes" (1.1.213), perhaps he will have better luck this time.

After a series of gently parried thrusts toward Juliet's body, and after learning that the feud will inhibit conventional courtship, Romeo—"bewitched by the charm of looks" (2.Chorus.6)—lurks "bescreen'd in night" (2.2.52) while the Capulet household readies for bed. For forty-nine lines after Juliet appears in her window (doing what?), he says nothing, only stares in secrecy. Twice at least, the text suggests, Romeo prolongs his advantage by overcoming an urge to reveal his presence—"I will answer it. / I am too bold" (13–14) and "shall I speak at this?" (37)—and instead remains in hiding as Juliet exposes more and more (of her feelings, at least). Romeo assures himself "'Tis not to me she speaks" (14), and thus, by the peculiar logic of this etiquette, he need not reply but can remain concealed to listen further.

To accuse Romeo of voyeurism here may seem mean-spirited, both toward the character and toward the play, but to exonerate him seems premature (or retroactive), and deprives us of yet another level on which the play traces the growth from immature to mature eroticism. Nor is there anything inherently ahistorical about the accusation. Despite what may have been a lesser standard of bodily privacy across many sections of Renaissance society, the possibility of voyeurism is verified by the persistence of scopophilic lyrics and sexual jokes. Many comedies in this period tease their spectators with an imminent exposure of women's genitalia—all the more provocatively because those spectators knew, on another level, that such exposure was impossible, since the women were played by boys. This dropping of the suspenders of disbelief is the underlying trick of Jonson's *Epicoene* and the ironic point of the interrupted puppet-show in his *Bartholomew Fair*. The works of Shakespeare and his contemporaries also frequently allude to the myth of Actaeon: a hunter who gazes on the virgin moon-goddess Diana as she bathes unclothed, and who is then destroyed when she turns him into a stag to be pursued by his hounds.[2] That Romeo here vows by the moonlight—which in Arthur Brooke's *The Tragicall Historye of Romeus and Juliet* (1562) is what exposes him to Juliet's view—may be romantic, but it is also plausibly an evocation of Actaeon's story: especially since the wary virgin, Juliet, warns him that he may be hunted down and torn apart by a pack if he is noticed there (2.2.64–70).[3]

Hapless Actaeon's glimpse of Diana was, by most accounts, initially accidental; yet Romeo's immediate precursor is more aggressive and willful. In

Brooke, Romeus casts "his greedy eyes" toward Juliet's window, and "In often passing so, his busy eyes he threw, / That every pane and tooting hole the wily lover knew."[4] In Shakespeare, Romeo's metaphors beneath Juliet's balcony imply similar motives. Gazing up at the "fair sun" Juliet, he immediately urges her to throw off her servitude to the virginal moon, and does so in terms that suggest he has a specific interim request of her: "Her vestal livery is but sick and green, / And none but fools do wear it; cast it off" (2.2.8–9). It is worth noting here that—though it may strike modern readers as a remarkable displacement—English law as well as classical mythography judged men's eyes primarily responsible for sexual crimes. Edward Coke notes that "of old time rape was felony, for which the offender was to suffer death, but before this act the offense was made lesser, and the punishment changed, *viz.* from death, to the losse of the members whereby he offended, *viz.* his eyes, *propter aspectum decoris, quibus virginem concupivit.*"[5]

Romeo's plea "that I were a glove upon that hand, / That I might touch that cheek" (2.2.24–25) is generally taken as a lovely moment of exalted courtship, if charmingly puerile. By wishing to be the glove, rather than the invasive hand or phallic finger, Romeo stays a decorous arm's length from, say, the sardonic De Flores of *The Changeling*—whose possession of Beatrice's glove leads him to consider "thrust[ing] my fingers into her sockets here"[6]—or from Shakespeare's own Tarquin, who seizes Lucrece's glove on his way to her bedchamber (316–322). But Romeo's imaginings here are akin to Parthenophil's increasingly vulgar wishes in Barnabe Barnes's Sonnet 63 (1593). After a quatrain citing Jove's predatory metamorphoses—becoming a bull to abduct Europa, an imposter-Diana to rape Callisto, and a shower of gold in Danae's lap—Parthenophil indulges in some fantasies of his own:

> Would I were chang'd but to my mistresse' gloves,
> That those white lovely fingers I might hide;
> That I might kisse those hands, which mine hart loves,
> Or else that cheane of pearle, her necke's vaine pride,
> Made proude with her necke's vaines; that I might folde
> About that lovely necke, and her pappes tickle,
> Or her to compasse like a belt of golde;
> Or that sweet wine, which downe her throate doth trickle,
> To kisse her lippes, and lye next at her hart,
> Runne through her vaynes, and passe by pleasure's part.[7]

It is a slippery slope to the clowns who wish they were fleas so that they might inhabit the undergarments of the kitchen-maid Nan Spit in Marlowe's *Doctor Faustus,* or to the various smirking personae of Cavalier verse who lasciviously imagine transforming themselves into their mistresses' garters: it is only too easy to degenerate from Lovelace's "Elinda's Glove" to his later "Her Muff." Romeo mopes into the vicinity of those degrading analogues in the balcony scene, and at 3.3.30–41, where he details the small creatures, including flies, who will have access to Juliet's body (from which he himself is banished).[8] And what might we deduce is on Romeo's mind in his very next speech, when he compares himself to a mortal whose "white-upturned wond'ring eyes . . . gaze on" an angel who "bestrides the lazy puffing clouds, / And sails upon the bosom of the air" (2.2.26–32)? Gazing up at a bestriding form tends to offer an intimate view; two scenes later, the "smock" of the Nurse—who is herself enduring the "ropery" (2.4.146) of Mercutio's verbal assault—is called "a sail" (102–103).[9] These offenses may seem mild, but they raise the question whether Romeo intends to earn or steal the erotic commodities he seeks from Juliet. In the anonymous *The Puritan* (1607)—which at moments looks like a comic parody of *Romeo and Juliet*—Moll comes out on her balcony "lacing of her clothes," and her prospective boyfriend Penny-Dub offers to climb up to her bedchamber. She refuses: "Ile keepe you downe, for you Knights are very dangerous if once you get above."[10]

Juliet promptly (and quite sensibly) devalues Romeo's oaths, since "at lovers' perjuries, / They say, Jove laughs" (2.2.92–93); Ovid's *Ars Amatoria* had advised young men not to "be timid in your promises; by promises girls are caught; call as witnesses to your promise what gods you please."[11] She therefore reacts to his subsequent "O, wilt thou leave me so unsatisfied?" with a testing, and arguably testy, question of her own: "What satisfaction canst thou have tonight?" (125–126). Even what she has already given has cost her "a maiden blush" (86). There is fear, not just girlish generosity, in her wish that she could retract her gift of love so she could "give it thee again" (131)—an anticipation of the problem of virginity as an erotic commodity.

Juliet's best alternative to that impossible retraction is to render Romeo's own commitment unretractable, and—as throughout this scene, where she wonders about high walls and worries about armed guards while he blithely, even blitheringly, claims love can somehow easily transcend such things—she answers his vague Petrarchan formulas with practical details:

> Three words, dear Romeo, and then goodnight indeed.
> If that thy bent of love be honorable,
> Thy purpose marriage, send me word to-morrow,
> By one that I'll procure to come to thee,
> Where and what time thou wilt perform the rite. (2.2.142–146)

The possibility that this Romeo is merely an amorous predator clearly crosses the minds of both Juliet, who worries that he "meanest not well"

(2.2.150), and her protective Nurse, who warns him not to "lead her in a fool's paradise" (2.4.165–166) before inviting him back for the second (2.4.165–166). 2.3 begins with the Friar, too, fearing that Romeo is just another young man inclined to seduce and abandon, one who believes he is fulfilling body and soul when he is merely reciting a clichéd and destructive script; 2.4 begins with Mercutio offering a similar—though more blunt and more approving—analysis, and ends with the Nurse worrying the same point. Indeed, by delaying her report about Romeo, the Nurse seems to demonstrate the coquettish techniques that Juliet has dangerously failed to practice: increasing male desire by deferring it, mixing a feigned dislike with liking, and indignation with playfulness, and demanding protracted bodily ministrations (in the Nurse's case, a backrub) before surrendering the main thing desired (in the Nurse's case, news of Romeo's reply).

Having long (and unhappily) refrained from imposing phallic violence on Rosaline—and, more recently, on Juliet—Romeo stabs their cousin Tybalt: Shakespeare's contemporaries did not need Freud to help them recognize stabbing as a version of rape.[12] As in *Othello*, the swordfight on the street looks very much like a displacement of the confrontation in the newlyweds' bedroom.[13] In the confrontation with Tybalt, Romeo is at first too affectionate to draw his sword, then—feeling his manhood compromised by his gentle passivity—returns with reckless violence against Juliet's flesh and blood: "Now I have stain'd the childhood of our joy / With blood remov'd but little from her own" (3.3.95–96). Instead of a confirmatory showing of the wedding night sheets, spotted with the blood of maidenhead, the wedding is compromised by the public display of a bloody shroud.[14]

News that "Romeo's hand shed Tybalt's blood" makes Juliet cry out, "O serpent heart, hid with a flow'ring face" (3.2.71, 73); this, however, is only an amplification of something she might have cried had Tybalt and Romeo never fought, something she must already (however unwillingly) have suspected. The fears that Juliet intermittently voices in the play can be readily located in Brooke, where they are, if anything, even more conspicuous.[15] Brooke's Juliet suspects the phallic serpent of treachery:

> What if his suttel brayne to fayne have taught his tong,
> And so the snake that lurkes in grasse thy tender hart hath stong?
> What if with friendly speache the traytor lye in wayte,
> As oft the poysond hooke is hid, wrapt in the pleasant bayte?[16]

These images of satanic ambush and deceit may seem overly dire, but they clearly establish the idea that Juliet's specific fear (in Brooke) is of a sexual fall—a fear she then elaborates by noting those Renaissance poster-boys of misogyny, Aeneas and Theseus:

Oft under cloke of truth, hath falshod served her lust
And toorned theyr honor into shame, that did so slightly trust.
What, was not Dido so, a crouned Queene, defamd?
And eke for such an heinous cryme, have men not Theseus
blamd?[17]

Later, after Romeus kills Tibalt, Juliet returns to her former suspicions that Romeus gave her merely "paynted promises" and "with veile of love" hid from her his "hatreds face."[18] Disingenuous seduction may lack the triumph of men's violence over women's will by which modern culture identifies rape—especially since it involves at least an illusory consent—but for women (and indeed for the law) it has long represented one more middle case in the spectrum between rape and love-making. Limiting one's interpretive aperture to the rosier hues of that spectrum does no service to the love story, because it does no justice to the dangers Juliet must accept in pursuing it.

The fear of callous abandonment, or even murder, is predictably subtler in Shakespeare's version, yet it persists.[19] Though 2.2 of *Romeo and Juliet* is generally known as "the balcony scene," there are actually two balcony scenes: one on the way up, one on the way down. We arrive at 2.5, the second balcony scene, with Romeo in obvious jeopardy, but Juliet hardly less so. As the wedding night ends, her first words are the archetypal complaint of the soon-to-be-abandoned woman: "Wilt thou be gone?" (3.5.1). It is easy enough for us to know she is not Dido, but how can she be confident that her dreamboat will not float off in the manner of Aeneas, or something even worse? (Similar fears occur to Jessica about her feud-crossed elopement with Lorenzo in *The Merchant of Venice* [5.1.1–20].) A potentially disturbing feature of the first balcony scene is that Romeo enters; a potentially disturbing feature of the second is that he exits.

In 2.2 Juliet questioned in the practical voice: who are you, how did you get in, how are you going to get out, what are we going to do about all this, how will I get a message to you, where, and at what time? Romeo is full of empty clichés about the moon and her eyes and eternity. In 3.5, however, the roles appear to have been reversed, perhaps because the balance of power has shifted in the aftermath of sexual consummation. Romeo is the one focused on business, while Juliet is lost in romantic dream and hyperbole, wanting to pretend it to be midnight. What satisfaction can she have this morning from his rather formal, proverbial, and seemingly complacent responses to her passionate entreaties and her worries about her continuing attractiveness to him? The contrast of tones is striking:

JULIET: Art thou gone so, love, lord, ay, husband, friend!

I must hear from thee every day in the hour,

For in a minute there are many days.

O, by this count I shall be much in years

Ere I again behold my Romeo!

ROMEO: *[From below]* Farewell!

I will omit no opportunity

That may convey my greetings, love, to thee.

JULIET: O, think'st thou we shall ever meet again?

ROMEO: I doubt it not, and all these woes shall serve

For sweet discourses in our times to come. (3.5.43–53)

His speeches here are as formally clothed as hers are emotionally naked.

The fictive spaces and physical arrangements of the two balcony scenes thus take us from the verticality of courtship idolatry (balcony as pedestal) to the horizontal parity of the consummated marriage (balcony as bed). The scenes also take us from the extremely tenuous privacy of the lovers' isolation from their families to a relationship that is no longer entirely secret, and that is pressured in increasingly drastic ways by the circumstances of the public world of the play. Indeed, the much shorter farewell episode records that pressure by its very brevity: fifty-nine lines to Romeo's exit, in contrast to the 189 lines of 2.2, which keeps not ending. The Nurse provides another index of this change. In the first she is a minor and invisible irritant—perhaps even helpful, giving occasion to renew the farewells and resistance to sharpen the desires. Her entrance into the second scene, however, brings with it not just her usual bawdy-comic energies, but also a sharp note of danger. Her warnings to "be wary, look about" (3.5.40) remind us that, from the perspective of the feud, the lovers' clandestine marriage remains illicit and vulnerable. At that instant Romeo descends from Juliet, and they are never again together in life.

The differences between the scenes are also recorded metrically, if we take John Barton's point that "a shared verse line says, 'pick up the cue.'"[20] In the first balcony scene, Romeo and Juliet divide pentameter lines eight times. Their mutual interruptions and self-interruptions—signaled by syntax as well as meter—and the uneven lengths of their speeches create a feverish pace on stage and establish an intimate connection between them. In contrast, the second balcony scene opens with Romeo and Juliet taking turns in an orderly fashion in speeches of similar lengths. The awkward, ecstatic energies of 2.2 are depleted. There are no incomplete sentences and only one shared line, and a rather chilly one it is. No wonder the word "fickle" now winds itself into three consecutive lines of Juliet's speech (3.5.60–62), though she diligently applies the word to Fortune rather than to Romeo.

Is the fuel gauge of this passion, though surely not on "Empty," already showing that first little flicker of the low-tank warning light? Our traditions and desires in reading the story resist such suspicions, but Juliet cannot know the traditions, or trust the desires. Accordingly, the language of this abbreviated aubade is strongly charged with regret on her part, and with exhaustion on his. Telling Romeo that the nightingale's song "pierc'd the fearful hollow of thine ear" (3.5.3) articulates Juliet's own pierced virginity. (That the "hollow" is "fearful" also suggests, retroactively, Juliet's ambivalence toward her own sexual desires.) His refusal, also expressed with anatomical precision, is based on the fact that "night's candles are burnt out" (9). How can she be sure that Romeo has not taken his pleasure knowing full well that he would be gone the next day anyway, and (because of the illicit nature of their clandestine marriage) that no one could profitably say anything to call him to account? The laws were generally quite clear that a woman who failed to cry out immediately for help—therefore, any woman who (like Juliet) was within earshot of potential rescuers—forfeited any right to claim rape thereafter. Brooke's Juliet voices that very fear:

> And thou, the instrument of Fortunes cruell will,
> Without whose ayde she can no way, her tyrans lust fulfill,
> Art not a whit ashamed, (as farre as I can see)
> To cast me of, when thou hast culd the better part of me.[21]

Although it is Fortune to whom she attributes this Tarquinian cluster of cruelty, will, tyranny, and lust, these seem barely disguised accusations of Romeus himself as one who shamelessly "culls" her and then casts her aside. Indeed, when Romeus explains why Juliet must not depart with him—a decision modern students of Shakespeare's play certainly recognize as questionable—his arguments seem far-fetched, and include the expectation that he will be executed "as a ravishor" of "a careless childe."[22]

A further fear awaits both Juliets, one that would make such a betrayal at once more explicable and more terrible, and would align the betrayal with the modern perception that rape is a crime based more in power than in sexuality. Might not this offer Romeus/Romeo the last laugh on a family he hates—a dirty joke for his Montague pals and a dark stain on the Capilet/Capulet honor?[23] In Shakespeare's "The Rape of Lucrece" the tyrant Tarquin actually wishes that he had some familial grudge against Lucrece's husband, because it might give him an "excuse" for committing the rape, "As in revenge or quittal of such strife" (232–236); indeed, as in many other Renaissance rape-stories, the main motive for the victim's suicide is to protect her family from shame by proving that the intercourse was in no way consensual.[24] In Brooke, Juliet explicitly worries that Romeus will seduce and then defame her as part of the feud, giving the Capulets an affront which they will find unanswerable in kind:

> Perhaps, the great revenge he cannot woorke by strength,
> By suttel sleight (my honor staynde) he hopes to worke at length.
> So shall I seeke to finde my fathers foe, his game,
> So I defylde, Report shall take her trompe of blacke defame,
> Whence she with puffed cheeke shall blowe a blast so shrill
> Of my disprayse, that with the noyse Verona shall she fill.
>   Then I, a laughing stocke through all the towne becomme,
>   Shall hide my selfe, but not my shame, within an hollowe toombe.[25]

Shakespeare's Juliet will find herself in a tomb soon enough, in an effort to conceal the truth about that amorous night.

Shakespeare connects the polemically cautionary world of Brooke to his own play early in the very first scene, when the Capulet servant Sampson—whose behavior is about to be mimicked by his betters—boasts that "I will show myself a tyrant: when I have fought with the [Montague] men, I will be civil with the [Montague] maids; I will cut off their heads . . . their maidenheads" (1.1.21–126). The implication that this interfamilial war might spill over into sexual exploitation prepares us to recognize the further threat of deception and humiliation that Juliet must evaluate.

The unpleasant possibilities we have raised would bring into focus another pair of ominous classical allusions. Juliet opens the second balcony scene with rape-references so indirect that they seem to have escaped commentary by the play's countless editors and critics, yet distinct enough to conspire with Ovidian anxieties elsewhere in the play.[26] As usual, it is difficult and perhaps unnecessary to judge whether these allusions should be taken as conscious on Juliet's part, as reflecting a subconscious anxiety she dares not quite confront, or as imposed by Shakespeare—exterior to the character—to warn the audience. It is worth noticing, though, that she is evidently inventing the nightingale, whether as an oblique expression of her own fears or as a provocation to Romeo. Although neither the nightingale nor the pomegranate tree appear in Shakespeare's known sources, they appear together in her aubade, carrying considerable emblematic weight:

> Wilt thou be gone? It is not yet near day.
> It was the nightingale, and not the lark,
> That pierc'd the fearful hollow of thine ear;
> Nightly she sings on yond pomegranate tree.
> Believe me, love, it was the nightingale. (3.5.1–5)

This draws on a sequence of bird references in their previous encounters: 2.2.22, 158–183; 2.5.7, 74. John Lyly's *Campaspe,* a prominent play in the previous decade, signals the ominous associations of this avian pairing:

> What Bird so sings and yet does wail?
>   O 'tis the Ravish'd Nightingale.
> Jug, jug, jug, jug, Tereu, she cries,
>   And still her woes at midnight rise.
> Brave prick-song! Who is't now we hear?
>   None but the lark so shrill and clear.
> Now at heaven's gate she claps her wings,
>   The morn not waking till she sings. [27]

In Ovid's *Metamorphoses,* the nightingale was once Philomel, transformed after Tereus raped her and cut out her tongue to prevent her testimony against him. The bird's melodious song is therefore both lamentation and compensation for Philomel's brutal silencing. The nightingale was said to press a thorn against its breast to give its tune a lyric accusing the rapist: "Tereu, Tereu!"

Wherefore might Romeo be Tereu? Suppose what Juliet thinks she hears is neither nightingale nor lark, but the proverbial fat lady singing, marking an ending, an undignified if operatic defeat. Tybalt would clearly want to offer his young cousin a warning resembling what Marcus tells Lavinia, after the fact, in Shakespeare's preceding tragedy, *Titus Andronicus:* "A craftier Tereus, cousin, hast thou met."[28] These stories usually seem to be on Shakespeare's mind when a woman is about to be violated, even when the violation is by trickery rather than force. In *Cymbeline,* Jachimo compares himself to Tarquin as he sneaks into Imogen's bedchamber to steal the sight of her uncovered breast, and notes that "She hath been reading late / The Tale of Tereus."[29] In *A Midsummer Night's Dream,* the chorus of the singularly ineffective fairy spell — designed to protect the sleeping Titania, who is about to be deluded into the embrace of the transformed Bottom — begins each time by calling on "Philomele" to provide the song.[30] Tereus's wedding with Procne was illuminated by "Furies snatching Tapers up that on some Herce did stande" (matching Shakespeare's insistent blending of wedding and funeral); Tereus tried "to corrupt hir servants" and "to bribe hir Nurse to prosecute his vice"; finally, he hid his captivity of Philomel by telling everyone she had died.[31] All these features draw that then-famous rape story into the mental field of spectators at the now-famous love story of Romeo and Juliet.

Our familiarity with *Romeo and Juliet* leads us to assume we are in the scenario of Keats's "The Eve of St. Agnes," where young Madeline wants young Porphyro to sneak into her chamber and seduce her, and he fully intends to marry her. But we cannot—or at least Juliet cannot—absolutely put aside an alternative scenario, which Shakespeare recorded as "The Rape of Lucrece." There Shakespeare repeatedly cites the figure of Philomel because Lucrece wants to replace the birdsong of day with the voice of the nightingale, to prevent day from shedding light on her shame in the aftermath of the rape (1079–1148). Juliet does not say that she has been abducted and raped by Romeo, but she does imply that, were Romeo to leave now, instantly, then what has happened between them will have been little better than that. Indeed, to have married the young noblewoman Juliet without her parents' consent places Romeo in a murky legal category associated with rape; by making Juliet even younger than she is in Brooke, Shakespeare assures the criminality of the match by Elizabethan standards, which also means that neither the Nurse nor the Friar—both of whom will lack the courage to defend the couple in other moments of crisis—could support Juliet's claim of marriage without risking jail.[32] The crime that first populated Rome (the rape of the Sabine women) and that later made Rome a republic (the rape of Lucrece that provoked the overthrow of the Tarquins) hovers uneasily around a Veronese youth with the exotic name of Romeo.[33]

2. The Underworld

Juliet's imaginary nightingale sings from a pomegranate tree, surely directing our attention to a second classical story: Hades' rape of Persephone, who was obliged to remain as his bride part of every year because she ate some seeds from an Underworld pomegranate tree. That story will resurface in Shakespeare's late plays: in both *The Winter's Tale* (4.4.116–118) and *The Tempest* (4.1.89) it serves to warn that even such princes among men as Florizel and Ferdinand might become rapists, rather than fiancés, to young women who love too much and trust too far.

In the first balcony scene, Juliet is already rehearsing for the role of Persephone: "Sweet, good night! / This bud of love, by summer's ripening breath, / May prove a beauteous flow'r when next we meet" (2.2.120–122). What presses the seasonal floral reference toward the classical myth is Juliet's suggestion, at the end of the Capulet ball, that the only alternative to marrying Romeo would be a marriage to death and the Underworld: "If he be married, / My grave is like to be my wedding-bed" (1.5.134–135). That suggestion resounds through the remainder of the play: "earth hath swallowed all my hopes but she," says her father (1.2.14); "I would the fool were married to her grave!" adds her mother (3.5.140).

In his associations with sycamore trees and westward darkness, and in his vampire-like aversion to the light, Romeo from the beginning seems to belong in the classical Underworld to which "dusky Dis" dragged Persephone (1.1.121–122, 138; *The Tempest*, 4.1.89) because he knew that her mother,

Demeter, would never otherwise permit the marriage. Juliet's famous soliloquy anticipating the wedding night—"Gallop apace, you fiery-footed steeds, to Phoebus' lodging" (3.2.1–2)—reinforces that impression. "Phoebus' lodging" was generally understood to be the Underworld (where the solar chariot had overnight parking privileges); so while Juliet's principal reference is unquestionably to that chariot, her desire for these steeds to hurry her to her deflowering hints that she may instead be boarding the chariot of Hades which rushed Persephone across the burning Phlegethon. As later with her eroticized version of Lucrece's suicide, Juliet here seems to be recapturing a rape story as, instead, her own passionate will. In contrast to the suave irony with which Thomas Carew's "The Rapture" transforms the classic rape victims into lascivious partners, Juliet's summoning of these steeds suggests her determination to make something positive out of the worst-case scenarios that implicitly haunt her throughout this courtship. "Give me my Romeo, and when I shall die . . ." (3.2.21), says Juliet, anticipating his arrival upon their wedding night and yet intimating a link, beyond the erotic pun, between Romeo and her own mortality. When Juliet is told, shortly thereafter, that he has indeed proven to be an agent of death, she says that news belongs "in dismal hell" (44), and then goes on to depict him as a "serpent heart" among the flowers, a "dragon" in a "fair . . . cave" (73–74), a potential Hades-figure destroying an Edenic garden scene, invading innocent flesh, dragging nature down into the dark Underworld: "O nature, what hadst thou to do in hell / When thou didst bower the spirit of a fiend / In mortal paradise of such sweet flesh?" (80–82). So it is appropriate for her to conclude, despairingly, "death, not Romeo, take my maidenhead" (137): symbolically, there is not much difference.[34]

These Hades-Persephone references culminate when Lord Capulet finds Juliet, seemingly dead, on her wedding morning:

> Death lies on her like an untimely frost
> Upon the sweetest flower of all the field. . . .
> O son, the night before thy wedding-day
> Hath Death lain with thy wife. There she lies,
> Flower as she was, deflowered by him,
> Death is my son-in-law, Death is my heir,
> My daughter he hath wedded. (4.5.28–29, 35–39)

Even Romeo, who earlier dreamed of being "an emperor" among the dead (5.1.9), echoes the allusion when he finds her beautiful body down in the Capulet tomb:

>   Shall I believe
> That unsubstantial Death is amorous,

And that the lean abhorred monster keeps
Thee here in dark to be his paramour?
For fear of that, I still will stay with thee,
And never from this palace of dim night
Depart again. (5.3.102–108)

Death, too, begins to look like a rapist, stealing women's bodies in the darkness, erasing their will. Henry Chettle's *Englands Mourning Garment* (1603)
urges the shepherd to "remember our Elizabeth, / And sing her Rape, done
by that Tarquin, Death."[35]

In the Persephone story, the messenger god Hermes arrives moments
too late to redeem her completely from the "palace of dim night," the royal
family of the dead: she has already tasted its fruit.[36] But the seasonal solution
to Persephone's death is implicit in the play's metaphysical and metatheatrical suggestion that she may spring back up to life in some next cycle, as Juliet
does in the tomb—and also in every new production of the play—precisely
because of her willingness to die for love. In other words, the associations
with the rape of Persephone amplify the noble, as well as ignoble, possibilities of a play where undying love and violent death are constantly striving to
surround and suppress each other, where comedy and tragedy compete for
the authority to frame this as a story either of renewal or of termination. The
notion of Romeo as Hades may suggest that he is a ravisher who destroys his
bride, but it also contributes to a pattern of redemptive hints that he carries
her—or rather, they carry each other—to another world on the far side of a
mortal barrier. This would be not rape, but rapture.

In this world, however—according to Shakespearean drama—Italy's the
right place for rape.[37] Even prospective husbands are sexual suspects. In *Titus
Andronicus,* when Lavinia's gallant young fiancé Bassianus carries her away
to prevent a dynastic marriage that her father was imposing, he is accused of
rape, and has to answer, "Rape call you it, my lord, to seize my own, / My true
betrothed love, and now my wife?" (1.1.405–406).

The discrepancy between Lord Capulet's protestations to Paris and his
practices with Juliet in 3.5.141–195 remind us only too clearly of the element
of coercion behind even seemingly consensual matches for aristocratic young
women in this period. Like several other prominent dynastic-marriage dramas
in the period, from *The Spanish Tragedy* to Webster's great tragedies, *Romeo
and Juliet* effectively unravels the myth of "consent" (e.g. 1.2.17), hinting that
marriage often entailed a degree of rape.[38] In Robert Mead's *The Combat of
Love and Friendship* (1654) Melesippus tells his daughter that, though he
hopes she will accept his choice, it is "No Marriage; but a well nam'd Rape,
where friends / Force Love upon their Children; where the Virgin / Is not so
truly given, as betraid" (1.4.9–11). Sebastian in Cyril Tourneur's *The Atheist's*

Tragedie (1611) makes the point even more directly: "Why what is't but a rape to force a wench / To marry, since it forces her to lie with him she would not?" (1.4.129–131). George Rivers's *The Heroinæ* (1639) observes that "Dido refused marriage, shee could not love. Marriage to her had been a rape, another had enjoy'd her against her will: if a rape must bee avoyded with the losse of life; through how many death[s] must she flie a loathed bed, where every night she shall be ravished?" (87–88). This enforcement makes an even more disturbing spectacle when the enforcer is the father, often insisting (as in classical comedy) that the daughter marry someone close to himself in age; it is hard to say whether the tradition of powerful theatrical fathers—such as Theophilus Cibber in the 1740s and Charles Kemble in the 1830s—playing Romeos to their daughters' Juliets was an effort to exploit or to preclude the transgressive aspects of the play's sexuality.

Conceivably playing in Shakespeare's mind, as he imagined Lord Capulet's anguish about Juliet, was Agamemnon's anguish about his daughter in Euripides' *Iphigenia at Aulis*: "And for this poor maid—why maid? Death, methinks, will soon make her his bride—how I pity her! . . . Alas! to what utter ruin Paris, the son of Priam, the cause of these troubles, has brought me. . . ."[39] In the history of sexuality as told to the Renaissance, a princely figure named Paris carried a lovely young woman off from her legitimate husband. In both stories, Paris thus occupies a middle category: not exactly a rapist in the obvious criminal sense—though he was often listed alongside more egregious rapists—but someone using force to take a woman to his bed, with destructive consequences, as "The Rape of Lucrece" reminds us at some length (1471–1568).[40] Lucrece reproves him for committing this violation out of "lust" (1473), while *Troilus and Cressida* calls him "wanton Paris" sleeping with "the ravish'd Helen" (Prologue, 9–10). For both Helen and Juliet, though in inverse ways, the figure of Paris ultimately asks at what cost a woman can—by giving or withholding consent—defy the marriage demanded by the social order.

Brooke's poem emphasizes this onomastic connection. When Romeus attends the Capilets' Christmas party (not to be confused with the Capulets' midsummer feast), he glimpses Juliet: "At length he saw a mayd, right fayre of perfect shape / Which Theseus, or Paris would have chosen to their rape."[41] This couplet seems especially abrupt if we come to it, as most all of us do, from Shakespeare's tragedy. What Theseus (whose notorious perfidy with women is recalled in *A Midsummer Night's Dream*) or Paris (tampered jurist, wife-abductor, war-inciter) should be doing here, at the precise moment of origin of this exemplary relationship of true love, is therefore disturbing to contemplate.[42] Several versions of Helen's story report that, as a very young woman, she was carried off—long before Paris did the same—by Theseus, who later went on a disastrous expedition to kidnap Persephone (with whom we have seen Shakespeare persistently associating Juliet) from Hades. George Turberville's 1567 version of *The Heroycall Epistles of . . . Publius Ovidius Naso* offers this tale in a way that again blurs the boundary between rape and Paris's abduction of Helen:

> Cause Theseus wrongde me once,
> well worthie am I deemde
> To be a Ruffians rape againe,
> and so to be esteemde?
> The guilt was mine if I
> allured were to yll:
> But so I rapted were by force,
> what coulde I doe but nill? (Epistle 16, 41–48)

Drawing on all these strands of cultural legacy, Shakespeare evokes the tangle of consent and coercion for a young woman in his society.

Brooke does not exactly say that Romeus is like-mindedly a rapist, but the energies released by the classical references—and by the rhyme that joins the perfection of Juliet's body with the idea of its violation—suggest that characteristics within Romeus are here being emblematically expressed. Later in Brooke's poem, when Juliet has feigned agreement with the plan to marry Paris, she tells her mother that she will seek to please her new husband by wearing "the bravest garments and the richest jewels" she owns—"for if I did excel the famous Grecian rape, / Yet might attire helpe to amende my bewty and my shape"—echoing the rhyme that communicated Romeus's love at first sight, and expressing Juliet's awareness of her bigamous predicament.[43]

Now, clearly, evidence against Brooke's Romeus should not be admissible in a trial of Shakespeare's Romeo any more than Trojan Paris's actions should be held against County Paris. Nonetheless, an array of details from the *Tragicall Historye* confirms the cultural reasons why Juliet, in both poem and play, might well be wary of any wooer, let alone a gatecrashing Montague. Interpreting Shakespeare through his sources is, of course, a tricky task. Finding the secret meaning of a Shakespeare play precisely in what he chooses to mute or omit seems perverse, though there could be an ironic production of meaning in the audience if the source's story was well-known—as Brooke's poem was—and value for the self-delighting playwright's mind even if the source were obscure.[44] Some subliminal residue seems plausible in this heavily allusive artistic culture. Since this residue needs to suggest nothing more than a repressed impulse in Romeo or repressed fear in Juliet, a thin association may nonetheless be sufficient and noteworthy. Indeed, scholarly exposition of the plays may resemble (though many suspect quite the opposite) the normal workings of the human mind, which navigates through the internal and external complexities of human experience by a layering of allusions, stories of varying degrees of proximity and vividness, most of them indirectly inherited, that tell us what to want and what to fear.

In thus naming and situating Paris, Brooke and Shakespeare pass on their sources' conflation of the notorious classical seizer of women with the general figure of the unwanted husband.[45] Furthermore, in the fights over Juliet Shakespeare conflates the two main ways Renaissance women were denied subjectivity and choice in the process of courtship: by their treatment as objects of exchange and competition among men, and by deprivation of their consent in their choice of spouses—though this was a problem for men also—and in their sexual relations with those spouses.[46] According to Ovid, Venus actively promotes Persephone's rape as advantageous to Venus's dynastic ambitions, ordering Cupid to aim at Dis: "And wherefore then should only Hell still unsubdued stand? / Thy mothers Empire and thine own why doste thou not advaunce?"[47] As if to focus on the element of rape in the enforcement of marriage, Juliet's solution to the proposed match with Paris echoes the pleas of most women faced with rape in classical and Renaissance literature:

> O, bid me leap, rather than marry Paris,
> From off the battlements of any tower . . .
> Or hide me nightly in a charnel house,
> O'ercover'd quite with dead men's rattling bones . . .
> Or bid me go into a new-made grave,
> And hide me with a dead man in his shroud. (4.1.77–78, 81–85)

The Friar does then give her death and entombment as the only way to stave off Paris's amorous intentions.[48] From there on her body becomes an object of adoration while she remains absolutely passive, though actually inwardly alive; the necrophiliac appeal of the ending is another force drawing the audience into fantasies of something like rape.

Even Paris's attack on Romeo at the Capulet tomb seems founded on the suspicion that Romeo intends to perform some necrophiliac violence (or vandalism) against Juliet's helpless corpse, "to do some villainous shame / To the dead bodies" (5.3.52–53). It is not an unfounded fear, given the commonplace association between womb and tomb, and especially if (as happens so often in Shakespearean tragedy) he partly overhears the worst of Romeo's words. Romeo tells Balthasar that he has come "partly to behold my lady's face, / But chiefly to take thence from her dead finger / A precious ring—a ring that I must use / In dear employment" (29–32). The final scene of *The Merchant of Venice* shows that Shakespeare assumed an association between wedding rings and female genitalia; in *Titus Andronicus* he has Martius say, of the corpse of a man whose wife has just been raped, "Upon his bloody finger he doth wear / A precious ring that lightens all this hole" (2.3.226–227); and Middleton's *The Changeling* confirms what sexual import English Renaissance playwrights could convey by amputated ring-bearing fingers.[49] The same rather banal synecdoche appears here in the gendered pair of suicides, one by cup and one by sword; the Capulets have every reason to believe, at 5.3.205, that Romeo has stabbed her, and even our knowledge that this was suicide rather than murder makes her destiny, her choice, only further resemble that of Lucrece. The way Romeo continues from there is, however, even more ominously vague:

> But if thou, jealous, dost return to pry
> In what I farther shall intend to do,
> By heaven I will tear thee joint from joint,
> And strew this hungry churchyard with thy limbs.
> The time and my intents are savage-wild. (33–37)

So dark a secret must surely suggest, to a half-informed observer such as Paris—as to Fernando at a notably parallel moment in John Ford's *Love's sacrifice*—the prospect of Juliet's posthumous rape by the prying Romeo.[50]

3. The Academy

Rape is thus the threat encompassing and permeating the physical actions, the psychological tensions, and the classical allusions of what is widely deemed the ultimate love story. Even among the male characters, the relationships (particularly in performance) seem to take on strong overtones of sexual aggression, ranging from sexual teasing and playful wrestling to the deadly serious phallic violence of swordfights.[51] The problem is that rape is hardly less complex or historically determined than sexuality in general: it appears in various guises and various degrees. Modern commentators have been understandably reluctant to address this problem, but Renaissance playwrights—negotiating a culture whose notions of rape were multiple and changing—repeatedly juxtapose the different forms and severities of compulsion (including prostitution) by which women were deprived of sexual choice. Compare, for example, the way *Romeo and Juliet* places socio-economically compelled marriage alongside dishonest seduction and more direct physical violence, with the various impingements on women's erotic will in Middleton's *Women Beware Women* and *The Changeling,* Jonson's *Volpone, The Alchemist,* and *Bartholomew Fair,* Marston's *Sophonisba,* and Ford's *'Tis Pity She's a Whore.*

Shakespeare's Paris—named after a famous quasi-rapist, and himself unwittingly attempting a quasi-rape—may either point up or channel off Romeo's associations with rape. Similarly, one could either defend or prosecute Romeo by acknowledging that standard courtship, manipulative seduction, underage marriage, offensive peeping, actionable stalking, and criminal rape are parts of a continuum of male sexual aggression, however sharply and rightly we might want to moralize and legislate the difference between the extremes of that continuum. It is not just by chance, then, that Friar Lawrence's observation about how the same herbs can be medicine or poison, depending on the dosage, leads directly into his efforts to evaluate Romeo's sudden passion for Juliet. There is certainly a crucial difference between "grace" and "rude will"—indeed, they are "opposed"—but both "encamp them still / In man" (2.3.27–28). Later in the scene, "grace" becomes Romeo's euphemism for erotic requital (2.3.86), whereas "rude will" suggests, in Elizabethan slang, male sexual aggression. Romeo is undeniably announcing a deep—and, more importantly, a requited—love when he tells the Friar:

> but come what sorrow can,
> It cannot countervail the exchange of joy
> That one short minute gives me in her sight.
> Do thou but close our hands with holy words,
> Then love-devouring death do what he dare,
> It is enough I may but call her mine. (2.6.3–8)

Yet, apart from line 6, Tarquin or Tereus could sincerely have said the same.

Of course we are not claiming that Romeo—even to the extent one deems him a complete and independent being rather than a mere dramatic character—is guilty of rape in the modern sense; only that Juliet might have reason to doubt his innocence and to question the honor of his intentions. Our understanding of this latent guilt is much like Edward Snow's more psychoanalytic perception that a fantasy of violence against the female body "does not so much enter Romeo's psyche as take its place in the haunted male background which the gentleness of his own love stands out against but never entirely exorcises."[52] Robert Appelbaum observes that, "because of our current difficulty in discussing the structure of masculinity without putting it on trial and pronouncing it guilty, our experience of tragic subjectivity in Shakespeare has been unable to find a suitable critical vocabulary."[53] The same problem hinders the search for a vocabulary of erotic aggression.

Much more could be said here to historicize the crime of rape.[54] But what about historicizing our discussion of it? What here could not have been written thirty years ago, when feminist scholars began excavating analyses of sexist violations from the depths of Shakespearean drama?[55] Perhaps it is enough to say that, for whatever reason, this particular piece of that story went (to the best of our knowledge) unwritten; perhaps the implication that specters of rape hover over even the most youthful and charming courtships would have been so unpopular and deterministic as to undermine the social advocacy such criticism often sought to perform. But even the most transcendently romantic reading of the play's bloody ending may remind us that, in the biological scheme, the necessary prelude to new birth may look disturbingly like an act of physical violence.

Why, then, has Romeo remained a fugitive from gender justice so long, while Leontes, Hamlet, and several Claudios sat glumly in the dock hearing their indictments? The easy answer is that Romeo is innocent. The hard truth, though—however prettily the nightingale may sing it—is that the world is not, and that the lover and the rapist are often separated by exactly the kind of reassuring conventional boundary that Shakespearean drama is always threatening to blur. The plays are part of an unacknowledged legislation of the world that takes account even of those crimes that occur only in the desiring and fearful minds of potential perpetrators and victims, where they appear as uneasy dreams of a personal future that can be articulated only in terms of the collective past, in the great stories of love and death.

The feud has trapped these lovers outside the social rules, leaving them dangerously, exhilaratingly free to invent their own; but they are not outside the culture, whose landmarks they still must use to orient themselves. There is nothing so unusual about the ways Juliet (at 1.5.110) and Friar Lawrence (at 2.3.88) try to tease Romeo out of his bookish wooings; anti-Petrarchan satire was commonplace. What makes this instance unusually compelling is the persistent question of whether the lovers, having broken free from the scripts of facile erotic complaint, can also pull free from more grandly tragic precedents. Like Lorenzo and Jessica at the beginning of act 5 of *The Merchant of Venice,* they can test their own situation only by brushing against tragic erotic touchstones such as Troilus and Cressida, Pyramus and Thisbe, and Dido and Aeneas—maybe even against Tarquin and Lucrece, Hades and Persephone, and Paris and Helen.

Our main critical point, then, is how often *Romeo and Juliet* alludes to rape, in all the different ways Renaissance law and literature defined it; our metacritical point is how diligently commentary on the play has looked away from those allusions. Not much in a major Shakespeare play has gone unexamined by simple carelessness; so this gap in the discussion of a play in which a young woman is about to be forcibly carried off to a bigamous bed by a man named Paris, and is then repeatedly associated with Persephone carried off to bed against her will by Hades, seems worth remarking, even if Juliet did not also echo Philomel and Lucrece. A small but representative instance of the averted (or distracted) gaze of criticism is the fact that neither the *Variorum* nor any standard modern edition of *Romeo and Juliet* remarks upon the special Ovidian charge Shakespeare achieves by locating an (imaginary) nightingale on a pomegranate tree in the Capulet orchard on the morning after the couple's sexual initiation. Commentary instead looks to ornithology, folklore, travelers' tales, or "poetic tradition" for an explanation of this line.[56]

A meta-metacritical incident may help to explain this blind spot. This article was previously submitted to another distinguished journal, where a reader's report scoffed at our reference to "phallic violence"—"I think they mean 'sex,'" the report suggested, though our point was that Romeo's deeds with Juliet blur into his deeds with Tybalt—while deciding that, by the "sexual aggression" involved in mating, we must really have meant "rape." This determination to push all male sexual activity into one of two perfectly distinct categories (for which we must simply have forgotten the words) is exactly the kind of erotic essentialism we were trying to resist and what we were arguing that the play resists. The other reader more openly objected to our failure to assert clear divisions among things called lovers, husbands, and assailants: "It really is important to recognize the distinction between seduction, courtship, and rape, even, or especially, when arguing that the culture works to elide them." Yet we had been quite explicitly arguing exactly the opposite: that the culture, as is morally imperative, works to distinguish these things, which in experience can often be murky and shifting—especially for a young person alone in the middle of them, deciding from moment to moment what to attempt and what to permit, how to send and how to read the often intricate and paradoxical signals of the human mating dance. The play persistently reminds its audience that people have to try to navigate by clear cultural markers—Is my suitor Petrarch or Tereus?—even while knowing that neither is likely to tell the whole story reliably. As a Caroline handbook for English gentlewomen would warn, "Your *True-love* may prove a *Jason* or a *Theseus,* and leave you in the bryers for all your confidence."[57] Whether Romeo is to be regarded as lover, husband, or rapist, depends on what each onstage observer knows and does not know at that particular moment; exactly the same can be said of his rival Paris (and of the Trojan Paris as well).

Since we had tried not to write obscurely, we conclude that something else was obscuring our argument. This something sounded like indignation, not only at our failure to emphasize the romantic aspect of the play, which we thought hardly needed reiterating, but also at our rejection of the fantasy that there is no third alternative between the benign melting-together of angelic lovers—as in Donne's "Air and Angels" and Milton's *Paradise Lost,* devoid of any element of physical aggression or potential exploitation—and sub-bestial attacks, such as those upon Lucrece and Lavinia.[58]

Acknowledging middle cases which can be viably erotic while still entailing physical aggression is risky, because many rapists have doubtless exploited it to escape their due punishment; we trust it is clear that we are neither denying nor justifying the fact of rape. But do these risks really justify steadfastly or reflexively averting our eyes from the deep questions this play so forcefully raises? As with so many of Shakespeare's other politically disquieting moments (on race and class as well as gender), perhaps it is time we moved from silent censorship to an open confrontation with the issues— issues which the plays doubtless raise for their audiences whether or not scholars like or admit it. In the Renaissance the availability of a romantic reading did not automatically exclude the threat of what they called rape; indeed, rape often led to marriage with a complacency now hard to fathom.[59] Moreover, it is hard to imagine a more gorgeous evocation of poetically conventional male erotic desire than the one Shakespeare provides for Tarquin as he prepares to rape Lucrece.

Renaissance literature reflected a legal principle that women slip into complicity with a rapist if they experience any pleasure, or conceive a child, during the act.[60] Though we now find that idea quite objectionable, scientifically as well as politically, it does mirror an important feminist argument that consensual sex can become rape during the act; and this kind of psychological vacillation of consent does not disappear from erotic experience just because we fear the consequences of acknowledging it. In an influential Renaissance analysis, Coluccio Salutati explained Lucrece's suicide as partly the result of her anguished recognition that she found some pleasure, however unwilling, in the rape, and therefore partook of its guilt. The pain of the sword serves to renounce and thus cancel any pleasure from the phallus:

> Because rape takes place physically and psychologically *inside*, it is, as Mieke Bal explains, "by definition imagined; it can only exist as experience and as memory, as image translated into signs, never adequately objectifiable. . . . Because of this difficulty in representing rape, its depiction is often displaced; it is then depicted as self-murder, as in Lucretia's case where self-murder stands for rape, the suicide becoming its metaphor." The figuring of rape through the image of suicide is perhaps most conspicuous in the paintings of the period. Although paintings depict separately the rape and the suicide, the weapon with which Tarquin initially threatens Lucrece always prefigures the weapon she will later use in her suicide, just as the weapon of suicide represents or stands in for Tarquin's weapon and the phallus it symbolizes.[61]

Juliet finally takes command of this destructive legacy, as she earlier had appropriated Tarquin's and Hades' impatience for the dark night and its sexual energies (3.2.1–31). She reclaims pleasure by consensual death with Romeo; she brings together the phallus and the sword, welcoming Romeo's "happy dagger" into what she calls—as Shakespeare's Lucrece did in a parallel moment, 1723–1724—the "sheath" (5.3.169–170) of her body. By attending to rather than trying to deny the complex weave of sex, power, and violence in the play, we can see Juliet forcibly rearranging it to meet the needs of the moment: her moment, but one shared—if only in metaphorical or milder form—by many other women, then and now.

The same blurring of the boundaries distinguishing courtship, seduction, rape, and marriage is a prominent feature of *A Midsummer Night's Dream*, the play Shakespeare was most likely writing simultaneously with *Romeo and Juliet*. When Shakespeare revises "The Knight's Tale" into *The Two Noble Kinsmen*, Chaucer's clear "distinction between licit sexual intercourse and rape is virtually obliterated."[62] Do we know that Caliban's actions toward Miranda were any more violent than, say, Silvius's toward Phoebe? The difference between the heroically/romantically persistent wooer and the criminally persistent one is rightly in the eyes of the person being courted, but may be hard—or, in cases of racism, too easy—for others to see. Did Katharine in *Henry V*, or even Isabella in *Measure for Measure*, have much more choice about her sex partner than Lucrece in "The Rape of Lucrece" or Lavinia in *Titus Andronicus?* Does it resolve the problem to assume that the wives will find more pleasure in and after the consummation than the rape victims, or does that push us back toward the repugnant old suggestion that a woman should seek pleasure even in imposed sex acts, and the hardly-less-repugnant old legality that acquitted men of rape if the woman ended up taking any pleasure or bearing any progeny from those acts?

If we do not acknowledge the ancient specter of rape haunting this story, we cannot recognize what Juliet does to exorcise it. The insistence that male erotic desire is always categorically either perfectly inoffensive or a criminal offense finally serves some urgent feminist causes no better than the division of women into madonnas and whores. Nor does it serve very well the cause of this great Shakespearean tragedy, which depends for both its pity and its fear on the recognition that Juliet must find her own way into the uncertain meaning of her own uncertain story, and pay for her final triumph over such categories with her life.

The Nurse's recollection of her late husband's bawdy joke and the toddler Juliet's strangely equanimous reply suggests that Juliet's destiny rests in her character, and that it is not a purely tragic destiny:

> "Yea," quoth he, "dost thou fall upon thy face?
> Thou wilt fall backward when thou hast more wit,
> Wilt thou not, Jule?" and by my holidam,
> The pretty wretch left crying and said, "Ay." (1.3.41–44)

This may seem mere comic patter, but Shakespeare has the Nurse tell the whole story three more times within ten lines, ending each time with Juliet's "Ay," like James Joyce allowing Molly Bloom finally to lift sexual consent free from ambivalence: "yes I said yes I will Yes." In a play laden with foreshadowings, and fates adumbrated since birth, Juliet here shows her precocious and prodigious determination to see what others might perceive as a dangerous fall as instead a positive choice; to take what the conventional elders see as mere injury and affirm it as her erotic will; "to lose a winning match, / Play'd for a pair of stainless maidenhoods" (3.2.12–13); to look ahead, stop her tears, and say unflinchingly to the "perilous knock" (1.3.54) of sexual experience, through pain and blood, "Ay."

Notes

1. All references to Shakespeare's works follow *The Riverside Shakespeare*, ed. G. Blakemore Evans et al., 2nd ed. (Boston: Houghton Mifflin, 1997).

2. References to Actaeon are especially noticeable in Shakespeare's Elizabethan comedies. As Barkan has shown, Shakespeare draws on the Actaeon myth clearly in *The Merry Wives of Windsor* and extensively in *A Midsummer Night's Dream*. *Twelfth Night* 1.1.18–22 conspicuously alludes to Actaeon's transformation (without naming him directly); Watson argues for the importance of the myth in *As You Like It*.

3. See Brooke, 468–469. (All subsequent references to Brooke will be by line number; references to Bullough's editorial material will be by page number.) Thinking of himself as the even more tongue-tied Actaeon would allow Romeo partly to excuse his obvious prying into Capulet affairs. Because Actaeon's glimpse of Diana was inadvertent—he was out hunting and, as Juliet might say, stumbled on Diana's counsels—his punishment was the result not of "desart / But cruell Fortune" (Golding, 3.164–165; all subsequent references to Golding's translation will be to book and line number). Such a formulation later proves attractive to Romeo after he kills Tybalt and exoneratingly proclaims himself "Fortune's fool" (3.1.136).

4. Brooke, 440–441. Bullough, 297, glosses "tooting" as "peeping."

5. Coke, chap. 13: "with which he desired the virgin, because of the sight of her beauty." Subsequent references add castration to the blinding, but that the initial reference is to blinding seems remarkable.

6. Middleton and Rowley, 1.1.230.

7. M. Evans, 164, ll. 5–14.

8. When Romeo specifically imagines "carrion flies" that "may seize / On the white wonder of dear Juliet's hand, / And steal immortal blessing from her lips" (3.3.35–37) it is difficult to avoid seeing her as a flyblown corpse that is simultaneously the object of courtship. We have moved, here, disturbingly graveward from the frolickings of Lesbia's sparrow and its avian descendants in amorous verse, where the wooer envies the bird's access to the beloved. The fuller implications of Romeo's necrophiliac nuance, and of the idea of a Juliet who is always in some sense dead, will be developed later in this article.

9. Franco Zeffirelli's film of 1968 develops this confrontation in strongly physical ways when an initially flirtatious Nurse undergoes what is arguably a stylized, slapstick stripping and gang-rape by Mercutio and other not-so-gentle

men of Verona. Mercutio lifts her skirt from behind, feigns the escape of malodors therefrom, yanks her huge veil about during the "hoar"/"hare"/"whore" flyting, then removes it altogether and wears it as a kind of false bosom, as though having exposed and captured her body. The Nurse is left with a kiss, knocked down on the stairs in the public square. The scene as a whole visually and performatively foreshadows the duel between Mercutio and Tybalt, fought in the same place and similarly surrounded by onlookers, thus linking sex, violence, and intermittent comedy—riot and laugh-riot—much as the play's opening dialogue does.

10. Sig. H2r, lines 31–32.

11. Bate, 179. Certainly the well-read Juliet of Brooke's *Tragically Historye* worries that the literary odds almost assure her wooer's treachery: "A thousand stories more, to teache me to beware, / In Boccace, and in Ovids bookes too playnely written are" (393–394).

12. See Gorges, bk. 4, 359–360: "If they by fight away would scape, / With your sharp blades their bosomes rape."

13. A more extended version of this parallel occurs in *Twelfth Night*, where two unmanly suitors flee a duel in 3.4 before blood can be shed—suggesting the fears preventing Orsino and Olivia from achieving marital consummations—only to yield to true bloodshed and marital consummation in 4.1 when the truly masculine Sebastian replaces the faux-masculine Cesario in brawl, and then in bed.

14. Capulet's horrified "O heavens! O wife, look how our daughter bleeds!" (5.3.202) similarly registers the confusing and tragic simultanity of Juliet's maturation, consummation, and demise. While much of the language of the play's end shows the characters trying to lodge Romeo and Juliet in the sterilized past of narrative, Capulet's present tense directs public attention to the ongoing, active messiness of the catastrophe.

15. Such fears echo onward into John Quarles's "Tarquin Banished: or, the Reward of Lust" (1655), where Lucretia finds that her "table fed a Serpent, not a Dove" (2)—terms Juliet applies to Romeo at 3.2.73–76—and where Tarquin's response to banishment markedly resembles that of Romeo in 3.3. It is decided that Tarquin's sentence "should not be speedy death, but . . . a sad and lasting banishment": "This news arriving unto *Tarquins* ears / He soon begins to argue with his fears: / Must I be sent, cryes he, into a place / Of no society, and there imbrace / Perpetual woe? Oh! how could Hell contrive / So great a plague to keep me still alive? / What shall I doe in this extreme abysse / Of woe and torments? Death had been a blisse / Beyond expression . . ." (7). Romeo also claims to prefer death as "merciful" compared to banishment, which he likens to "purgatory, torture, hell itself" (3.3.12–18; cf. 47–48). This cluster of associations, established by verbal and circumstantial allusion, may suggest that, by the seventeenth century, aspects of Romeo and Tarquin have become conflated within the cultural memory.

16. Brooke, 385–388.

17. Ibid., 389–392.

18. Ibid., 1114, 1126.

19. For fears of murder in Brooke, see ibid., 1123–1128.

20. Barton, 32.

21. Brooke, 1591–1594.

22. Ibid., 1651–1654.

23. Burks, 769, quotes *Aristotle's Master-Piece*—a notably "popular text on reproductive biology" translated into English just before Shakespeare wrote *Romeo*

and Juliet—which warns parents to raise their girls carefully, "most of all the Virgins, when they grow up to be marriageable, for if through the unnatural severity of rigid Parents they be crossed and frustrated in their love, many of them, out of a mad humour, if temptation lies in their way, throw themselves into the unchaste Arms of a subtle, charming Tempter, being through the softness of good Nature, and strong Desire, to pursue their Appetites, easily induced to believe Men's Flatteries, and feigned Vows of promised Marriage, to cover the shame; and then too late the Parents find the effects of their rash Severity, which brought a lasting stain upon their Family." Notice again how poorly the boundaries separating ordinary sexual desire and destructive sexual violation appear to have been marked.

24. Stimpson, 58, cites "political or familial revenge" as "the common justification for rape"; see "Shakespeare and the Soil of Rape." In Renaissance culture generally, the woman's willing death is the surest, perhaps the only, proof that she really had been raped; see Williams, 105–108.

25. Brooke, 395–402.

26. Williams, 93, begins her impressive study by observing that "Brief allusions to rape occur throughout Shakespeare's work, combining maximum effect with minimum critical perturbation." She does not, however, mention *Romeo and Juliet,* despite her recognition that "For Renaissance readers, the best-thumbed guide to ancient riots, incests, and rapes is Ovid's *Metamorphoses*" (97).

27. Lyly, 5.1.35–42.

28. *Titus Andronicus,* 2.4.41.

29. *Cymbeline,* 2.2.12, 44–45

30. *A Midsummer Night's Dream,* 2.2.13, 24

31. Golding, 6:550; 589–590.

32. Dalton, 248, explains that "The taking away of a maide under sixteene yeares of age, without the consent of her parents or governors, of contracting marriage with her, or deflowering her, is no felony, but yet shall be punished with long imprisonment, without baile, or with grievous fine." Coke concludes his chapter on rape by noting that marrying a woman below the age of consent without her parents' endorsement falls under the same category. John Donne discovered unhappily that society would not forbear punishing a seducer of an aristocratic young woman just because he was willing to marry her. In his complaint that "Young beauties force [y]our love, and that's a rape"—"The Autumnal," 3—Donne shows another way the category is elastic in this period.

33. Livy, bk. 1, chap. 9, describes the mass rape of the Sabine women as Romulus's ultimately successful tactic to populate Rome; Detmer-Goebel, 76, asserts that "rape is the centerpiece of Shakespeare's fictional history of Rome."

34. Farrell, 144, observes that "Romeo imagines Juliet sexually enslaved in the 'palace' of a 'monster' who is also a warrior-king. This fantasy projects the long-denied dark side of the patriarchal forms in which the lovers have construed each other. Romeo dissociates from himself as Death the part of him that would be made an emperor by Juliet's kiss. In this final moment of tenderness he rejects the devouring triumphalism latent in all patriarchy. . . . Otherwise, loving such an emperor-Romeo, Juliet would be submitting to rape like the women Sampson fancies 'ever thrust to the wall.'"

35. Chettle, 35–36.

36. Porter, 80–81, 104, 127, 192, explores the pertinence of Mercury (or Hermes) to Mercutio in, among other ways, his role as conductor of souls to Hades' Underworld.

37. Stimpson, 57.

38. It is important to remember, however, that modern concerns about marriage as a way of achieving rape were less noticeable, four hundred years earlier, than concern about rape as a way of achieving marriage, since a woman known to have been violated became hard to wed to anyone but her violator, and widows could sometimes be compelled to marry their attackers—both facts which men used to enforce profitable matches. Coke, chap. 11, reports this misfortune befalling two widows; cited by Burks, 768, n. 23.

39. Jones, 110–118, argues that Shakespeare drew on *Iphigenia at Aulis* in writing *Julius Caesar;* a Latin translation had been published by Erasmus at the start of the sixteenth century. There is also reason to believe that Shakespeare knew the other Euripides play that Erasmus translated, *Hecuba*.

40. For example, see Robert Chester's "To the kind Reader" in the 1601 *Loves martyr,* which lists "Hellan's rape" and "Lucrece rape" in parallel. The crimes are similarly run together in Johnson, chap. 15: "What became of Hellens rauishment, but the destruction of renowned Troy? What of Romane Lucresiaes rape, but the bannishment of Tarquin? and what of Prognies foule deflowrement by her sisters husband, the lustfull King of Thrace, but the bloudie banquet of his yong Son Itis, whose tender bodie they serued to his table baked in a Pie?"

41. Brooke, 197–198.

42. For *A Midsummer Night's Dream,* see especially 2.1.74–80; furthermore, the entire opening scene of the play emphasizes that Theseus is taking a bride by force.

43. Brooke, 2235, 2237–2238.

44. See Bullough, 1:275, on Brooke's wide readership.

45. Levenson, 7, notes that in Bandello's version of the tale, "in a rare moment of wordplay, Giulietta describes Count Paris of Lodrone as a thief ('ladrone') who steals another's property."

46. English legal history indicates that rape itself was evolving in the later sixteenth century from a theft of male property toward a violation of female erotic will. Williams, 99–100, reports that "The late sixteenth century is a watershed in rape law. From Anglo-Saxon times, rape was defined as the abduction of a woman against the will of her male guardian. Consent was often irrelevant; violation was a side-issue: the crime was essentially theft." Statutes in 1555 and 1597 broke rape and abduction into distinct offences; Detmer-Goebel, 75–78, explores the growing authority of women's testimonies as rape, and the victim of rape, became thus redefined in law. Though her discussion focuses on Lavinia in *Titus Andronicus,* it also indirectly illuminates the way Juliet's relatively isolated predicament informs her rhetorical choices in articulating both her desires and her fears. For more on these legal changes, see Bashar.

47. Golding, 5:466–467.

48. Any wedding-night intercourse with Paris would be both unwilling and extramarital, thus placing it firmly in the category of rape, a charge from which marriage often gave husbands immunity. However decorously floral Paris's presence in the graveyard may be, it disquietingly displaces his deflowering intentions for the

wedding-night, when—according to the Nurse's bawdy speculation—Paris would let her "rest but little" (4.5.7), and not in peace.

49. In 3.4 De Flores continues his digital assault on Beatrice by presenting her with Alonzo's severed finger, on which sparkles the diamond ring she had been forced to send her unwelcome wooer. A complex sexual bargaining ensues: though De Flores gets the ring for his murderer's fee, his symbolic castration of a rival—and his demand for Beatrice's virginity—turns the scene into, among other things, the parodic wedding of a couple "engag'd so jointly" (89) by guilt, for which the unfortunate Alonzo serves as best man.

50. Romeo here closely resembles the penitent Duke in act 5 of *Loves sacrifice*, who returns to the tomb of the beloved he has killed sounding oddly like Romeo: "Peace and sweet rest sleep here; let not the touch / Of this my impious hand, prophane the shrine / Of fairest purity, which houers yet / About those blessed bones inhearst within"—returns to the tomb of the beloved he has killed, only to be confronted by Fernando in the role Paris feels he must play. He is then confronted by Fernando in the role Paris feels he must play: "Forbeare; what art thou that dost rudely presse / Into the confines of forsaken-graues? / Has death no privilege? Com'st thou, *Caraffa*, / To practise yet a rape upon the dead? Inhumane Tyrant; / Whats' ever thou intend'st, know this place / Is poynted out for my inheritance: / Here lyes the monument of all my hopes. / Had eager Lust intrunk'd my conquered soule, / I had not buried living ioyes in death: / Goe, Revell in thy pallace, and be proud / To boast thy famous murthers: let thy smooth / Low-fawning parasites renowne thy Act: / Thou com'st not here" (395–407). That Ford seems to allude—extensively, if parodically—to *Romeo and Juliet* in his *'Tis Pity She's A Whore* may lend extra weight to these comparisons.

51. Though it is obviously a further reach, Romeo's speech to the Apothecary is oddly reminiscent of the sexual bullying in Lovelace's poem "The Fair Beggar"—a speech to a starving woman where seduction is again inextricable from extortion. Associating the young men's fights with sexual aggression has become standard practice in recent productions.

52. Snow, 187, argues that Romeo's "metaphors of grief" suggest "a fantasy of oral retaliation against the withdrawn, depriving maternal breast."

53. Appelbaum, 257.

54. See, for example, Helms, especially 77–91; Ray; Catty; Wolfthal; Bamford; Belsey; and Saunders.

55. Dworkin represents an extreme but noteworthy instance of radical-feminist conflation of eroticism with rape; a more recent wave of theory—including what has been called "lipstick feminism"—objects that Dworkin's position tends to exclude or occlude heterosexual women's desire in a way that Shakespeare, here and in *Othello*, clearly does not.

56. Evans's and Levenson's editions briefly discuss the possible Philomel reference, but only to account for why Juliet's bird is female when it is, in nature, the male who sings. Levenson does note how thickly the play is textured with "allusions to unrelated Ovidian stories" (16), but confines the Persephone legend to Romeo's speech about the unconscious Juliet as Death's "paramour" (5.3.105).

57. Brathwait, 350.

58. For an example of the way this neat dichotomy hides (even from a leading Shakespeare scholar) the play's disturbing suggestion that, as the violence has a sexual component, so the sexuality has a violent one, see Kahn, 173: "*Romeo and*

Juliet plays out a conflict between manhood as violence on behalf of fathers and manhood as separation from fathers and sexual union with women."

59. See the instances explored by Gossett. Coke, chap. 13, discusses the problems—arising from the class system—with allowing a man to escape rape charges by offering to marry his victim.

60. Foreste in D'Avenant's *The cruell brother* (1630) argues that "'If compulsion doth insist, untill / Enforcement breed delight, we cannot say, / The femall suffers. Acceptance at the last, / Disparageth the not consenting at the first: / Calls her deniall, her unskilfulnesse; / And not a virtuous frost i'th' blood'" (5.1). For the legal version of this argument, see Dalton, 248: "If the woman at the time of the supposed rape, doe conceive with child, by the ravishor, this is no rape, for a woman cannot conceive with child, except she do consent." Burks, 789, n. 42, cites several other instances of this belief from the earlier seventeenth century.

61. Baines, 90, quoting Bal, 81.

62. Baines, 87; see also her discussion (76) of the way rape and seduction can be mistaken for each other by ahistorical readers. Baines cites Lefkowitz, who argues that what have been called rapes in Greek myth are often to be understood (within the terms of their culture) as abduction or seduction instead. For an opposing view, see Curran.

Works Cited

Appelbaum, Robert. "'Standing to the wall': The Pressures of Masculinity in *Romeo and Juliet*." *Shakespeare Quarterly* 48 (1997): 251–272.

Aristotle's Master-Piece. London, 1595.

Baines, Barbara. "Effacing Rape in Early Modern Representation." *English Literary History* 65.1 (1998): 69–98.

Bal, Mieke. "The Rape of Lucrece and the Story of W." In *Reclamations of Shakespeare*, ed. A. J. Hoenselaars, 75–104. Amsterdam, 1994.

Bamford, Karen. *Sexual Violence on the Jacobean Stage*. New York, 2000.

Barkan, Leonard. "Diana and Actaeon: The Myth as Synthesis." *English Literary Renaissance* 10 (1980): 317–359.

Barton, John. *Playing Shakespeare*. London, 1984.

Bashar, Nazife. "Rape in England between 1550 and 1700." In *The Sexual Dynamics of History: Men's Power, Women's Resistance*, ed. The London Feminist History Group, 28–42. London, 1983.

Bate, Jonathan. *Shakespeare and Ovid*. Oxford, 1993.

Belsey, Catherine. "Tarquin Dispossessed: Expropriation and Consent in *The Rape of Lucrece*." *Shakespeare Quarterly* 52 (2001): 315–335.

Brathwait, Richard. *The English gentleman and the English gentlewoman*. 3rd ed. London, 1641.

Brooke, Arthur. *The Tragicall Historye of Romeus and Juliet*. In Bullough, ed., 1:284–363.

Bullough, Geoffrey, ed. *Narrative and Dramatic Sources of Shakespeare*. 8 vols. London, 1957.

Burks, Deborah G. "'I'll Want My Will Else': *The Changeling* and Women's Complicity with the Rapists." *English Literary History* 62 (1995): 759–790.

Catty, Jocelyn. *Writing Rape, Writing Women in Early Modern England: Unbridled Speech*. New York, 1999.

Chettle, Henry. *England's Mourning Garment*. London, 1603.

Coke, Edward. *The Institutes of the Laws of England*. London, 1644.

Curran, Leo C. "Rape and Rape Victims in *The Metamorphoses*." *Arethusa* 11 (1978): 213–239.

Dalton, Michael. *The Countrey Justice*. London, 1618.

D'Avenant, William. *The cruell brother*. London, 1630.

Detmer-Goebel, Emily. "The Need for Lavinia's Voice: *Titus Andronicus* and the Telling of Rape." *Shakespeare Studies* 29 (2001): 75–92.

Donne, John. *The Major Works*. Ed. John Carey. New York and Oxford, 1990.

Dworkin, Andrea. *Intercourse*. New York, 1997.

Evans, G. B., ed. *Romeo and Juliet*. 2nd ed. Cambridge, 2003.

Evans, Maurice, ed. *Elizabethan Sonnets*. London, 1977.

Farrell, Kirby. *Play, Death, and Heroism in Shakespeare*. Chapel Hill, 1989.

Ford, John. *Loves sacrifice*. London, 1633.

Golding, Arthur. *Ovid's Metamorphoses*. 1567. Ed. John Frederick Nims. Philadelphia, 2000.

Gorges, Arthur. *Lucans Pharsalia*. London, 1614.

Gossett, Suzanne. "'Best Men Are Molded Out of Faults': Marrying the Rapist in Jacobean Drama." *English Literary Renaissance* 14 (1984): 305–327.

Helms, Lorraine. *Seneca by Candlelight and Other Stories of Renaissance Drama*. Philadelphia, 1997.

Johnson, Richard. *The seven Champions of Christendome*. Part 1. London, 1608.

Jones, Emrys. *The Origins of Shakespeare*. Oxford, 1977.

Kahn, Coppélia. "Coming of Age in Verona." In *The Woman's Part* (1980), 171–193.

Lefkowitz, Mary R. "Seduction and Rape in Greek Myth." In *Consent and Coercion to Sex and Marriage in Ancient and Medieval Societies*, ed. Angeliki E. Laiou, 17–37. Washington, D.C., 1993.

Levenson, Jill L., ed. *Romeo and Juliet*. Oxford, 2000.

Livy, Titus. *The History of Rome*.

Loves martyr. London, 1601.

Lyly, John. *Campaspe*. Ed. G. K. Hunter. Manchester, 1991.

Mead, Robert. *The Combat of Love and Friendship*. London, 1654.

Middleton, Thomas, and William Rowley. *The Changeling*. Ed. George Walton Williams. London, 1967.

Porter, Joseph. *Shakespeare's Mercutio: His History and Drama*. Chapel Hill, 1988.

The Puritan. London, 1607.

Quarles, John. *Tarquin Banished: or, the Reward of Lust*. London, 1655.

Ray, Sid. "'Rape, I fear, was root of thy annoy': The Politics of Consent in *Titus Andronicus*." *Shakespeare Quarterly* 49 (1998): 22–39.

Rivers, George. *The Heroinæ*. London, 1639.

Romeo and Juliet. Videocassette. Directed by Franco Zeffirelli. 1968; Paramount: Hollywood, CA, 2003.

Saunders, Corinne. *Rape and Ravishment in the Literature of Medieval England*. Rochester, NY, 2001.

Shakespeare, William. *The Riverside Shakespeare*. Ed. G. Blakemore Evans et al. 2nd ed. Boston, 1997.

Snow, Edward. "Language and Sexual Difference in *Romeo and Juliet*." In *Shakespeare's Rough Magic*, ed. Peter Erickson and Coppélia Kahn, 168–192. Newark, DE, 1985.

Stimpson, Catharine. "Shakespeare and the Soil of Rape." In *The Woman's Part* (1980), 50–64.

Tourneur, Cyril. *The Atheist's Tragedie*. Ed. Irving Ribner. Cambridge, MA, 1964.

Turberville, George. *The Heroycall Epistles of . . . Publius Ovidius Naso*. London, 1567.

Watson, Robert N. "As You Liken It: Simile in the Wilderness." *Shakespeare Survey* 56 (2003): 79–92.

Williams, Carolyn D. "'Silence, like a Lucrece knife.'" *Yearbook of English Studies* 23 (1993): 93–110.

Wolfthal, Diane. *Images of Rape: The "Heroic" Tradition and its Alternatives*. New York, 1999.

The Woman's Part: Feminist Criticism of Shakespeare. Ed. Ruth Swift Lenz, Gayle Greene, and Carol Thomas Neely. Urbana: 1980.

JENNIFER A. LOW

"Bodied Forth": Spectator, Stage, and Actor in the Early Modern Theater

Picture the original staging of these two death scenes:

In *Bussy D'Ambois,* the title character fights off a host of assassins, then turns to combat the man who has hired them. Upon conquering his enemy, Bussy grants mercy to him just as a pistol shot from an assassin standing off-stage wounds him mortally. Amazed that his body is "but penetrable flesh," Bussy swears to die standing, like Emperor Vespasian, and then apostro-phizes his sword: "Prop me, true sword, as thou hast ever done! / The equal thought I bear of life and death / Shall make me faint on no side; I am up / Here like a Roman statue! I will stand / Till death hath made me marble. O, my fame, / Live in despite of murder" (5.4.78, 93–98).[1] In contrast, the hero-ine of *Romeo and Juliet* rises from her catafalque only to learn, as the Friar gestures toward Romeo's body, that "A greater power than we can contradict / Hath thwarted our intents" (5.3.153–154).[2] The Friar almost immediately leaves Juliet. Seeking a means of suicide, she finds Romeo's dagger: "Yea, noise? Then I'll be brief. O happy dagger, / This is thy sheath *[stabs herself]*; there rust, and let me die" (5.3.169–170).

Bussy's death is a public one—Monsieur and Guise look on from above—and his final speeches demonstrate his concern with his position in the social hierarchy rather than with his private life. The action foregrounds his wounded but upright body which, because of the crowd of murderers,

Comparative Drama, Volume 39, Number 1 (Spring 2005): pp. 1–29. Copyright © 2005 Western Michigan University.

must necessarily be located at the forefront of the stage; similarly, because of the combat with Montsurry, he must be close to or at center stage. Although Bussy is surrounded by others, his opponent and the assassins would be sure to stand well out of reach of his sword. Turned to watch him, Montsurry's face would reflect the audience's own interest in the extent of Bussy's injury. Tamyra and the shade of the friar might clutter up the visual tableau by approaching Bussy—or strengthen it by allowing Bussy to stand unimpeded until his death. Audience involvement would have been affected by two extra-dramatic factors: intensified, perhaps, by their proximity to the indoor stage of St. Paul's and distanced, perhaps, by the fact that the actors were children: the Children of Paul's.

Produced by the Lord Chamberlain's Men almost a decade earlier, *Romeo and Juliet* was performed on the public stage. The tomb to which the stage directions refer several times would, logically, have been represented by the tiring-house, receding from the facade at the back of the large platform stage.[3] Audiences might even have had to squint or lean forward to see Juliet's exact gesture in that shadowy recess. Aside from the prone bodies of Romeo inside and Paris just on the threshold, Juliet would have been quite alone as she stabbed herself. The visual focus would have emphasized the narrowing perspective created by distance and detail: a significant but not broad gesture, staged in a visually uncluttered space, far back from the audience. Such staging would have pulled the audience in, forcing their involvement by making them strain to see the action.

Both stagings enclose the death scene. Bussy's is enclosed by the watching actors who mirror for the audience their spectatorial involvement. The death scene is also enclosed mimetically (though not visually) by the scene's setting: Tamyra's closet, the small room where she has already received Bussy and the Friar as they rise through a trapdoor. The necessary staging suggests Chapman's enjoyment of visual paradox. Everything about Bussy's death emphasizes its public nature: his concern with fame, the watchers above, the presence of the tangentially involved assassins, the hero's steadfast insistence on dying on his feet (to impress whom if not those watching?); yet it occurs in a private place, the one in which Tamyra has engaged her lover in intimate acts and her husband in intimate conversations.[4] By his theatrical mode of dying, Bussy transforms Tamyra's private room into his showplace, the site of his final enactment of epic fortitude. By reconfiguring its function, Bussy pushes the limits of the imagined space outward. Ringed by the other characters, he is enclosed by the space, but by his words he broadens it, dissolving Tamyra's bedroom into the larger frame of the playhouse of St. Paul's. (Smaller than that of Blackfriars, the stage of St. Paul's was perhaps twenty feet wide and fairly shallow, since the entire auditorium was less than sixty-six feet long.)[5]

In the death scene, Chapman has his theatrical cake and eats it too: he concludes the play in the kind of intimate setting that functioned so effectively on the stage of the private playhouse,[6] yet he permits Bussy the rhetorical gestures that transform Tamyra's closet into an orator's platform. While the setting and the staging of the scene isolate the hero, his performance simultaneously reminds the watchers of their collectivity and their role—as watchers —in apotheosizing him beyond a mere malcontent or bedroom cavalier. His expectation that death will "make [him] marble" alludes to the permanence of statuary and evokes both the vertical space of the statue and the horizontal space of the tomb's carved effigy.[7] Thus, the setting becomes a metatheatrical forum for Bussy's aspirations to epic heroism: the rhetorical equivalent of a modern stage blackout with a spotlight on the face of a soliloquizing actor.

Juliet's death scene is also enclosed—by the setting of the tomb and its stage equivalent, the tiring-house. Shakespeare uses Romeo to emphasize the claustrophobic nature of the place in several ways: by having the youth pry open the door with a mattock and a crowbar (5.3.22 and 48 s.d.); by having him allude to Death as a monstrous Cupid who reenacts the myth's bedroom scene with Juliet (or Romeo himself) as a new Psyche; by vividly evoking the tomb through Romeo's references to "worms that are thy chambermaids" (5.3.109). For a straight Freudian interpreter, this Liebestod is clearly a return to the womb.[8] Romeo returns to his home in Verona and buries himself, his last gesture an orgasmic kiss. Juliet ecstatically stabs herself; like Romeo, her last word is *die*, with its obvious double-entendre, and her final gesture transforms her entire body into a sheath (punning on the Latin *vagina*) for Romeo's phallic dagger. The site of her budding fertility becomes a place of death.

Both death scenes complicate the nature of the place in which they occur, going well beyond the usual complication of a stage set. Bussy's speech dissolves the fictional place in which the hero dies; Juliet's tomb metonymizes her body. Theorist Anne Ubersfeld asserts that

> By virtue of the multiplicity of its concrete networks, stage space can simultaneously convey the image of a metaphorical network, a semantic field, and an actantial [activating or energizing] model. . . . Likewise, once stage space can be simultaneously the figure of a given text, of a sociocultural or sociopolitical network, or of a topography of the mind, we can be sure that there are substitutive crossovers between these different shaping structures.[9]

As the penetration of Juliet's body has been thematized by imagery and represented in her manner of death, it is more generally figured in Romeo's violent entrance into her tomb. Just as he has forced his way into the Capulet home and the Capulet family, he now violates another stronghold of the dynasty: their burial vault. Each of these family structures—including Juliet's body—is figured in Romeo's final, frantic violation of the inner room. Juliet symbolically repeats the process of violation when she stabs her own body. The same symbolic structure appears to operate, though more subtly, throughout *Bussy D'Ambois,* only concluding with Bussy's death. The hero has always entered Tamyra's room (the site of several trysts) by rising up out of a trapdoor from a secret passageway suggesting (to a classic Freudian theorist, at least) the vagina. While Tamyra has blocked her husband throughout the play in every way possible, refusing to grant him the information he asks for even when he stabs her and racks her, she is open to Bussy, even arranging his first visit to her through a transparent stratagem:

> And he I love will loathe me when he sees
> I fly my sex, my virtue, my renown
> To run so madly on a man unknown.
> See, see, a vault is opening that was never
> Known to my lord and husband, nor to any
> But him that brings the man I love, and me.

                                                             (2.2.124–129)

The "vault" she refers to is literally the machinery raising Bussy and the Friar from the cellarage below. But this is where Freud fails us: though it is tempting to see the passage as female genitalia, there is no evidence to suggest that Tamyra denies her husband access to her body. The vault, then, represents something more sophisticated: an aspect of Tamyra hidden to the world, one revealed only to her father confessor. Despite the focus on access to Tamyra's body, the true emphasis is on her subjectivity.[10] As in *Romeo and Juliet,* the playwright uses the fictional space as a figure for the heroine; the hero's penetration of that space, however, is a multivalent act.

The symbolic framework of such stagings, in which the stage space represents the self of a character in either physical or psychological terms, was by no means an innovation. Such a framework is well known to dramatic scholars today and was quite familiar to the early modern theatergoer as well. Its precedent exists in the morality play, which allegorizes the Christian's struggle against worldliness as a series of external events. In the morality play, while each psychological aspect of the protagonist is personified as a separate character in a classic psychomachia (a representation of the conflict of the soul), the stage serves as a map of the protagonist's self, often drawing on symbolic meanings of the compass points to justify a character's entrance from a specific direction. In such a play, the Christian figure is staged twice:

once as an actor in the play's events and once as the performance site upon which the struggle between good and evil is enacted. In Catherine Belsey's words, the Christian figure is "the momentary location" of a cosmic struggle.[11] Though the diagram of the Macro manuscript figures the stage of *The Castle of Perseverance* as a circle, that circle, a microcosm of the world, is also a macrocosm of the Christian himself. Throughout the play, the stage is the site for the wanderings of Mankind, who is enticed by various temptations that stand upon scaffolds set at the stage's perimeter. But these temptations, like the figure of God, can also approach Mankind on the stage, thus penetrating the space representing his self—what is alternately presented as his soul and his consciousness.

At certain moments, early modern plays also use the stage (or part of the stage) to embody the main character. Belsey has pointed out that, at moments of particular tension, early modern playwrights tended to draw on the morality tradition, engendering what she calls a "tension between realism and abstraction" a moment when psychological drama reverts to almost archetypal patterns.[12] Such a pattern often develops in plays that thematize penetration or repeatedly stage penetrative acts. I use the term *penetration* advisedly. The word *penetrate* is etymologically related to the phallic *penile* (suggesting a sexual, if not an erotic, component to the act) but also to the geographical *peninsula,* deriving from the Latin *penetrare,* which could be used to mean "to place within," "to enter within," or "to pierce." These related terms emphasize the spatial, almost geographical aspect of penetration. "To penetrate" means "to make or find its (or one's) way into the interior of, or right through (something): usually implying force or effort".[13] And even by Shakespeare's time, the word had developed its figurative meaning: "to pierce the ear, heart, or feelings of; to affect deeply; to 'touch.'" The Latinate word was a latecomer to English; decried as an inkhorn term, it was defended by Puttenham, who argues, "Also ye finde these words, *penetrate, penetrable, indignitie,* which I cannot see how we may spare them . . . for our speach wanteth wordes to such sence so well to be vsed."[14] I want to bring the multiple valences of the word to bear on various dramatic and thematic instances of penetration in order to suggest the subjectivity inherent in the human being's consciousness of embodiment.

In these dramatic instances, the penetration of space serves as a complex representation of the act of gaining access to a character's interior self. The physical space that is penetrated may be the personal space of a character, the space created by a grouping of actors, the space of the stage as a whole, or even the personal space of the audience. The putative self represented by these spaces may signify, variously, a purely corporeal body; a body part (such as a vagina or a penis); a mind (or subjectivity); or a heart (either the physical organ or the conventional symbol of the desiring self). The varied meanings of the "self" suggested in these spatial intrusions indicate the complexity of the early modern experience of selfhood. We can see the partial nature of each possibility as we move toward developing a view more thoroughly grounded in embodiment.[15]

In Belsey's view, the model of self presented in the morality play precludes the possibility of a speaking subject, since even the main character lacks agency. Belsey not only dismisses the morality play as a possible locus of subjectivity but also presents the links between Renaissance drama and the morality in a way that undermines longstanding critical arguments that literary subjectivity was born on the English Renaissance stage. Belsey draws her definition of subjectivity from a liberal humanist model. Based on language and the ability to speak itself, the subject that she envisions, a "discursive hero . . . independent of providence and of language," is wholly identified by intellectual apparatuses; the subject's corporeal status is entirely ignored.[16] The Cartesian structures that define such a model also limit it, eliding the phenomenological *habitus,* the experience of being in the body. Despite numerous studies of the body, the interiority of physical experience—Gail Kern Paster's "subjective experience of being-in-the-body"—has been neglected in favor of an "objective" examination of the appearance of experience.[17] This lacuna has only recently been addressed by theorists, and their work is only beginning to be applied to the drama.

In fact, the physical experience of corporeality also generates a type of subjectivity, one that is responsive to constant interaction with the physical world—with the environment, as well as with both animate and inanimate objects. This aspect of subjectivity is key to my argument, both because it renders the "penetration" I see visible and because it broadens the significance of that penetration, enabling us to recognize simultaneous, multiple meanings of "the self." In his volume *Production de l'espace,* Marxist theorist Henri Lefebvre initiated the reintroduction of the physical self into our understanding of subjectivity. He argues that Descartes' theories marked a crucial dissociation between self and body and led the understanding of the self in the wrong direction, instantiating the germs of an eventual crisis: "With the advent of Cartesian logic . . . space had entered the realm of the absolute."[18] As Lefebvre explains, the idea of space became entirely abstract, as if the subjective could be eliminated from our perceptions:

> The scientific attitude, understood as the application of "epistemological" thinking to acquired knowledge, is assumed to be "structurally" linked to the spatial sphere. . . . Blithely indifferent to the charge of circular thinking, that discourse sets up an opposition between the status of space and the status of the "subject," between the thinking "I" and the object thought about. . . . Epistemological

thought . . . has eliminated the "collective subject," the people as creator of a particular language, as carrier of specific etymological sequences. . . . It has promoted the impersonal "one" as creator of language in general, as creator of the system. It has failed, however, to eliminate the need for a subject of some kind. Hence the re-emergence of the abstract subject, the *cogito* of the philosophers.[19]

In other words, scientific thought, in its dependence upon Descartes, has permitted a longstanding rift between our (i.e., Western culture's) *quantification* of space and our (i.e., each individual's) *experience* of space. Philosophical thought, too, by following Descartes in its examination of selfhood, has lost a fundamental component of the self, accepting the "impersonal 'one'" as a substitute for the social subject and the concrete subject, the individual. Recent theorists of space as varied as Yi-Fu Tuan and Edward T. Hall have reminded us that space *as we know it* is shaped by the perception of our senses: sight, sound, and touch all play a part. Moreover, as each individual shapes his concept of space, his sense of where he is affects his sense of self. Although space is commonly used in such metaphors as "the social hierarchy" and "the great chain of being," space is a literal experience—an experience of tactility. It is dry or wet, crowded or empty, expansive or compressed, and so forth. Even this brief list of expe-riential alternatives indicates the extent of the awareness based on physical feeling, an awareness quite separate from one's command of language or will. Like the literary scholar Cynthia Marshall, who sees in early modern culture "any number of signs indicat[ing] an experiential slippage from [the conscious, self-determining individual]," I posit a sense of self that is not at all dependent on reason or will.[20] This experience of subjectivity is located in the unmediated experience of physicality, specifically of proprioception, the interpretation of stimuli concerning one's sense of position and one's experi-ence of the movements of one's limbs and other body parts. As Paster asserts, "bodiliness is the most rudimentary form of self-presence."[21] Everyone's sense of existence comes first from the physical sense of one's own body.

One's experience of one's own physical presence is partly determined by biological factors. Twentieth-century social scientist Edward T. Hall builds on several studies of mammals by such animal psychologists as Hediger, C. R. Carpenter, and A. D. Bain in order to develop his analysis of human be-ings' territoriality. He extensively examines how the nerves in different parts of the body help us to develop a sense of space through auditory, olfactory, and thermal information. As Hollis Huston explains, Hall's theory "describes not a particular code of manners, but an invariant scale of stimulant thresh-olds, to which individuals and peoples may respond in various ways."[22] The scale refers to physiological experiences consistent across cultures and even across mammalian species; however, different creatures or cultures may respond differently to their stimuli. Hegemonic institutions may attempt to restructure the way that certain groups respond to specific spatial experiences, distinguishing women from men or aristocrats from the underclass or the middling sort, thus dividing a culture along lines of gender or social rank; in such a situation, those involved are engaged in structuring the *doxa* that underlie a psychological response to physiological stimuli. Thus, beliefs may intersect with action, and even sensation, though what is true for *doxa*—that, as Bourdieu points out, "[t]he principles embodied in this way are placed beyond the grasp of consciousness, and hence cannot be touched by voluntary, deliberate transformation, cannot even be made explicit"—is even more true of the experience of bodiliness.[23] Such an attempt at imposing rules upon a specific social group is evident in the many early modern conduct books for women: the body of the gentlewoman was no sooner distinguished as her own than it became the subject of many social strictures intended to impose a *habitus* that would become internalized. Women were taught to keep their eyes downcast; timidity was encouraged and the blush considered a sign of reverence and maidenly virtue.[24] Women were also taught not to perceive the physical proximity of others as an intrusion. Adult women, even those of high status, were expected to endure the approach of others, and even to endure disciplinary violence enacted upon their bodies.[25] They were discouraged from physical resistance to aggressive seduction or even sexual coercion.[26]

This thoroughly Foucauldian discipline almost certainly achieved the goal of imposing a sense of self-abnegation upon the women who manifested the demeanor considered appropriate for their sex and status. One aspect of physical experience is the sense of owning or possessing the space around ourselves, what we colloquially call "personal space." Edward Hall developed the term *proxemics* to refer to study of the individual's structuring of and perception of space. Hall's research indicates that our sense of the extent of the space we possess is structured by such elements as the perception of heat as well as by more purely tactile and visual information. Hall theorizes that "[u]ntil recently man's space requirements were thought of in terms of the actual amount of air displaced by his body. The fact that man has around him as extensions of his personality the zones described . . . has generally been overlooked."[27]

In *'Tis Pity She's a Whore,* John Ford's representation of the female *habitus,* or experience of being in the body, manifests a significant confusion about the nature of female selfhood. The play's male characters so often allude to Annabella in stock terms that they almost render the heroine a mere plot device: a receptacle, an object of erotic desire that male characters wish to enter. Staging of the erotic object in early modern drama often makes use of mimetic forms such as entrance onto the stage, in fact: physical and/or aggressive intrusion may be enacted in such a way as to suggest erotic bodily penetration. But entering may also, depending on the setting, represent penetrating a character's subjectivity—entering into direct communication with a character's mind, heart, or soul. Though Annabella's body is the focus of several characters in Ford's play, the author himself manifests a concern with the relation between Annabella's body and her "inwardness"; this concern is literally staged throughout the play, as textual images force our attention to connections between metaphor, staging, and plot.

Throughout *'Tis Pity*, there are a plethora of metaphors about various containers, and many of these figure Annabella as the container.[28] But other images of containment metaphorize the body more generally to express subjectivity in ways that were common during the early modern period. After the siblings have had sexual intercourse, Annabella tells Giovanni, "Go where thou wilt, in mind I'll keep thee here" (2.1.39).[29] The idea that the beloved is contained as an image within the mind or the mind's eye of the lover frequently recurs (and is read today as a sign of subjectivity) in Shakespeare's and Sidney's sonnet sequences. Later, Ford strikingly echoes Antony's opening lines in *Antony and Cleopatra* (as well as the lyrics of John Donne, his contemporary) when Giovanni says, "Let poring book-men dream of other worlds, / My world, and all of happiness, is here" (5.3.13–14). It would be false and reductive to suggest that this reference to Annabella is purely sexual.

Related imagery appears when other characters anxiously examine Annabella's motives. After advising Annabella, the Friar comments, "But soft, methinks I see repentance work / New motions in your heart" (3.6.31–32). Her heart represents her interior state; his vision, his ability to see beyond her physical appearance. This reference to Annabella's interiority is repeated when Soranzo discovers his new wife's pregnancy. Eventually, dissembling his rage, Soranzo distinguishes between himself and her supposed lover: "Well might he lust, but never lov'd like me. / He doted on the pictures that hung out / Upon thy cheeks ... Not on the part I lov'd, which was thy heart, / And, as I thought, thy virtues" (4.3.125–129). These characters evince a desire for a different, nonsexual penetration: discovery of the truth of Annabella's heart. Her consciousness, her subjectivity become as much of a focus of the play as her body.

This concern is dramatized by staging and by verbal references to stage action. In a play that begins with a speech about bodily space and continues with a complaint about violent intrusions upon one's space of private property, we might expect to see intrusion staged repeatedly. Indeed, one of the characters, Annabella's maidservant, actually states this expectation: "How like you this, child? Here's threat'ning, challenging, / quarreling, and fighting, on every side, and all is for your / sake; you had need look to yourself, charge, you'll be / stol'n away sleeping else shortly" (1.2.63–66). Yet there are few, if any, scenes in which Annabella's suitors aggressively enter upon her solitude.[30] When Giovanni and Annabella discover their mutual affection, they do so in their father's hall. This space, which is neutral ground to each, enables them to meet without intrusion on the part of either. (Indeed, one could read Annabella's willingness to make her brother her erotic choice as an extreme example of endogamy that makes it unnecessary for her ever to leave the family circle.) When the two have pledged their love, they exit, presumably to consummate their vow. But the next scene stages not their act of love but the low comedy of Bergetto's indifference to Annabella. Directly following that scene, Giovanni and Annabella enter "as from their chamber"; they renew their vows and agree to remain faithful to one another. Thus, the audience is denied the revelation of Annabella's body. Instead, it enjoys a parodic inversion of Giovanni's courtship. The staging seems to reflect back on the audience its prurient desire for the unveiled sex scene that the play initially seemed to promise. As Patricia Fumerton argues, the subject at this time

> lived in public view but always withheld for itself a "secret" room, cabinet, case, or other recess locked away (in full view) in one corner of the house. . . . the aristocratic self [enacted] a sort of reflex of retreat, an instinct to withdraw into privacy so pervasive even in the most trivial matters that there never could be any final moment of privacy.[31]

It seems that this private room will never be revealed. Even to Putana, Annabella pointedly refuses to offer any confidence about the details of what has passed.

Despite their urgent desire to win the prize, Annabella's other suitors gain little access to her. Almost the only contact that Grimaldi achieves occurs when Annabella and Putana enter "above" after his fight with Vasques. The stage direction strongly implies that the two women peer down at the fight from an upper window or a balcony overlooking the street. Annabella remains "above" the violence, and apart from it—never seriously threatened. Her meeting with Bergetto is only recounted, not staged; true, Annabella is later summoned by her father to read the youth s letter, but after doing so, she is permitted to dismiss the suitor without further ado. When Soranzo courts Annabella, they walk in her father's hall; her sense of security is evident in her raillery. Even when her husband discovers her previous sexual activity, Annabella remains calm. Stage directions indicate their entrance: "Enter Soranzo unbrac'd, and Annabella dragg'd in" (4.3.1 s.d.). We can deduce that they enter from a shared bedchamber after their mutual disrobing reveals Annabella's condition. The fact that Ford does not stage the scene in the bedchamber itself emphasizes that Soranzo fails to penetrate Annabella's defenses. She steadfastly refuses to name her lover and sings a song that indicates her indifference to death. Despite their wedding, Soranzo never gains access to Annabella's interior self.

Annabella's bedchamber is not represented onstage until the scene of her repentance. The stage direction says, "Enter the Friar sitting in a chair, Annabella kneeling and whispering to him: a table before them and wax-lights: she weeps and wrings her hands" (3.6.1 s.d.).[32] The scene plunges *in medias res* as the Friar comments, "You have unripp'd a soul so foul and guilty . . . I marvel how / The earth hath borne you up" (3.6.2–4). He dominates the scene with speeches punctuated only occasionally by exclamations from Annabella, graphically describing hell and its torments until Annabella asks, "Is there no way left to redeem my miseries?" (3.6.33).[33] His answer persuades her that marrying Soranzo is the right choice: when the Friar asks if she is content, she replies, "I am" (3.6.42).[34]

Though the stage direction indicates that Annabella and the Friar appear onstage together, the pose described and the speeches that follow indicate that Annabella's concealed subjectivity has finally been revealed. The scene depicts what we have long desired to see: Annabella's bedchamber. This feminized space is indeed penetrated by an aggressive male—the Friar, whose coercive speeches constitute an assault upon Annabella's privacy. But what is exposed inside this *sancta sanctorum* is not Annabella's body but her soul. The long-awaited revelation of Annabella's self presents not an overly-willing woman but a thoughtful one. The Friar's concerns gain him access to a purely spiritual interior.

Yet this understanding of Annabella is undermined by the play's conclusion. Ford parts the bed curtains in 5.5, revealing Giovanni and Annabella in bed once again.[35] There is no need for Giovanni to make an aggressive entrance; he has already taken possession of Annabella's body. Now, on this bed, Annabella's inner space is reconstituted, this time in an erotic guise, and, as the lovers use the time they have, they re-enact the primal act, staging Annabella as a body entered and conquered by a male. Stabbing her, Giovanni penetrates the body violently as well as sexually, killing the fetus, the interloper whose presence brought Soranzo into Annabella's sphere ("The hapless fruit / That in her womb receiv'd its life from me / Hath had from me a cradle and a grave" [5.5.94–96]). Annabella's interiority is turned inside out, as the staging places her body on display and the script suggests that what matters for Giovanni is not his sister's soul, but her body. The space of the stage represents Annabella's interior once again, but that interior seems more appropriately figured by her genitalia than by her heart.

The heart itself reappears at the end. Shrunk down to the actual organ, however, interiority retains unknowability. What is internal is, as Katharine Maus says, "beyond scrutiny, concealed where other people cannot perceive it.

And it *surpasses* the visible—its validity is unimpeachable."[36] When Giovanni enters the stage "with a heart upon his dagger" (5.5.7 s.d.), the tableau inevitably recalls the scene in which Giovanni urged Annabella to discover the truth of his, feelings by cutting open his body to see his heart. The trope of the heart as the seat of love, so common in the verses of Sidney, Shakespeare, and Donne, is here literalized. Thus, Giovanni presents to all his triumph:

> The glory of my deed
> Darken'd the midday sun, made noon as night.
>
> . . .
>
> I came to feast too, but I digg'd for food
> In a much richer mine than gold or stone
> Of any value balanc'd; 'tis a heart,
> A heart, my lords, in which is mine entomb'd:
> Look well upon't; dee know't?
>
> (5.6.22–29)

The speech leads us to expect a bawdy pun—surely the "richer mine" must refer to Annabella's *queynt*. But Ford surprises us by altering the meaning of the container once again: Giovanni is proud that he has conquered Annabella's *affections*. The "case" is not the vulva but the heart, which Giovanni believes will offer the pure, unequivocal sign of authentic feeling that he desires. But, of course, it does not. Even Giovanni's father fails to recognize Annabella's heart (as Giovanni says, "Why d'ee startle? / I vow 'tis hers" [5.6.31–32]). When presented onstage, the heart is just a bloody hunk of flesh: it lacks any identifying trait, let alone the symbolic value that it has for Giovanni himself.[37]

On a theatrical level, one that comprises both plot and staging, the revelation of Annabella's interiority, though deferred for a while, is finally reached—and is reached, in fact, more than once. Annabella's interiority is not only visible, but actually staged when her room and her bed are revealed onstage. As Georgiana Ziegler has said in her discussion of *The Rape of Lucrece*, "the chamber metaphorically represents her 'self,' her body with its threatened chastity."[38] But in this play, the "self" is represented as several different constructs. It may be the soul, the conscience, the genitals, the womb. Is fancy bred in the heart, in the head, inside the vagina? Ford cannot decide: his stagings shift the seat of the self from one thing to another. Annabella's interiority remains a moving target; her characterization is nowhere more ambiguous than at the play's end.

'Tis Pity draws on the conventions of the morality play to stage the female aristocratic body and to examine the nature of the subjectivity represented by that body. It also resembles the morality play in the psychological

distance that it maintains between the characters and the audience. Despite, or perhaps because of, the play's sensationalism, 'Tis Pity remains largely an intellectual exercise for the audience member, a quest for the nature of Annabella's subjectivity. Unlike Macbeth, for example, 'Tis Pity offers no entrance into the focal character's experience but remains a cautionary lesson not unlike morality plays themselves.

If 'Tis Pity does offer the audience a role, it is that of the onlooker, the peeping Tom whose desires have been legitimized because commodified. What aspect of Annabella do we desire to see? Giovanni's desire may awaken our prurience, but the incestuous nature of his desire makes us experience any touch of kinship with Giovanni as distasteful. Even more than its gore and its subject matter, the position in which it places its audience members may be the element that links 'Tis Pity with an Artaudian Theatre of Cruelty. Do we watch with Giovanni or over his shoulder? And in which of these capacities are we more (or less) akin to him? This challenge to the spectator's role—when we are both enticed and sickened by our willingness to be enticed—leads to larger questions about theatrical transactions between actors and spectators. What draws us into the action? And how are our relations with the characters altered when we are? Do we empathize with each character seriatim or with only one, enjoying a dual viewpoint as we relate to the other characters through the lens that "our" character provides? No matter what the action, it is evident that as soon as one actor establishes a relation to another, he alters their spatial relations and realigns the audience with each of them. As Hollis Huston explains,

> To transfer Hall's comprehensive analysis of behavior directly to the stage [would be] a catastrophic mistake. A stage differs from real life in a way that is essentially proxemic. . . . [T]he fundamental relationship of the theater is not between two actors, but between the two of them and those who watch: when the contract of mutual responsibility is broken, the stage dies and the theater is void.[39]

Any consideration of staging is incomplete without discussion of its effect upon the spectators. By extension, discussion of the body and its use in the theater should also include the spectator as a third element, forming a triad of related concerns.

Many antitheatrical pamphleteers who feared that dramas could have a bad effect upon audience members inveighed against what they perceived as a loss of control that resulted from watching plays. Stephen Gosson, for example, writes repeatedly of the danger of "gazing." In Playes Confuted in Five Actions, he alludes four times to the effect of the spectacle—or, more exactly, to the effects of gazing upon a spectacle:

Yf we be carefull that no pollution of idoles enter by the mouth
into our bodies, how diligent, how circumspect, how wary ought we
to be, that no corruption of idols, enter by the passage of our eyes
& eares into the soule? . . . that which entreth into us by the eyes
and eares, muste bee digested by the spirite.[40]

Phillip Stubbes perceives the theatrical experience similarly: "For such
is our grosse and dull nature, that what thing we see opposite before our eyes,
to pearce further, and printe deeper in our harts and minds, than that thing,
which is hard [sic] onely with the eares."[41] Both these writers characterize
sight as a way of opening up the body, as if the eye were a mouth that in-
gests visual stimuli. Sight becomes an invitation for stimuli to enter into the
body: a "piercing," or penetration. To make sense of the assault upon the self
that these writers see in the very experience of play-watching, I revert to the
relation between what Hall calls "distance receptors—those concerned with
examination of distant objects—the eyes, the ears, and the nose" and "immediate receptors—those used to examine the world close up—the world of
touch, the sensations we receive from the skin, membranes, and muscles" for
early modern theatergoers.[42]

How would early modern audience members have experienced the drama at the physiological and visceral levels? At the sensorial level? Based on
the contract for constructing the Fortune Theater, Bruce Smith asserts that
"no one in the Fortune or the 1599 Globe was more than fifty feet from an
actor standing downstage, at the focal center of the space."[43] Though this distance may have been small in terms of auditory experience, it is experienced
proximically as somewhat remote, falling under the category that Hall calls
"public distance" the distance at which people lose a sense of connectedness
with one another.[44] According to Hall's research, actors attempting to make
their performance touch the spectator work with the limitations established
by that distance:

Most actors know that at thirty or more feet the subtle shades of
meaning conveyed by the normal voice are lost as are the details of
facial expression and movement. Not only the voice but everything
else must be exaggerated or amplified. Much of the nonverbal
part of the communication shifts to gestures and body stance. In
addition, the tempo of the voice drops [and] words are enunciated
more clearly.[45]

But for groundlings already in intimate contact with the stage, the actor's
approach onto the *platea* (downstage area) of the stage would intensify the
experience of closeness resulting from the actor's approach within social

distance. Hall characterizes the physical experience of such intimacy as somewhat uncomfortable—certainly, it takes active observation to form an impression of what is nearby. At a close social distance,

> the area of sharp focus extends to the nose and parts of both eyes; or the whole mouth, one eye, and the nose are sharply seen. Many Americans shift their gaze back and forth from eye to eye or from nose to mouth. . . . At a 60-degree visual angle, the head, shoulders, and upper trunk are seen at a distance of four feet.[46]

Perhaps most significantly, Hall notes that "to stand and look down at a person at this distance has a domineering effect."[47] One can easily extrapolate from this (and from one's personal experience) that craning one's neck upward to watch a performance would render one submissive to impressions.

In the public theaters, the thrust stage aggressively appropriated the standing room of the audience. A raised platform jutting forty feet out into a bare area, the stage must have served as a physical intrusion upon the personal space of those spectators pressed close to it. Despite the excitement of proximity, those who stood around its actual perimeter would have been uncomfortable at being pressed against the hard wooden platform—more so than those more distant spectators who were pressed back against the walls of the amphitheater. Surrounded by groundlings on three sides, an actor could not possibly achieve the same visual effect as one performing toward only one side. Yet in this case, the audience would be much more affected by actors' entrances, particularly when they passed from *locus* (upstage area) to *platea* (downstage area) for greater intimacy. These paired concepts are particularly suggestive in this context. Robert Weimann argues that the *platea* "becomes part of the symbolic meaning of the play world, and the *locus* is made to support the dialectic of self-expression and representation." In moving from one to another, actors employed "transitions between illusion and convention, representation and self-expression, high seriousness, and low comedy—each drawing physically, socially, and dramatically on the interplay." Further, Weimann suggests, an early modern actor "uses certain conventions of speech and movement that roughly correspond to *locus* and *platea*, conventions by which the audience's world is made part of the play and the play is brought into the world of the audience."[48]

How might specific scenarios or stagings further compel the audience to open themselves up in the way that Gosson and Stubbes describe? Can the audience themselves be *penetrated* by their experience of the theater? Not, one might suspect, in seats of the nineteenth-century proscenium arch theater, watching actors in the crowded Victorian setting of the typical box set—but perhaps in the crowd surrounding the early modern amphitheater's thrust stage, when a bare stage awaits the actor's entrance, which will shape the area into meaningful space.

Not all theatrical entrances convey a sense of aggressive penetration, of course (least of all when characters enter in the midst of conversation), but a solitary actor might achieve this effect, particularly when the scene was set for aggressive entry by previous imagery, conversation, setting, or the mode of earlier entrances.[49] Further, in moving from *locus* to *platea*, an actor not only penetrates an empty stage but also steps into and above space that the audience would experience as their own. Gurr seems to support this view when he argues, "The chief feature of the staging and its interaction with the audience was the intimate connection between them. The spectators were as visible as the players, and even more potently they completely surrounded the players on their platform."[50]

More than once throughout his dramatic career, Shakespeare created a representative body onstage that stands in for the audience, thereby enabling him to use the material conditions of his theater to manipulate the spectator's proxemic experience. How might the linkage of stage entrances to thematic concerns with penetration and invasion of the body have brought the audience to share the proxemic experience of the onstage (intradramatic) spectator?

Shakespeare's *Coriolanus* not only makes use of a mob as an intradramatic spectator, it constantly thematizes the relationship between crowds and individuals, parts and wholes, closed bodies and open bodies. Piercing and penetration remain an underlying theme of the play, as Shakespeare constantly draws our attention to openness, vulnerability, autonomy, and the necessity for solidarity. In *Coriolanus*, the hero wins his name by penetrating and opening up the town of Corioles, but he refuses to render himself vulnerable to figurative penetration. He resists the traditional theatrical vulnerability of the soliloquizer, in itself a metaphorical openness to penetration;[51] he refuses to show his wounds to the populace, blocking their gaze (a visual and symbolic form of penetration); and he ignores the needs of both the metaphorical stomach (the desires of the Roman populace) and those of the literal stomach (food as fuel for the body), thereby refusing to acknowledge that the body can be affected by external, or even internal, stimuli.[52] Martius's refusal to acknowledge his vulnerability is most notable in the showstopping scene in which he successfully penetrates the town of Corioles entirely alone.

Entrances and exits almost immediately become symbolic of thematic concerns throughout the play. *Coriolanus* begins with action, possibly reinforced by confused sound: "Enter a company of mutinous Citizens, with staves, clubs, and other weapons."[53] This is, as Arden editor Philip Brockbank notes, the only play of the period to open with public violence.[54] And, as critic Jarrett Walker points out, the audience experiences this beginning as "a frontal assault of bodies."[55] From an empty stage, we change to a confused milling about of hostile, angry characters—as many extras as the King's Men had on hand. This would have been experienced as violence, as attack; the audience would have felt the shock of reverberating boards, of crowdedness very different from that of the spectators crammed together.[56]

Indeed, Zvi Jagendorf suggests that Shakespeare purposely contrasts the "isolated and discrete body of the man who stands alone" with the common body of the people:[57]

> Both are prominent features of the play's spectacle. The crowd—the citizens in the street and marketplace, the common soldiers on the battlefield—is a constant feature of the action. We hear their shouts on and offstage. We are encouraged to imagine them jostling for space in the victory parades, and we both see and hear them in the mob scenes.[58]

Shakespeare, I am suggesting, brings together crowds and the figure of the body by creating scenes in which crowds and (ultimately) the whole stage come to "stand in" for a body, as Ford does through different techniques in 'Tis Pity She's a Whore. Throughout the play, the thrust stage and the actors create situations in which penetration of groups of bodies occurs. The opening is a case in point: after the unruly multitude have assembled, they are called to order by the First Citizen, who addresses the crowd. Whether they stand in small clusters or assemble in a circle or semicircle, it is natural for the next character who appears, Menenius, to enter from the back and push through to the center of a crowd that then surrounds him. His penetration of the crowd is his first move toward controlling and dispersing it. In entering and taking center stage, in fact, he seems to provide a visual emblem of the belly in his fable. He becomes the visual center, around which there would be a circle of empty space because the plebeians would have to stand far enough off so that they could turn their eyes upon him.[59] When Caius Martius enters, he too would necessarily thrust his way through the crowd of plebeians, but his presence would confuse the effect of the tableau. The conversation would cease to be a dialogue between individual and crowd; it would become more diffuse, less of a clear exchange, as Martius quarrels both with Menenius and with members of the crowd.

Entering and exiting become the subject of discussion a scant two scenes later, when Virgilia insists, "I'll not over the threshold till my lord return from the wars" (1.3.74–75). Although Valeria argues, "Fie, you confine yourself most unreasonably," Virgilia stands firm (1.3.76). Refusing to visit "the good lady that lies in" (1.3.77), Virgilia insists on her own enclosure, her own containment. Walker actually comments that Virgilia's silence itself is visual and emblematic when framed by her talkative friend and her mother-in-law:

She is never fully separable from the women who surround her.
Accordingly, when I refer to Virgilia as a presence onstage, it is
with the understanding that Volumnia and Valeria are essential to
draw our attention to that presence and are thus, in phenomenal
terms, inseparable from it.[60]

Even in this scene, a closed circle is more than once broken in upon: Volumnia and Virgilia enter together, their paired-ness making us focus on their
interaction rather than on their penetration of the empty stage. But the
stage directions (which textual critics as venerable as Greg and as recent as
Werstine believe to have been written by Shakespeare himself) indicate that
the pair seat themselves on stools and begin to sew silently, creating a sense
of intimacy and community broken by Volumnia s first words: "I pray you,
daughter, sing, or express yourself" (1.3.1–2). The circle is again disrupted
when a servant enters to announce Valeria's arrival and Virgilia is with difficulty prevented from exiting the stage. When Valeria appears with an Usher
and a Gentlewoman (presumably Valeria's servant), the previous intimacy is
dissolved by the presence of too many bodies on stage.

In the next scene, the sense of the stage space that I have described is
reversed. Scene 1.4 stages the Roman attack upon Corioles. As well as the
main actors, the stage directions specify "Drum and Colours [extras], with
Captains and Soldiers . . . to them a Messenger." The army of the Volsces,
which soon pours out of the tiring-house door, further confuses the visual
picture. They beat the Romans "to their trenches," and then Martius appears,
"cursing"; he pursues the Volsces, who flee back to the gates of Corioles (the
doors of the tiring-house), and he follows them in. As the gates are shut and
the Roman general Titus Lartius immediately focuses on the possible loss of
Martius, the characters and the audience can only speculate on what is going
on behind the door in "Corioles." Martius's own powers of penetration are
best perceived by the audience not when he is fighting onstage but now, when
he is absent and all eyes are fixed upon the door through which he has passed.
Ironically, our attention is not directed toward the penetration of swords
piercing bodies behind the door; instead, we see the city of Corioles itself as
the thing that Martius has penetrated by entering it. Thus, the city becomes a
larger emblem of the cutting, wounding, and opening up of individual bodies
that Martius traditionally enacts in battle. As I have shown elsewhere, the
penetration indicated by the wound's blood is a matter for shame, as it reveals
masculine vulnerability—a vulnerability associated, according to Gail Paster,
with a woman's menstrual flow.[61]

When Martius emerges, "bleeding, assaulted by the enemy" (1.4.61
s.d.), the general Titus Lartius exclaims, "O, 'tis Martius! / Let's fetch him
off, or make remain alike," and the company of Roman soldiers rush toward

Martius, who turns and leads them all back into the city (1.4.61–62). This action inverts the more usual sense of the stage as an area that can be penetrated; instead, it focuses the watchers' attention on a single point of exit or entry. The possibility of forced penetration is outward—through the tiring-house doors—but yet away from the audience. Thus, as Titus Lartius enters, the extras pause, facing toward the door through which Martius has passed. When he re-enters and turns about, they all follow him, and the flow of actors abruptly pushes toward the single, central door, leaving the stage as empty as if it had been evacuated. I hypothesize an effect as of tumescence and detumescence—not in literal terms, but in the audience's experience of the stage.[62] As the circulation of bodies onstage focuses on action occurring directly behind the doors, the audience would not only focus on what the doors concealed, but would experience the cessation of action as an abrupt slowdown—one that they might even understand as resembling a sudden chill to flowing blood. They would feel the stage's detumescence as a sudden emptying out, an absence of tension in the immediate vicinity and a sense of closure to the scene that is suggested by the outflow, which, on a primitive level, would carry a sense of the Romans' attack as almost inevitably successful.

In architectonic terms, the staging implied by the action of *Coriolanus* manifests two different ways of dwelling in space. Edward S. Casey characterizes two extremes of architectural experience as "hestial" and "hermetic": "Any built place that aims at encouraging hestial dwelling will . . . tend to be at once centered and self-enclosed. The implicit directionality will be from the center toward the periphery and will thus obey the architectural counsel to 'extend inner order outward.'"[63] In contrast, "the hermetic moves out resolutely"; it "represents the far-out view, a view from a moving position."[64] Shakespeare offers both these experiences to his audiences through the proxemics inherent in the staging examined here. Each form of *experience* affects watchers viscerally, and each develops a sense of self substantially different from that of the region "between or behind the eyes."[65]

The staging of the body affects the audience's experience on many levels. While related to proxemic concerns, the effect of entrances and exits goes beyond that single dimension; it depends not only on proximity but on the design and use of the stage within the theater itself. Thus, the stage space, whether that of the thrust stage or the proscenium arch, organically affects the experience of the spectator, as each stage design creates a different relation between the audience and the action.

The self implicated by early modern metaphors of the body is not easily defined, any more than is the self that comes into being through proxemic experience. Yet the validity of applying proprioceptive analysis to staging should be evident. Freud's paradigms have so thoroughly infused our culture that one is likely to describe the audience's proprioception as an unconscious response to the staging of the action. Such a term denies the nature of the experience, which is unrelated to psychic structures or intellectual activity. The "bodiliness" if you will, of the individual is an important constitutive element of subjectivity—a subjectivity that must be recognized as a broader experience than has been understood hitherto.

Scholars who have written about the early modern spectator's experience have often intuitively done so in the context of considering bodily, even proprioceptive, elements onstage. Not only does Belsey discuss the uses of psychomachiae in *The Subject of Tragedy,* she treats similar issues in her analysis of *The Duchess of Malfi,* a play whose focus could be defined as the question, "Who controls the body of the Duchess?" When Huston Diehl addresses audience experience, she does so in the context of her discussion of stage violence.[66] We must continue to examine how spatial elements construct the subject, using the drama both as a mimetic form and as an intraperformative transaction between actors and audience members. The staged nature of dramatic theater offers a unique opportunity to examine this dimension of human experience.

NOTES

1. Quotations from *Bussy D'Ambois* refer to George Chapman, *Bussy D'Ambois* ed. Robert J. Lordi (Lincoln, Nebr.: Nebraska University Press, 1964). This edition is based on Q2, published in 1641.

2. Quotations from *Romeo and Juliet* and other Shakespeare plays (unless otherwise noted) refer to William Shakespeare, *The Riverside Shakespeare,* ed. G. Blakemore Evans (Boston: Houghton Mifflin, 1974).

3. At 5.3.48 s.d., Q1 states, "Romeo begins to open the tomb." At 5.3.87, Theobald includes the stage direction, "Laying Paris in the tomb." Q1 also specifies at 5.3.139 the stage direction "Friar stoops and looks on the blood and weapons" directly before the Friar's line, "Alack, alack, what blood is this, which stains / The stony entrance of this sepulchre?" (140–141). Two lines later, the Douai MS offers the stage direction, "Enters the tomb." The many references to the tomb indicate that it was represented by a physical structure, for which the obvious choice would have been the tiring-house. Based on similarly circumstantial evidence, Gurr confidently asserts that the tiring-house front "served as the Capulet house when Romeo climbed to its balcony" (Andrew Gurr, *The Shakespearean Stage, 1574–1642* [Cambridge: Cambridge University Press, 1992], 182).

4. This point may be somewhat negated by the argument about bedchambers espoused by Michael Danahy in "Social, Sexual, and Human Spaces in *La Princesse de Cleves,*" *French Forum* 6, no. 3 (Sept. 1981): 212–224. Yet Danahy's point is also mine: when female courtiers lack any private space, and even lack the ability to decide who may enter their bedroom and who may not, they may fail adequately to develop an interior space, a sense of self that is distinct from the directions and wishes of others.

5. See Andrew Gurr, *The Shakespearean Stage,* 160. As Gurr points out, "after the adults took [the Blackfriars playhouse] over in 1608 swordplay was confined to

the occasional fencing bout and . . . battles and what Shirley called 'target fighting' were never tried there" (157). The size of the stage provides one explanation for why Bussy's epic duel in act 2 is described, not staged.

6. Consider the "boudoir atmosphere" (to coin a useful anachronism) of such settings as Clerimont's dressing room in Jonson's *Epicoene*, the Duchess's closet in Webster's *Duchess of Malfi*, and Tamyra's closet in this play.

7. Indeed, the line may even have been intended as a reference to the golden statues that apotheosize the lovers at the close of *Romeo and Juliet*.

8. Sigmund Freud, *Introductory Lectures on Psychoanalysis*, trans. and ed. James Strachey (New York: Norton, 1966), 156.

9. Anne Ubersfeld, *Reading Theatre*, trans. Frank Collins, ed. Paul Perron and Patrick Debbeche (Toronto: University of Toronto Press, 1999), 110.

10. These symbolic structures persist beyond Bussy's death. After her lover's decease, Tamyra begs to depart from her husband's house. Having failed to keep her affair hidden, her bedroom matters private, she urges her husband to let her depart until her stab wounds—"that never balm shall close / Till death hath enter'd at them, so I love them, / Being opened by your hands"—heal (5.4.194–196). Having been grotesquely penetrated by her husband's phallic knife, Tamyra promises to bear lovingly these signs of his ownership, his right to enter her body exclusively, and in any way he wishes. She pledges, "I never more will grieve you with my sight, / Never endure that any roof shall part / Mine eyes and heaven; but to the open deserts, / Like to a hunted tigress, I will fly" (5.4.197–200). Leaving behind the empty shell of a place that failed to offer her protection, she seeks the promise of nakedness that the wilderness seems to offer. After Bussy's death, she no longer needs any private place. Violated by her husband's knife and by his base murder of her lover, Tamyra becomes a walking emblem of a woman who has nothing to hide, a woman whose interiority contains nothing but a bleakness that she is willing to share with the world.

11. Catherine Belsey, *The Subject of Tragedy: Identity and Difference in Renaissance Drama* (London: Methuen, 1985), 13. Michael Hattaway looks to the future, borrowing the term gest from Brecht to characterize "moments when the visual elements of the scene combine with the dialogue in a significant form that reveals the condition of life in the play" (*Elizabethan Popular Theatre: Plays in Performance* [London: Routledge, 1982], 57).

12. Catherine Belsey, "Emblem and Antithesis in *The Duchess of Malfi*" *Renaissance Drama* 11 (1980): 117.

13. As an example, the *OED* cites Hall's *Chronicles*, from *Richard III*, 56: "With out resistence, [we] have penetrate [sic] the ample region . . . of Wales." The French cognate was also commonly used at this time to mean "to enter into a space."

14. George Puttenham, *The Arte of English Poesie* (Kent, Ohio: Kent State University Press, 1970), 159.

15. Many critics, following Gail Kern Paster's groundbreaking book, *The Body Embarrassed: Drama and the Disciplines of Shame in Early Modern England* (Ithaca: Cornell University Press, 1993), have investigated the relation between selfhood and early modern humoral theory. My approach attempts to focus on actual physical perception rather than on the physiological discourse of the time.

16. Belsey, *The Subject of Tragedy*, 14.

17. Paster, *The Body Embarrassed*, 3.

18. Henri Lefebvre, *The Production of Space*, trans. Donald Nicholson-Smith (Oxford: Blackwell, 1991), 1.

19. Ibid.

20. Cynthia Marshall, *The Shattering of the Self: Violence, Subjectivity, and Early Modern Texts* (Baltimore: Johns Hopkins University Press, 2002), 14.

21. Paster, *The Body Embarrassed*, 5.

22. Hollis Huston, *The Actor's Instrument: Body, Theory, Stage* (Ann Arbor: University of Michigan Press, 1992), 112. For more specifics, see Edward T. Hall, *The Hidden Dimension* (Garden City, New York: Doubleday, 1966). Hall discusses different cultures in Europe (123–138), Japan (139–144), and the Middle East (144–153).

23. Pierre Bourdieu, *Outline of a Theory of Practice*, trans. Richard Nice (Cambridge: Cambridge University Press, 1977), 94.

24. Ruth Kelso, *Doctrine for the Lady of the Renaissance* (Urbana, Ill.: University of Illinois Press, 1956), 43–44.

25. In *The Family, Sex, and Marriage in England, 1500–1800* (New York: Harper, 1977), Lawrence Stone quotes Lady Jane Grey as complaining of her parents' rigorous and even apparently spiteful discipline:

> When I am in presence either of father or mother, whether I speak, keep silence, sit, stand or go, eat, drink, be merry or sad, be sewing, playing, dancing, or doing anything else, I must do it, as it were, in such weight, measure, and number, even so perfectly as God made the world, else I am so sharply taunted, so cruelly threatened, yea presently sometimes with pinches, nips and bobs, and some ways I will not name for the honour I bear them, so without measure misordered that I think myself in Hell. (167)

26. Jennifer A. Low, *Manhood and the Duel: Masculinity in Early Modern Drama and Culture* (New York: Palgrave, 2003), 73–74.

27. Hall, *The Hidden Dimension*, 121.

28. In 1.1, Giovanni asks the Friar whether "[a] customary form . . . [should] be a bar / 'Twixt my perpetual happiness and me?" (1.1.25–27). Since his happiness is in the enjoyment of Annabella's body, his reference to a bar implies that he conceives of his sister's body as a room with the entrance barred by the traditional prohibition against incest. Later, when Giovanni learns of Annabella's pregnancy, he asks Putana, horrified, "But in what case is she?" (3.3.17). In this instance, the double meaning is the author's, not the character's. The term clearly refers to Annabella's body as container—not, this time, an empty container with space for the phallus but a full container, bearing the child that is the result of his "filling" her.

29. All quotations from *'Tis Pity She's a Whore* refer to John Ford, *'Tis Pity She's a Whore*, ed. N. W. Bawcutt (Lincoln, Nebr.: University of Nebraska Press, 1966). This edition is based on Q1, authored by Ford himself.

30. In contrast, consider the scene in *The Duchess of Malfi* when Ferdinand enters the Duchess's chamber just as she, speaking to Antonio, says, "You have cause to love me, I ent'red you into my heart" (John Webster, *The Duchess of Malfi*, ed. Elizabeth Brennan, [New York: Norton, 1993], 3.2.61). As Judith Haber comments, "When Ferdinand enters that space, uninvited and 'unseen, he forcibly reappropriates her body/room/stage and defines it as his container—the empty, passive receptacle that is the ground of his existence. . . . At this point, understandably, the Duchess's

speech undergoes a radical change" ("'My Body Bestow upon my Women': The Space of the Feminine in *The Duchess of Mafi*," *Renaissance Drama* 28 [1997]: 144). Georgianna Ziegler also pursues this line of reasoning in her discussion of Cymbeline. "For Iachimo, a woman's body is part and parcel of her room and can be similarly violated. Though he does not physically rape Imogen, we nevertheless feel that a rape has been committed in his voyeuristic intrusion on her privacy" ("My Lady's Chamber: Female Space, Female Chastity in Shakespeare," *Textual Practice* 4, no. 1 [1990]: 82).

31. Patricia Fumerton, *Cultural Aesthetics: Renaissance Literature and the Practice of Social Ornament* (Chicago: Chicago University Press, 1991), 69.

32. The editor N. W. Bawcutt comments, "Q's *in his study* clearly seems an error, as the scene takes place in Annabella's bedroom (see 3.4.33)" (*'Tis Pity She's a Whore*, 57). At the cited line, Florio says to the Friar, "Come, father, I'll conduct you to her chamber."

33. According to editor Mark Stavig, the Friar's speech draws substantially on Ford's poem *Christ's Bloody Sweat*. See Stavig, introduction to *'Tis Pity She's a Whore* (Arlington Heights, Ill.: AHM, 1966), vii–xix.

34. Claudine Defaye sees the scene as a representation of psychological enclosure for which the Friar provides an egress: "It is as if, by conforming to the role of sinner assigned by religion, terrible and constraining though it be, Annabella succeeded in escaping from her own intimate and immediate torment, from a kind of existential anguish, where all issues seem blocked" ("Annabella's Unborn Baby: The Heart of the Womb in *'Tis Pity She's a Whore*," *Cahiers élisabéthains* 15 [1979]: 37).

35. The scene is almost surely set in the main bedchamber in Soranzo's house.

36. Katharine Eisaman Maus, *Inwardness and Theater in the English Renaissance* (Chicago: University of Chicago Press, 1995), 4.

37. Many critics have attempted to clarify the personal symbolism of Giovanni's sensationalistic gesture. Among them are Ronald Huebert, who argues that the gesture literalizes a flawed analogy between discovering a secret and ripping up a bosom (John Ford, *Baroque English Dramatist* [Montreal: McGill-Queen's University Press, 1977], 145); Michael Neill, who makes some of the same points that I do in his effort to sort out the "welter of competing definitions and explanations [that the gesture] invites" ("'What Strange Riddle's This?': Deciphering *'Tis Pity She's a Whore*," in *John Ford: Critical Re-Visions*, ed. Michael Neill [Cambridge: Cambridge University Press, 1988], 165); and Susan J. Wiseman, who asserts that Annabella's heart, for Giovanni, is "endowed . . . with all the private and confused meanings of incest" ("*'Tis Pity She's a Whore*: Representing the Incestuous Body," in *Revenge Tragedy*, ed. Stevie Simkin [New York: Palgrave, 2001], 222). Wiseman's article, excellent in many ways, nonetheless unthinkingly uses spatial concepts as metaphor in a way that runs directly contrary to my goal of noting how space shapes consciousness and vice versa. Most notably, Wiseman seems to collude with Ford's own rhetoric when she asserts that, in *'Tis Pity*, "the female body is represented as an ethical, financial, spiritual, amatory and psychological territory" and that Annabella's body "is located and relocated within these competing ways of looking at the body" (215). Like me, however, Wiseman asserts that "the significance of Annabella's body is repeatedly transformed during the play by the powerful discourses which . . . define it" (216).

38. Ziegler, "My Lady's Chamber," 80.

39. Huston, *The Actor's Instrument,* 113.

40. Stephen Gosson, *Playes Confuted in Five Actions,* (1582; reprint, New York: Garland, 1972), B8^v.

41. Phillip Stubbes, *The Anatomie of Abuses* (1583; reprint, New York: Garland, 1973), A Preface to the Reader, quoted in Marshall, *The Shattering of the Self,* 17.

42. Hall, *The Hidden Dimension,* 40.

43. Bruce R. Smith, *The Acoustic World of Early Modern England: Attending to the O-Factor* (Chicago: Chicago University Press, 1999), 206.

44. Hall, *The Hidden Dimension,* 120.

45. Ibid., 120.

46. Ibid., 114–115.

47. Ibid., 115.

48. Robert Weimann, *Shakespeare and the Popular Tradition in the Theater: Studies in the Social Dimension of the Dramatic Form and Function* (Baltimore: Hopkins University Press, 1978), 83.

49. As Gay McAuley says,

> The moment of entering the presentational space is extremely important for the actor as is evident from the fact that conventions have been developed in many different performance genres to heighten or mark the moment of entrance. These may involve the material reality of the performance (the drum roll, music flourish, and spotlight of circus or music hall) or be activated from within the fiction . . . but the function is similar: to draw the spectators' attention to the physical point of entrance into the space and to mark the moment in some way.

Space in Performance: Making Meaning in the Theatre (Ann Arbor: University of Michigan Press, 1999), 96.

50. *The Shakespearean Stage,* 179.

51. Cynthia Marshall alludes to this issue in "Wound-man: *Coriolanus,* Gender, and the Theatrical Construction of Interiority," in *Feminist Readings of Early Modern Culture,* ed. Valerie Traub, M. Lindsay Kaplan, and Dympna Callaghan (Cambridge: Cambridge University Press, 1996), 95.

52. *Penetration* is not the right word here, of course. Jarrett Walker's comment is useful: "Ultimately, [Coriolanus] does not distinguish between being nourished and being wounded. Both are kinds of incorporation, and in both cases he responds by 'spitting back' at the world in an automatic reciprocal action, a compulsive denial of receptiveness" ("Voiceless Bodies and Bodiless Voices: The Drama of Human Perception in *Coriolanus,*" *SQ* 43, no.2 [summer 1992]: 176). These terms enable us, I think, to perceive more accurately what mechanism is at work. *Starving,* a related term that invokes the process of digestion, is one of the principal foci of Stanley Cavell's groundbreaking essay "'Who does the wolf love?' *Coriolanus* and the Interpretation of Politics," in *Shakespeare and the Question of Theory,* ed. Patricia Parker and Geoffrey Hartman (New York: Routledge, 1985), 245–272.

53. William Shakespeare, *Coriolanus,* ed. Philip Brockbank (New York: Arden, 1976; reprint, New York: Routledge, 1988), 95.

54. Ibid., 95.

55. Jarrett Walker, "Voiceless Bodies and Bodiless Voices," 172.

56. In discussing group experiential space, Yi-Fu Tuan asserts that crowds may "not detract, but enhance the significance of the events: vast numbers of people do not necessarily generate the feeling of spatial oppressiveness" if the people's reasons for being present are identical and are not directly opposed to the presence of others ("Space and Place: A Humanist Perspective," in *Philosophy in Geography*, ed. Stephen Gale and Gunnar Olsson [Dordrecht: D. Reidel, 1979], 404).

57. Zvi Jagendorf, *"Coriolanus:* Body Politic and Private Parts," *SQ* 41, no. 4 (winter 1990): 462. Similarly, Arthur Riss argues that the play develops a "nexus between the land and the body," establishing "a correspondence between the impulse to enclose public land and Coriolanus's urge to enclose his body" ("The Belly Politic: *Coriolanus* and the Revolt of Language," *ELH* 59, no. 1 (spring 1992): 55).

58. Jagendorf, "Body Politic and Private Parts," 462. For a different point of view, see Ralph Berry, who analyzes the opening and concludes "that the Roman crowd . . . is not the fearsome manifestation of the popular will that it might at first appear. There is nothing here like the brutal capriciousness of . . . the blood lust that Antony arouses during the Forum scene. On the contrary, we see a collective of indeterminate and variable characteristics" ("Casting the Crowd: *Coriolanus* in Performance," *Assaph* C4 [1988]: 114).

59. An alternative interpretation of the scene would present the dialogue between 1. Cit. and 2. Cit. center stage, surrounded by the mob. This staging would create a small bubble of intimacy that would either be broken by Menenius's entrance or dissolve as the two citizens faded into the crowd. Michael Warren considers various possibilities for staging the citizens in his article "The Perception of Error: The Editing and the Performance of the Opening of *'Coriolanus'*" in *Textual Performances: The Modern Reproduction of Shakespeare's Drama*, ed. Lukas Erne and Margaret Jane Kidnie (Cambridge: Cambridge University Press, 2004), 127–142.

60. Walker, "Voiceless Bodies and Bodiless Voices," 179, n. 16.

61. Paster, *The Body Embarrassed*, 92.

62. Janet Adelman strongly endorses this view, though she is quite uninterested in staging and uses a psychoanalytic framework for her argument. Adelman asserts that

> the scene at Corioli represents a glorious transformation of the nightmare of oral vulnerability . . . into a phallic adventure that both assures and demonstrates his independence. Coriolanus' battlecry as he storms the gates sexualizes the scene: "Come on; / If you'll stand fast, we'll beat them to their wives" (I.iv.40–41). But the dramatic action itself presents the conquest of Corioli as an image not of rape but of triumphant rebirth.

"'Anger's My Meat': Feeding, Dependency, and Aggression in *Coriolanus*," in *Representing Shakespeare: New Psychoanalytic Essays*, ed. Murray M. Schwartz and Coppelia Kahn [Baltimore: Johns Hopkins University Press, 1980], 134.

63. Edward S. Casey, *Getting Back into Place: Toward a Renewed Understanding of the Place-World* (Bloomington: Indiana University Press, 1993), 133.

64. Ibid., 137–138.

65. Edward Casey meditates on "hereness": "[E]ven within my lived body, I can distinguish a corporeally localized here from the here that is coextensive with my body as a whole. At this level, my here is often identified with my head, and

even more particularly with a region between or behind the eyes" (*Getting Back into Place*, 52).

66. See Belsey, *The Subject of Tragedy: Identity and Difference in Renaissance Drama*; Belsey, "Emblem and Antithesis in *The Duchess of Malfi*," 115–134; and Diehl, "The Iconography of Violence in English Renaissance Tragedy," *Renaissance Drama* 11 (1980): 27–44.

LINA PERKINS WILDER

Toward a Shakespearean "Memory Theater": Romeo, the Apothecary, and the Performance of Memory

Romeo's first reaction to the news of Juliet's death is not mourning but a lengthy and, according to some, unnecessary recollection of an apothecary and the contents of his shop:

> Well, Juliet, I will lie with thee tonight.
> Let's see for means. O mischief thou art swift
> To enter in the thoughts of desperate men.
> I do remember an apothecary—
> And hereabouts a dwells—which late I noted
> In tatter'd weeds, with overwhelming brows,
> Culling of simples. Meagre were his looks,
> Sharp misery had worn him to the bones,
> And in his needy shop a tortoise hung,
> An alligator stuff'd, and other skins
> Of ill-shap'd fishes; and about his shelves
> A beggarly account of empty boxes,
> Green earthen pots, bladders, and musty seeds,
> Remnants of packthread, and old cakes of roses
> Were thinly scatter'd to make up a show.
>
> (5.1.34–48)[1]

Shakespeare Quarterly, Volume 56, Number 2 (Summer 2005): pp. 156–175. Copyright © 2005 The Johns Hopkins University Press.

Critics have long complained that this speech is inappropriate to Romeo's situation both practically and in its affect, that the speech has little to do with the acquisition of poison (the scene's ostensible purpose) and nothing to do with the grief that one might expect Romeo to be feeling.[2] I argue here that the apothecary scene is appropriate, that it does express grief, and that it does so by means of what I will call a "performance of memory."

The apothecary scene in *Romeo and Juliet* is one of many performances of memory in Shakespeare's plays, moments in which one character's seemingly digressive recollection momentarily displaces dramatic action. Other examples include the first of Justice Shallow's scenes in *2 Henry IV* (3.2); reminiscences of Falstaff in *Henry V* (2.3); Hamlet's scenes with the Ghost (1.5), the First Player (2.2), and the skull of Yorick (5.1); Enobarbus's recollection of Cleopatra on the barge at Cydnus (2.2) and her "return" to Cydnus as she prepares for death (5.2); and Prospero's exposition (1.2), Miranda's half-memory of women (1.2), and Caliban's dream in *The Tempest* (3.2). The function of memory scenes in Shakespeare's plays seems to be similar to that of flashbacks in film: they give background and expand the work's narrative frame beyond its immediate physical and temporal borders. But the difference between what the audience sees onstage and the past events the character is recalling creates a dissonance not present in cinematic flashbacks: stage memory belongs to a register of experience separate from that of represented action. In addition to tying events from the play's or the character's past to those in the acted present, and to momentarily relaxing the pace of a play such as *Romeo and Juliet,* in which narrative drive is otherwise relentless,[3] the performance of memory interrogates early modern ideas about memory and about theater.

Looking backward over the action of the play and even toward events outside the play's scope, Shakespeare's memory theater may invite both audience and actors to see the play as a dramatic whole, an effect that Tiffany Stern claims was unusual in the early modern English theater. "Plays seem to have been watched," she writes,

> as they were performed, with the emphasis at least as much on parts as on the whole. . . . Part-oriented response is reflected in the way the audience might, for instance, take objection to single characters in plays as well as to plays themselves, and in the preponderance of actor-focused criticism over much of the period.[4]

She also notes:

> Plays often indicate that an actor has privately learnt his role, but does not know what parts his fellow actors are playing . . . , or

whom he is supposed to be addressing. . . . [M]any actors, having learnt to deal primarily with their own parts in private study, had not learnt to think of the play as a unity.[5]

But Shakespeare's performances of memory do more than counteract the isolating effect of part-based memorization through having actors "recall" events that took place earlier in the play or words spoken by other characters. They actually attempt to recreate events that are not witnessed by the audience or even, in some instances, by the rememberer.

I. The Performance of Memory

Shakespeare's performances of memory create a memory theater that draws on and then upends the imagery and the vocabulary of the memory theaters employed by such students of the art of memory as Giulio Camillo, Robert Fludd, and John Willis: Using the metaphor of theater, the memory arts imagine, and in some cases physically construct, a spatial and visible representation of memory. Shakespeare's memory theater returns memory to a state of invisibility, inaccessibility, even mystery by refusing to provide the spectacle that performed remembering implies, by not allowing us to see otherwise-visible objects (such as Romeo's "ill-shap'd fishes").[6] This is true not only for the theater audience, which is made to feel that it is witnessing an essentially private act made uncomfortably public, but for the rememberer himself or herself, for whom memory becomes not a tool for retaining information but a means by which forgotten or overlooked information is unexpectedly recovered or even "discovered," seemingly for the first time.

The element of the unexpected in Shakespeare's memory theater is the product of disorderly, even random recollection, a conceptualization of memory far from standard in the early modern period. Indeed an emphasis on order is so ubiquitous both in discussions of mnemonics and in physical treatises on the memory as to be more an assumption than a subject for argument, as we see in the work of such widely differing scholars of medieval and early modern memory systems as Frances Yates, Lina Bolzoni, and Mary J. Carruthers.[7] As John Sutton has ably demonstrated, however, the equation between memory and order in the period is not as simple as it seems. The attempt to order the memory through artificial means reflects a fear that memory could dissolve into complete disorder. The source of this disorder is the body.[8] It was generally accepted in the early modern period that memory takes place in the brain, collecting in the rearmost of three or four "ventricles" in which sensual impressions are formed, interrogated, and stored.[9] But the fluidity of this place, awash in the "animal spirits" that carry information through and from the brain, is not conducive to order. Sutton argues that the methods of the memory arts are a means of liberating the mind from "the dirt added to thoughts by the body," effected by imposing mental discipline and moral control.[10] Should this discipline fail, one could always turn the page: treatises on the art of memory are nearly always paired with treatises for improving the natural memory through physical means. These include lists of recipes for treatments that can alter the physical makeup of the brain or the humors that make the brain too hot, too cold, too dry, or too wet to retain information, along with what might be called lifestyle advice (avoid drunkenness, too much sleep, venery, and, according to one author, wearing dirty shoes to bed).[11] But despite the fact that these instructions are bound in the same volume as treatises on the memory arts, they seem to be viewed as a separate solution to the body issue, even as a kind of crutch.

The memory arts themselves reimagine the role of the physical body not as the location of memory but as an observer of external, well-ordered memory scenes. The method of ordering provided by the memory arts is particularly suggestive because it offers a model for joining memory and theater, one that Shakespeare does not consistently exploit. Avoiding the sticky process of humoral correction, localist models of memory extract recollection from the interior of the rememberer's body by imagining memory as an act of spectatorship.[12] Instead of contemplating a potentially volatile interior space, memory artists are advised to "walk" through towns, buildings, or rooms constructed in their minds and to observe them as spectators. For example, Johannes Romberch recommends constructing in one's mind a town composed of a series of memory *loci*, with places such as monasteries, restaurants, churches, chapels, houses, and theaters.[13] In many cases the memory *locus* is not an imaginary space: some memory artists advise their readers to memorize a real room, preferably empty, in which they can then imagine arranging memory objects. The influential memory artist Peter of Ravenna gives a list of rules for choosing a memory place: it should have windows and columns, and must be neither too close nor too distant, neither crowded nor too high.[14] Whether imagined or real, a memory place functions like a map on which information that might otherwise fall into disorder can be organized and easily recalled. The memory objects in a particular *locus* might represent the main points of a speech to be given in public; to stick to his text, the orator need only recall his path through the memory *locus* and visualize, one by one, the objects that he placed there, which will in turn evoke the words of his speech.

The ordering device of memory theater associates the memory artist's spectatorship overtly with the theatrical stage. The memory theaters designed by Shakespeare's contemporaries differ from their medieval predecessors in that they resemble London stages rather than classical amphitheaters. The seventeenth-century physician John Willis, for instance, imagines himself as a spectator in front of the theater of his own memory, as does his contemporary Robert Fludd. Willis's description of his imaginary "theater" is striking in its physical detail:

> A *Repository* is an imaginary fabrick, fancied Artificially, built of hewen stone, in form of a *Theater,* the form whereof followeth; suppose the Edifice to be twelve yards in length within the walls, in breadth six yards, and in height seven yards, the roof thereof flat, leaded above, and pargetted underneath, lying wholly open to view, without any wall on that side supposed next us: Let there be imagined a *Stage* of smooth gray Marble, even and variegated with a party coloured border, which *Stage* is to be extended over the whole length and breadth of the building, and raised a yard high above the *Level* of the ground on which the said Edifice is erected. . . .
>
> A *Repository* according to this fashion, is to be represented before the eyes of our minde, wheresoever we are, as oft as we intend to practise this Art; supposing our selves to stand about two yards distant, against the midst thereof.[15]

Although the accompanying diagram indicates that Willis's memory theater is a proscenium rather than a thrust stage, its dimensions, materials, and open construction, along with the fact that it is raised above the level of the spectator, suggest the influences of stages like the ones on which Shakespeare's plays would have been performed. Fludd's diagrams of his memory theater led Frances Yates to speculate that it was modeled on the Globe.[16]

For the purposes of the memory arts, theater is defined by its ability to make the internal external: as Bolzoni sees it, early modern memory internalizes that which theater "makes visible, . . . projects outward."[17] When the memory artist Giulio Camillo constructed a physical edifice of ordered boxes and shelves, Erasmus reports that he "called it a theatre *because* it can be seen with the eyes of the body."[18] Through the use of physical objects, real or imagined, this "memory theater" turns the mind inside out, places it on display. As Camillo argues,

> all the things that the human mind conceives but that cannot be seen with the eyes of the body can . . . be expressed with some bodily signs, so that everyone can see directly with his own eyes all that which otherwise is submerged in the depths of the human mind.[19]

But the question remains just how much this mnemonic theater has to do with the places where plays are performed, or with the idea—the process—of performance. Frances Yates's supposition that Fludd's drawings of his memory theater were modeled on the Globe has not met with much favor; other attempts to link the theatrical imagery of the memory arts with actual theaters and actual plays have had limited success.[20] Early modern memory theaters seem to have more in common with tableaux than they do with plays: images are arranged to be scanned by the inner (or outer) eye; they may be "animated," but their movement does not develop into narrative.[21] While tableaux, dumb shows, and images meant to shock the spectator do occur in early modern plays, they occur in the context of a larger process. It seems clear that early modern English plays and memory theaters share, at least to some extent, a visual appeal. But they do not share dramatic process; they do not share narrative.

Shakespeare's memory theater, in contrast, places memory in a narrative context or, more specifically, in the narrative context peculiar to the early modern English stage. Jill L. Levenson speculates that early modern English audiences and players would have had a much more dynamic concept of dramatic structure than the one we have now. Rehearsing (if one did rehearse) or performing a play in Shakespeare's theater, she writes,

> meant locating one's character—second by second—on the fluid, unlocalised stage, in relation to the other players, and without the guidance of a director. . . . [T]he first productions of *Romeo and Juliet*—or any English Renaissance drama—were performances in the making: processes which integrated all parts of the dramatic whole in view of a large, responsive audience.[22]

Like Stern, Levenson sees the stage as embracing the uncertainty that memory theaters seek to avoid. Levenson invokes the very metaphor of "fluid[ity]" that is resisted by students of the art of memory because of their fears of bodily disorder. "Ideals of powerful executive control," Sutton writes, "sat well with local memory, for independent ordered items in their places were already passive, waiting for the active executive to hunt them out."[23] The early modern English theater, lacking even "the guidance of a director," is a "hunt" of a very different sort, a hunt without an executive.[24]

Shakespeare's performances of memory reflect and invite the "integrat[ion]" of structural elements on the part of the players as well as the audience. Romeo's extended memory of the apothecary gives audience, character, and actor time to perceive the parallels in Romeo's actions. Working from individual parts rather than complete scripts, the actors playing (for example) Romeo, the apothecary, Friar Laurence, the Nurse, and the Chorus might not recognize the implications of their lines until they heard each other speak, and, as Stern and Levenson point out, limited rehearsal time could mean that they heard each other's lines for the first time in front of an audience.[25] For each of the groups involved, the process of discovery outlined in Romeo's performed remembering might have been entirely genuine. As I will demonstrate, that process of discovery moves from the identification of Friar Laurence with the apothecary to the more shadowy identification of the Nurse with both figures and the incorporation of Romeo's "defiance" into the Chorus's predetermined plot summary.

But the performance of memory requires more than a drawing of structural lines through a series of events that everyone—player, character, audience member—witnesses at once. Romeo's performance of memory evokes a scene that he alone saw—and this "he" is Romeo the character, not the actor playing Romeo. When Romeo remembers this absent scene, the theatrical community described by Levenson dwindles to a single person, if he can be called a person. Audience participation in Romeo's "experience" of Mantuan roads is limited to what the performance of memory can bring us. The memory emblems and the tableaux of memorable objects that William Engel finds in early modern plays invite the audience to participate in the play by remembering its images. (Shakespeare does this occasionally: the dumb show that precedes the Mousetrap in *Hamlet* is one example.[26]) In Shakespeare's memory theater, though, the audience and indeed the actors participate along with the characters only to a certain extent in the process of remembering. We see Romeo seeking poison, not the evocative interior of the apothecary's shop; we see the aging Justice Shallow, not the (perhaps fictional) "lusty Shallow" of his past (3.2.15);[27] we see Yorick's skull, not the lips that Hamlet remembers kissing; we see Cleopatra's suicidal "return" to Cydnus, not her first appearance there; we see Caliban cursing, not dreaming. The door in the wall remains, essentially, closed; we see only quick flashes of the space behind it.

II. "I Do Remember": Memory Theater in *Romeo and Juliet*

Two of Shakespeare's clearest examples of memory theater occur in *Romeo and Juliet*—one of them the apothecary scene (5.1), the other the Nurse's recollection of Juliet's weaning (1.3). Both demonstrate many of the qualities that I have described above: the disruption of dramatic action, the physical absence of otherwise vividly sensual remembered objects, the extended performance of memory, the element of discovery. Romeo and the Nurse create memory theater from objects that, because they are in the past or because they are outside the capabilities of an only intermittently spectacular theater, are not visible to the audience: the interior of a shop with the dusty remains of an inventory and desiccated fish hanging in the window, a shaking dovehouse, a child fussing over the taste of a nipple daubed with wormwood. Romeo's and the Nurse's recollections draw on the iconography of the memory arts. Romeo in particular seems to have internalized the principles that would lend order to his stored impressions. (Romeo describes the apothecary's shop as a place "which late I noted"; a habit of "noting" was recommended as a way to create memory *loci* and to practice memorization.[28]) But the process of recollection, it seems, disrupts any system imposed during storage.

The Nurse's speech at 1.3.20–44 anticipates, through the reactions of her onstage listeners, the impatience and embarrassment with which critics would greet Romeo's performed remembering in the apothecary scene. More importantly, it introduces the device of performed remembering into the play as the Nurse famously recounts the earthquake of Lammas Eve eleven years earlier and Juliet's weaning. The images animated by her performance of memory draw her own interest, but as they multiply, they test the patience of her auditors: Lady Capulet's "Enough of this" (l. 49) is quickly followed by Juliet's "stint thou" (l. 58).[29] Like the earthquake, the shaking dovehouse, the pratfall, and the husband's bawdy joke that punctuate the Nurse's performance of memory, the furniture of the apothecary's shop is in accord with the objects recommended by memory artists: the "merye, cruell, iniurious, merueylous, excellently fayre, or exceedinglye foule thynges" which William Fulwood claims "do chaunge and moue the senses, and . . . styrre vppe the Memorye."[30] Romeo remembers an apothecary who is himself grotesque and who is surrounded by grotesque objects: a man "[i]n tatter'd weeds, with overwhelming brows, / Culling of simples," who has been "worn . . . to the bones," and whose shop is filled with decayed reminders of death: the stuffed carcasses of alligator and tortoise, "ill-shap'd fishes," and stores that have grown "musty" and "old." But although they resemble objects placed to stimulate the memory, the sparseness and disorganization of the apothecary's wares suggest a more haphazard version of memory than the one usually advocated by memory artists.

The seemingly arbitrary dilation on the apothecary's shop, which is Shakespeare's innovation,[31] underlines the role in this scene of the memory arts, in which apothecaries have a long history. The apothecary's shop, first of all, recalls the imagined cities filled with shops arranged in alphabetical order by means of which some memory artists memorized words and phrases. Johannes Romberch, for example, provides an engraving in which alphabetized shops distinguished by simple images—a man dispatching a steer in the *Bovicida*, books in the window of the *Bibliopola*—provide a mental path that the memory artist could follow in order to collect remembered objects left in each place.[32] A few memory artists include *apothecarius* and related words in their lists of alphabetized shops and professions.[33] Further and more significantly, the word *apothecary* is both etymologically and metaphorically related to the organization of memory. As Carruthers notes, "storehouse," usually rendered in Latin as *thesaurus* or *arca*, is one of the conventional metaphors for memory. *Apotheca* also "means 'storehouse,' originally for wine, but extended . . . to mean something like a 'shop,' a store full of precious things laid away in order, any of which the *apothecarius* can bring forth immediately in response to a request, and indeed, bring forth a host of related things too."[34] Carruthers then cites the memory treatise by Hugh of St. Victor:

> This ark [*arca*, memory repository] is like to an apothecary's shop, filled with a variety of all delights. You will seek nothing in it which you will not find, and when you find one thing, you will see many more disclosed to you. Here are bountifully contained the universal works of our salvation . . . [and] the condition of the universal Church. Here the narrative of historical events is woven together, here the mysteries of the sacraments are found, here are laid out the successive stages of responses, judgments, meditations, contemplations, of good works, virtues, and rewards.[35]

The differences between the apothecary's shop in *Romeo and Juliet* and the one described by Hugh are as striking as the similarities. Compared to Hugh's apothecary shop, Romeo's is disorganized and poorly stocked, and its owner's "penury" is predictive of his willingness to sell Romeo poison; but this shop also reflects the qualities of Romeo's memory. The items in the shop in Mantua are not "laid away in order," but "scatter'd." The apothecary is not present to "bring forth immediately" the items Romeo wishes to purchase (or remember) and to produce associated items from neighboring shelves but must be summoned from his shop ("What ho! Apothecary!" [5.1.57]). Under normal circumstances the objects on the shelves of an apothecary's shop, like those carried by a modern drugstore, existed as much to distract the patron into adding a few unnecessary items to his shopping bag as to heal his ailments: as Hugh says, "when you find one thing, you will see many more disclosed to you." This is not the case in Romeo's apothecary shop. Romeo's memory does not contain the easily reached *copia* of texts or objects with which memory artists crammed their minds. The shop is not "full of precious things"; in fact, as Romeo says, the apothecary's inventory has reached desperately low levels, and there are only a few images set out in his *apotheca*.

The shop's low inventory and the difficulty with which Romeo gains access to what it does contain mirror the challenge of translating Romeo's past experience into his present situation. The performance of memory is an act of self-conscious negotiation between present and past, a "repetition with revision" (as Joseph Roach calls both memory and performance) that gives the rememberer an increasingly precise orientation in the dramatic present.[36] Remembering the shop's contents brings Romeo physically into the scene as he moves from a vague sense that the apothecary lives "hereabouts" (l. 38) to the near certainty that "this should be the house" (l. 55):

Well, Juliet, I will lie with thee tonight.
Let's see for means. O mischief thou art swift
To enter in the thoughts of desperate men.
I do remember an apothecary
And hereabouts a dwells—which late I noted
In tatter'd weeds, with overwhelming brows,
Culling of simples. . . .
Noting this penury, to myself I said,
'And if a man did need a poison now,
Whose sale is present death in Mantua,
Here lives a caitiff wretch would sell it him'.
O, this same thought did but forerun my need,
And this same needy man must sell it me.
As I remember, this should be the house.

(ll. 34–40, 49–55)

Beginning awkwardly, with short sentences and numerous self-interruptions, Romeo traces the process of recollection from the initial and silent thought of poison back toward the remembered quip that produced it (ll. 50–52), the thought that "did but forerun my need." His memory of the apothecary finds Romeo in the same physical location in which he formed a memory of the shop's contents and their possible use, but his changing circumstances make it seem strange: "this *should* be the house," he says. (Memory by places, it seems, is not always as effective as memory artists would have us believe.[37]) It is important that the shop, often represented in performance by a door in the back wall, be left to Romeo's memory and the audience's imagination. Romeo does not actually enter the apothecary's shop; instead, he calls the apothecary to come forth. Since the shop is closed, shut behind a door that leads to the dust and timber backstage, negotiations between Romeo's past and present perceptions of the shop take place entirely in words, and the perspectives involved are exclusively Romeo's. The apothecary's shop, like a psychic prop-room, exists only in the backstage of Romeo's mind and is brought forward only through his performance of memory.

As the scene continues, Romeo finds himself increasingly and involuntarily caught up in the associative logic of recollection. The backward trail of Romeo's memory does not end with his unstaged walk through the streets of Mantua when he first arrived there, nor do his thoughts of poison begin there. The apothecary scene shows Romeo to be more observant than his previous behavior gives us reason to suspect and suggests that his habit of "noting" began before he encountered the apothecary shop. Romeo's description of the apothecary—a poor man "[i]n tatter'd weeds, with overwhelming brows, / Culling of simples"—becomes a recollection of another character's first appearance, that of Friar Laurence. The first time we see Romeo and the friar together, Friar Laurence is engaged in the activity by which Romeo later identifies the apothecary:

> Within the infant rind of this weak flower
> Poison hath residence, and medicine power:
> For this, being smelt, with that part cheers each part;
> Being tasted, stays all senses with the heart.
>
> (2.3.19–22)

The apothecary, as Dominick Grace convincingly argues, is a double for Friar Laurence.[38] Early in the play, Romeo sees Friar Laurence as he is performing the same task of culling simples that he remembers the apothecary performing.[39] Friar Laurence himself associates plant-cutting with the manufacture of poisons. Although he distinguishes "precious-juiced flowers" from "baleful weeds" early in the speech (1.4), medicinal and harmful qualities grow less distinguishable as the speech proceeds. Since Romeo enters just before Friar Laurence identifies the plant as half-medicine, half-poison,[40] he would hear most clearly not Friar Laurence's moralizing but his decidedly practical conclusion, in which the function of the plant is made explicit. The connection that Romeo makes in the apothecary scene between a man "Culling of simples" and that man's ability to provide him with poison may deliberately recall and certainly echoes his first scene with Friar Laurence.

Romeo's echo of Friar Laurence's words rebelliously sweeps away all the friar's careful distinctions. When playing apothecary, Friar Laurence concocts the "*borrow'd likeness* of shrunk death" (4.1.104, emphasis added); Romeo, though he addresses his vial as "cordial and not poison" (5.1.85), wants the real thing. His attempts at renaming—calling his gold "poison" and his poison "cordial"—reflect the mind of a man schooled under Friar Laurence and familiar with his multiple glosses, but the renamings do not conceal his un-Laurentian purpose. The swiftness of the death Romeo demands—he wants to die "[a]s violently as hasty powder fir'd / Doth hurry from the fatal cannon's womb" (ll. 64–65)[41]—justifies the friar's misgivings three acts earlier:

> These violent delights have violent ends
> And in their triumph die, like fire and powder,
> Which as they kiss consume. . . .
>
> (2.6.9–11)

Friar Laurence picks up the gunpowder metaphor again in 3.3 after Romeo's banishment. "Thy wit," he says,

Like powder in a skilless soldier's flask
Is set afire by thine own ignorance,
And thou dismember'd with thine own defence.

(3.3.129, 131–133)

As T. J. B. Spencer writes, "What the Friar had prophesied as the consequence of [Romeo's] impetuous love, and his equally impetuous despair,
Romeo himself now asks for the poison to bring about."[42]

Although Romeo could not be aware of the irony that he has, in effect, been "set afire by [his] own ignorance" that Juliet is not dead, he does, I
think, recognize how drastically he has departed from Friar Laurence's advice. Checked in his rush toward suicide by the apothecary's fear of Mantuan
law, Romeo finds himself repeating the past in a more subdued tone:

Art thou so bare and full of wretchedness,
And fear'st to die? Famine is in thy cheeks,
Need and oppression starveth in thy eyes,
Contempt and beggary hangs upon thy back.
The world is not thy friend, nor the world's law;
The world affords no law to make thee rich;
Then be not poor, but break it, and take this.

(5.1.68–74)

Romeo's world-weariness here recalls Mercutio's disillusioned voice, the
voice that tells the lovesick Romeo to "[p]rick love for pricking" (1.4.28)
rather than fall prey to romantic self-destruction. And Romeo's phrasing
echoes, once again, Friar Laurence. Perhaps half-hearing his own allusion
(5.1.64–65) to the gunpowder of the "skilless soldier" (3.3.131), Romeo
returns (at 5.1.72–73) to the Friar's advice in 3.3:

What, rouse thee, man. Thy Juliet is alive,
For whose dear sake thou wast but lately dead.
There art thou happy. . . .
The law that threaten'd death becomes thy friend
And turns it to exile. There art thou happy.

(3.3.135–137, 139–140)

Friar Laurence, the play's earlier apothecary figure, stopped Romeo from
committing suicide on more than one occasion. Romeo's determination not
to let the apothecary himself deter him from his purpose thus requires him
to negotiate not only with the man present before him but with his memory
of Friar Laurence's advice. But when Romeo finds himself in the position of

negotiator, he takes on Friar Laurence's role and reiterates the friar's words. Romeo says, quietly, "The world is not thy friend." The word *friend* as well as the rhythm of Romeo's line recall the friar's concluding argument: "The law . . . becomes thy friend / And turns [death] to exile." When Romeo recognizes this perhaps unconscious echo of Friar Laurence's diction and his sententious iambs, he turns and revises his own words. "The world is not thy friend," he says aloud and then, half to himself, "nor the world's law." The deliberate nature of Romeo's rejection of Friar Laurence is underlined by his departure from the metrical inevitability that marks Friar Laurence's advice: the trochee at the end of the line invites the actor playing Romeo to slow down, to emphasize the line's final words.

But before Romeo finds himself echoing Friar Laurence's advice, he also seems unconsciously to be echoing the Nurse's vivid and disorganized recollection of Juliet's weaning.[43] The Nurse's memory, like Romeo's, toys with and discards the imagery of the memory arts. As Carruthers and Stephen Greenblatt remind us, dovehouses are a potent image for memory theorists, and one with somewhat equivocal implications.[44] "Plato," Greenblatt writes,

> evidently felt obliged to supplement his primary image of the wax in order to convey what that image conspicuously misses: the sense that memories often seem alive, fluttering, and elusive. The aviary metaphor . . . eschews any notion of systematicity, the sense . . . that memory is like a treasure-house or strongbox with distinct compartments where one can look for particular objects. In the aviary, one must grope after memories that seem anxiously determined to fly out of one's grasp.[45]

The ordered nesting-places in which the Capulet doves rest are upset by the very event that anchors the Nurse's memory: the earthquake. Greenblatt's suggestion that avian memories are less systematic than memories inscribed in wax applies here, but the remnants of method that he finds in the aviary also lose their methodic character. The earthquake not only disturbs the evocative rows of doves in their "pigeon-holes,"[46] but causes the Nurse to move away from the dovehouse: "Shake! quoth the dovehouse. 'Twas no need, I trow, / To bid me trudge." The Nurse recalls the upheaval that troubles the orderly pigeonholes, relishing the memory of the trembling dovehouse and (one suspects) the squawking and squabbling doves inside it, whose peaceful cooing contemplation is interrupted by the shaking of the earth.[47]

In its partial rejection of the masculine and scholarly habits of the art of memory, Romeo's memory theater is in some sense a return to his "mother tongue," to the distrusted garrulity of a plebeian, uneducated nursemaid who is also a voice for random reminiscence.[48] The place where the Nurse situates her recollection of Juliet's weaning is as significant as the apothecary's shop and for largely the same reasons: it is both an evocation of memory systems and a violation of their principles. Weaning by wormwood, like Friar Laurence's gathering of simples, mimics an apothecary's activities. But both the history of the apothecary's profession and the order in which the characters appear in *Romeo and Juliet* suggest that the formulation should be reversed: the apothecary, rather than being a model for the Nurse, is himself modeled on her domestic example. As Wendy Wall points out, in the sixteenth century the medical profession and the profession of apothecary were both relatively new phenomena. Most people still relied on "clergy, wise women, and most commonly the housewife" for medical advice and treatment. Wall quotes Juan Luis Vives's *The Instruction of a Christen Woman:*

> Because the business and charge within the house lyeth upon the woman's hand, I wolde she shuld knowe medycines and salves for suche diseases as bee common, and reigne almost daily: and have those medicines ever prepared redy in some closette wherewith she maie helpe hir housebande, hir littell children, and hir householde meny [servants], whan any nedeth, that shee nede not ofte to sende for the phisicion, or bye thynges of the potycaries.[49]

In Vives's formulation, physicians and apothecaries are to be called in only when home remedies fail. Housewives' remedies were not always pleasant. The kitchen was, in an age before refrigeration, also a surgery: "Health," Wall writes, "smacked of licensed bloodshed."[50] The Nurse's breast as the source of food is replaced by a medicine that apes the working of poison. She, like Friar Laurence, gives Juliet what is and is not a poison, hoping to free her at this early stage from dependence on another person through a minor loss, a mimicked death.

The apothecary has been present throughout *Romeo and Juliet* in his wares (wormwood, simples, cordial, poison) and in the persons of the Nurse and Friar Laurence. He is as much a part of a recognizably domestic sphere as he is an alien element. Romeo's performance of memory, however strange it may seem to him, leads him homeward, toward the strangely familiar, the *Heimlich*, toward Juliet, whose voice is excluded from the apothecary scene. In that scene Romeo approaches her but does not reach her, turned aside toward the "means" to reach her (a role that has been filled in the course of the play by Friar Laurence and by the Nurse, as well as by the poison he is now seeking) instead of toward their end. Rather than seeing Juliet's face, Romeo sees "old cakes of roses," faded emblems of female beauty scattered on a poor apothecary's shelves.

The sense of the play's past, implied and staged through the performance of memory, is never complete. It is restricted not only by the absence of the remembered object (always absent or it would not have to be
remembered) but also by the rememberer's limited experience. "There is
nothing in the intellect that was not first in the senses," as memory artists
often remarked.[51] Romeo cannot remember scenes that he did not witness,
cannot recognize structural connections between events that he does not
understand and over which he has no control. The irony in his defiance of
the stars (5.1.24) is lost on him, since he did not hear the Chorus predict
that the "star-cross'd lovers" (1.Pro.6) would follow the course of action that
he now undertakes as if it were his own idea. The sense of structure generated by performed remembering is always, often tragically, defined by the
rememberer's experience and perspective. Performed remembering can create new things, new connections, but it occasionally ignores (literally, does
not know) old ones.

III. Conclusion

In Shakespeare's memory theater remembered objects are not always visible,
nor are the mechanics of memory. This is true not only of the mechanics
of other people's memories but also of the mechanics of one's own. Romeo's
astonishment at the working of his memory ("O mischief thou art swift") is
a more sinister counterpart to the Nurse's satisfaction at the way her memory
works separately from herself ("Nay I do bear a brain"). Reminiscent of the
recipes for salves, pills, and "gargarismes" (solutions for gargling) that were
attached to treatises on the art of memory are the pharmacological objects
remembered by the characters in *Romeo and Juliet:* the Nurse's wormwood,
the friar's simples, the apothecary's potions. These objects represent a series
of attempts to change or to manipulate the body through medicinal means
that accompany and sometimes coincide with manipulations of the plot.
Though involved in the language of physical exchange, the recollections
of these objects come to emphasize the barriers as much as the continuity
between the embodied experience of individuals. The poison around which
Romeo's performance of memory develops is gone when Juliet tries to follow
Romeo; he has "[d]runk all" (5.3.163). Because Juliet's sleeping potion—
among the play's most significant medicinal interventions—is missing from
Romeo's experience, all the detail in his recollection of the apothecary's shop
cannot lead him to discover it.

The visual precision with which the objects in Shakespeare's memory
theater are recalled suggests a desire to manifest the inaccessible—the past,
the internal, the unstaged. The emphasis on the visual points to a separate
mode of representation which transcends and embraces the physical limits of
the early modern English stage. As Julie Stone Peters argues:

As the stage poet says in Gabriel Chappuis's *The Celestial Worlds* (1583), "the thing represented live" in the theatre is represented "exactly as it was done." Because of its connection to the worldly icon, theatre was seen (as it often still is) as a more immediate form of representation than the purely verbal arts of the page. . . . Identical with its correlate phenomenon in the world, the stage icon seemed not to require of the spectator the same efforts of translation required of the reader or mere listener.[52]

Like Erasmus of Rotterdam, who explains that Camillo's memory theater is so called "because it can be seen by the eyes of the body," Peters argues that the early modern theater was primarily a visual environment, marked by a direct appeal to the "spectator." This view is not universally accepted: Cynthia Marshall, for example, has objected strongly to "the reliance on specular response that guides much current dramatic criticism"; others emphasize the rhetorical aspect of playacting, which also requires an audience more aurally than visually attuned.[53] What we find in Shakespeare's memory theater is neither the one nor the other; instead, it is a crossing of these two means of apprehension, an aural landscape coded in a visual language. By appealing to the sense of sight and then refusing to satisfy it, the performance of memory produces an atmosphere of unfulfilled desire. Shakespeare's memory theater, while placing memory in a narrative context, also uses memory to break the frame of that narrative, to gesture toward what the play does not show: Romeo's past and, later and more tantalizingly, in plays that space does not allow me to discuss here, Shallow's, Falstaff's, Hamlet's, Antony's, Cleopatra's, Miranda's, Caliban's past, the space and time outside the boundaries of the "two hours' traffic of our stage" (1.Pro.12), even a sense of inwardness. By evoking an extradramatic past, the performance of memory in Shakespeare's plays intimates that the rememberer's existence is not limited to the immediate physical present of the stage, and thus that he or she is to some degree separable from the play.

But Shakespeare's memory theater has to do with more than the vexed question of character. Recent critics have demonstrated in a variety of ways how deeply Shakespeare's art is implicated in a past (personal, cultural, or material) outside the action of particular plays.[54] I am suggesting that Shakespeare's concern with the past is also dramaturgical. It is no accident that scenes of performed remembering in Shakespeare's plays are often associated with excess: the rhetorical trope of *dilatio,* a departure from the plot. From Seneca and his Elizabethan imitators, Shakespeare learned that a past evoked but unstaged can enrich and motivate present staged action. The excessive intrusion of the past in Shakespeare's memory theater lays the groundwork for the romances and the mature tragedies, particularly *Othello, Macbeth,* and

King Lear, all of which have to do with perturbed or mutilated recollection. Ultimately this dramaturgical strategy leads toward a theater that is a crossroads of the physical present and an absent, immaterial, but inescapable past.

NOTES

I would like to thank Lawrence Manley, Annabel Patterson, and the readers (anonymous and otherwise) at *Shakespeare Quarterly* for reading and rereading drafts of this essay. Earlier versions were presented at the 2002 annual conferences of the Shakespeare Association of America and the Group for Early Modern Cultural Studies.

1. Quotations from *Romeo and Juliet* here follow Brian Gibbons's edition for the Arden Shakespeare (London: Methuen, 1980).

2. This passage from an anonymous eighteenth-century critic presents the typical response to the apothecary scene: "Shakespeare . . . makes [Romeo] in the midst of his affliction for the death of his wife, and while the horrible design of killing himself was forming in his mind, give a ludicrous detail of the miserable furniture of a poor apothecary's shop; a description which, however beautiful, is here ill-timed and totally inconsistent with the condition and circumstance of the speaker" ("An Account of the Novel and Play of *Romeo and Juliet*" [1764], quoted here from *Shakespeare: The Critical Heritage,* Brian Vickers, ed., 6 vols. [London: Routledge and Kegan Paul, 1974–1981], 4:538–539). For defenses of the apothecary scene, see Samuel Taylor Coleridge, *Shakespearean Criticism,* ed. Thomas Middleton Raysor, 2 vols. (London: Dent; New York: Dutton [1961–1962]), 1:11; Harley Granville-Barker, *Prefaces to Shakespeare,* 5 vols. (London: Sidgwick and Jackson, Ltd., 1927–1947), 2:56; G. Wilson Knight, *Shakespeare's Dramatic Challenge: On the Rise of Shakespeare's Tragic Heroes* (London: Croom Helm, 1977), 42; Clifford Leech, "The Moral Tragedy of *Romeo and Juliet*" in *English Renaissance Drama: Essays in Honor of Madeleine Doran and Mark Eccles,* Standish Henning et al., eds. (Carbondale: Southern Illinois University Press, 1976), rpt. in *Critical Essays on Shakespeare's* Romeo and Juliet, Joseph A. Porter, ed. (New York: G. K. Hall, 1997), 7–22, esp. 14–15; and James H. Seward, *Tragic Vision in* Romeo and Juliet (Washington, DC: Consortium Press, 1973), 183. For a recent extended reading of the apothecary scene, including a summary of its negative reception, see Dominick Grace, "Romeo and the Apothecary," *Early Theatre: A Journal Associated with the Records of Early English Drama* 1 (1998): 27–38, esp. 29.

3. On the role of time in *Romeo and Juliet,* see E. Pearlman, "Shakespeare at Work: *Romeo and Juliet*," *English Literary Renaissance* 24 (1994): 315–342; Lloyd Davids, "'Death-Marked Love': Desire and Presence in *Romeo and Juliet*," *Shakespeare Survey* 49 (1996): 57–67; Thomas Pughe, "'What an Unkind Hour': Time in *Romeo and Juliet*," *Q/W/E/R/T/Y: Arts, Littératures & Civilisations du Monde Anglophone* 2 (1992): 5–15; David Lucking, "Uncomfortable Time in *Romeo and Juliet*," *English Studies* 82.2 (2001): 115–126; Jill L. Levenson, *Shakespeare in Performance:* Romeo and Juliet (Manchester: Manchester University Press, 1987), 16 and passim; and James Calderwood, *Shakespearean Metadrama: The Argument of the Play in* Titus Andronicus, Love's Labour's Lost, Romeo and Juliet, A Midsummer Night's Dream, *and* Richard II (Minneapolis: University of Minnesota Press, 1971), 85–119.

4. Tiffany Stern, *Rehearsal from Shakespeare to Sheridan* (Oxford: Clarendon Press, 2000), 13–14.

5. Stern, 64, 98.

6. See "On Memory and Recollection" in *Aristotle: On the Soul, Parva Naturalia, On Breath,* ed. and trans. W. S. Hett (Cambridge, MA: Harvard University Press, 1957), 288–313, esp. 311, 313. On Aristotle and memory, see David Farrell Krell, *Of Memory, Reminiscence, and Writing* (Bloomington: Indiana University Press, 1990), 13–50; and Janet Coleman, *Ancient and Medieval Memories* (Cambridge: Cambridge University Press, 1992), 15–38.

7. See, for example, Helkiah Crooke: "Finally, all these [Ideas or Notions] are receyued by the Memory, which as a faithful Recorder or Maister of the Rolles doth preserue, store vp and dispose *in due order* all the forenamed Notions or abstracted formes" (*Mikrokosmographia, or, A Description of the Whole Body of Man* [London, 1615], 502, emphasis added). See also Frances A. Yates, *The Art of Memory* (London: Routledge and Kegan Paul, 1966), 2, 306, and passim; Lina Bolzoni, *The Gallery of Memory: Literary and Iconographic Models in the Age of the Printing Press,* trans. Jeremy Parzen (Toronto: University of Toronto Press, 2001), xxii, 155; Mary J. Carruthers, *The Book of Memory: A Study of Memory in Medieval Culture* (Cambridge: Cambridge University Press, 1990); Douwe Draaisma, *Metaphors of Memory: A History of Ideas About the Mind,* trans. Paul Vincent (Cambridge: Cambridge University Press, 2000); and Paolo Rossi, *Logic and the Art of Memory: The Quest for a Universal Language,* trans. Stephen Clucas (London: Athlone Press, 2000). For discussions of theater and the visual imagery of the art of memory, see William E. Engel, "Mnemonic Criticism and Renaissance Literature: A Manifesto," *Connotations: A Journal for Critical Debate* 1 (1991): 12–33; Engel, *Mapping Mortality: The Persistence of Memory and Melancholy in Early Modern England* (Amherst: University of Massachusetts Press, 1995); and Engel, *Death and Drama in Renaissance England: Shades of Memory* (Oxford: Oxford University Press, 2002).

8. John Sutton, "Body, Mind, and Order: Local Memory and the Control of Mental Representations in Medieval and Renaissance Sciences of Self" in *1543 and All That: Image and Word, Change and Continuity in the Proto-Scientific Revolution,* Guy Freeland and Anthony Corones, eds. (Dordrecht and Boston: Kluwer Academic Publishers, 2000), 117–150, esp. 117–121, 123, 127–128, 142n.

9. See Katharine Park, "The Organic Soul" in *The Cambridge History of Renaissance Philosophy,* Charles B. Schmitt et al., eds. (Cambridge: Cambridge University Press, 1988), 464–484; G. W. Bruyn, "The Seat of the Soul" in *Historical Aspects of the Neurosciences,* F. Clifford Rose and W. F. Bynum, eds. (New York: Raven Press, 1982), 55–81; and Walter Pagel, "Medieval and Renaissance Contributions to Knowledge of the Brain and Its Functions" in *History and Philosophy of Knowledge of the Brain and its Functions,* F.N.L. Poynter, ed. (Oxford: Blackwell Scientific Publications, 1958), 95–114.

10. Sutton, "Body, Mind, and Order," 121–130, esp. 129. See also Sutton, *Philosophy and Memory Traces: Descartes to Connectionism* (Cambridge: Cambridge University Press, 1998).

11. "To sleepe hosed and shued especially with foule sockes, doth hinder the Memorie, because of the reflection of ye vapours: feebleth the sight, and causeth the bodie to waxe hot and burne" (William Fulwood, *The Castel of Memorie* [London, 1573], sig. D2^v). Fulwood's treatise, first printed in 1562, is a translation

of Guglielmo Gratarolo's *De Memoria Reparanda, Avgenda, Servandaqve Liber vnus. De Locali vel Artificiosa Memoria Liber alter* (Rome, 1555).

12. I borrow the phrase "localist model" from Sutton; see "Body, Mind, and Order," passim.

13. Johannes Romberch, *Congestoriu[m] Artificiose Memorie* (Venice, 1520), sig. B7ʳ.

14. See Peter of Ravenna, *Foenix D[omi]ni Petri Rauenatis Memoriae Magistris* (Venice, 1491), sig. B3ʳ⁻ᵛ.

15. John Willis, *Mnemonica; or, the Art of Memory, Drained out of the pure Fountains of Art & Nature . . .* (London, 1661 [first published in Latin in 1618]), sigs. E2ᵛ–E3ʳ, E4ᵛ. Bolzoni draws an analogy between acting and the construction of memory images (173). See also Engel, *Death and Drama,* 52–53.

16. See Yates, 342–367. Yates reproduces both Willis's and Fludd's diagrams in her chapter on Fludd.

17. Bolzoni, 241.

18. Erasmus of Rotterdam, *Opus epistolarum,* ed. P. S. Allen (Oxford: Oxford University Press, 1941), 10:29–30, quoted here from Bolzoni, 159 (emphasis added).

19. Letter from Viglius Zuichemus to Erasmus, quoted here from Bolzoni, 159.

20. See Engel, *Death and Drama;* Nigel Alexander, "Hamlet and the Art of Memory," *Notes & Queries* 213 (1968): 137–139; Bernard Richards, "Hamlet and the Theatre of Memory," *N&Q* 233 (1981): 53; Adam Max Cohen, "Hamlet as Emblem: The *Ars Memoria* and the Culture of the Play," *Journal of Early Modern Cultural Studies* 3.1 (2003): 77–112.

21. See Bolzoni, 173.

22. Levenson, 14–15.

23. Sutton, "Body, Mind, and Order," 125.

24. On the lack of dramatis personae and other markers in early modern playtexts and performances, see, Margreta de Grazia and Peter Stallybrass, "The Materiality of the Shakespearean Text," *Shakespeare Quarterly* 44 (1993): 255–283, esp. 267.

25. Stern, 46–123, esp. 52–79; and Levenson, 14.

26. See Engel, *Death and Drama,* 37–45.

27. Quotations from *The Second Part of King Henry IV* follow A. R. Humphreys's edition for the Arden Shakespeare (London: Methuen, 1966).

28. Fulwood explains that "[t]he right way to haue artifical Memorie, is the collocation & diligent obseruation of thinges" (sig. F8ʳ). Willis emphasizes the importance of "noting": "Natural Memory is a faculty which every man hath naturally to apprehend and retain note-worthy things" (sig. K4ʳ); Willis also advises students that, among other disciplines (such as eating raisins for breakfast), "[t]he mind must be constantly exercised in learning some sentences by heart (yea though there be no need) that the faculty of remembring may be quickned by use and practice" (sig. L4ʳ).

29. On Juliet's and Lady Capulet's attempts to interrupt the Nurse, see Stern, 89–90.

30. Fulwood, sig. G4ʳ. This principle, drawn from classical Latin sources (Cicero, Quintilian, the anonymous *Ad Herennium*), recurs in most treatises on the memory arts. See Engel, *Death and Drama,* 53; and Yates, 10.

31. Jill Levenson points out that Bandello's novel does not contain an apothecary at all; the role is added in later versions of the story to explain Romeo's acquisition of poison ("*Romeo and Juliet* Before Shakespeare," *Studies in Philology* 81 [1984]: 325–347, esp. 340–341). Arthur Brooke's *Romeus and Juliet* includes the apothecary and much of the language from the scene but excludes the role of memory. Romeus's search for an apothecary's shop takes place in real time and space rather than in his memory; see Arthur Brooke, *Brooke's 'Romeus and Juliet', being the original of Shakespeare's 'Romeo and Juliet'*, ed. J. J. Munro (New York: Duffield and Co.; London: Chatto and Windus, 1908), ll. 2563–2567. See also Grace, 28.

32. Romberch, sig. D4ʳ. Yates points out that both Romberch and Giordano Bruno suggest shops as memory *loci* (112f [Pl. 5a], 250–251).

33. See Romberch, sigs. D6ʳ, F6ᵛ–F7ʳ; and the anonymous *Ludus artificialis obliuionis* (Leipzig, 1510), sig. B1ʳ.

34. Carruthers, 45.

35. Hugh of St. Victor, "De arca Noe morali," quoted here from Carruthers, 45.

36. Joseph Roach, *Cities of the Dead: Circum-Atlantic Performance* (New York: Columbia University Press, 1996), 3–4, 29–30; the term derives from Margaret Thomson Drewal's discussion of parody in *Yoruba Ritual: Performers, Play, Agency* (Bloomington: Indiana University Press, 1992), 4–5. See also Roach, "Reconstructing Theatre/History," *Theatre Topics* 9 (1999): 3–10. My thanks to Emily Hodgson Anderson for this reference.

37. According to Willis, "*particularly as to* Places, *their usefulness doth hence appear, that if a Traveller observe any remarkable thing in a cross way, or some noted place of his journey, returning the same way, he doth not onely remember the place, but calleth to mind what soever he had seen here, though at present removed. The same thing often happeneth in* Repetition *of* Idea's; *for the mind as it were walking through the same* Places . . . *is much assisted in recalling* Idea's *to mind there placed*" (sigs. A3ᵛ–A4ʳ).

38. See Grace, 30, 31, 33, 35.

39. Grace also notes this parallel: "Now, when Romeo describes the apothecary, he recalls he first saw the man 'Culling of simples'—that is, gathering herbs, just as Friar Laurence was doing when first we saw him" (35).

40. The stage direction that places Romeo's entrance immediately preceding line 19 comes from Q2 and is reprinted in the Folio.

41. His odd word choice—the "cannon's womb"—may also echo Friar Laurence's earthy womb-tomb at 2.3.5–6, although Romeo is not present to hear that part of the speech.

42. T.J.B. Spencer, ed., The Penguin Shakespeare *Romeo and Juliet* (London: Penguin Books, 1967), 31–32. See also Grace, 28.

43. In Brooke's *Romeus and Juliet*, Romeo is present when the Nurse recalls Juliet's childhood (ll. 651–662).

44. See Carruthers, 35–36; and Stephen Greenblatt, *Hamlet in Purgatory* (Princeton, NJ: Princeton University Press, 2001), 214–218.

45. Greenblatt, 214–215.

46. The earliest use of the word *pigeonhole* in English in its modern sense is in the eighteenth century, but the concept is present from antiquity onward. See Carruthers, 36.

47. The association of the *cella columbarum* with other memory *cellae* may or may not be the reason that so many memory theorists recommend that their readers

eat turtledove. Fulwood, for example, departs from his source to mention the fact that "[i]t is also sayde, that the flesh of a Turtle Doue doth encrease the wit" (sig. D5ʳ).

48. See Wendy Wall, *Staging Domesticity: Household Work and English Identity in Early Modern Drama* (Cambridge and New York: Cambridge University Press, 2002), 74.

49. Juan Luis Vives, *A Fruteful and pleasant boke called the Instruction of Christen Woman* (London, 1529), 108, quoted here from Wall, 164.

50. Wall, 195.

51. *Ludus artificialis obliuionis* is one of the many treatises to repeat the phrase "Et nihil est in intellectu nisi prius fuerit in sensu" (sig. C6ᵛ). Park identifies this as a "commonplace" (470).

52. Julie Stone Peters, *Theatre of the Book 1480–1880: Print, Text, and Performance in Europe* (Oxford: Oxford University Press, 2000), 171–172.

53. Cynthia Marshall, "Man of Steel Done Got the Blues: Melancholic Subversion of Presence in *Antony and Cleopatra*," *SQ* 44 (1993): 385–408, esp. 397; see also Hélène Cixous, "Aller à la Mer," trans. Barbara Kerslake, *Modern Drama* 27 (1984): 546–548, esp. 547 (cited in Marshall, 397). On theater and rhetoric, see Joseph Roach, *The Player's Passion: Studies in the Science of Acting* (Newark: University of Delaware Press, 1985), 32; Leo Salingar, "Uses of Rhetoric: *Antony and Cleopatra*," *Cahiers Élisabéthains* 55 (1999): 17–26, esp. 18–19. On the use of the terms *audience* and *spectators* in early modern English theater, see Andrew Gurr, *Playgoing in Shakespeare's London* (Cambridge: Cambridge University Press, 1987), 86–98.

54. See, for example, Greenblatt, passim; Michael Neill, *Issues of Death: Mortality and Identity in English Renaissance Tragedy* (Oxford: Clarendon Press; New York: Oxford University Press, 1997); Ann Rosalind Jones and Peter Stallybrass, *Renaissance Clothing and the Materials of Memory* (Cambridge and New York: Cambridge University Press, 2000); and Katharine Eisaman Maus, *Inwardness and Theater in the English Renaissance* (Chicago and London: University of Chicago Press, 1995).

THOMAS HONEGGER

"Wouldst thou withdraw love's faithful vow?": The Negotiation of Love in the Orchard Scene (Romeo and Juliet *Act II*)

1. Introduction

Shakespeare's dramatic dialogues have, for obvious reasons, been repeat-edly the subject of historical pragmatic studies.[1] *Romeo and Juliet*, however, may not strike one as the most obvious choice for historical dialogue analysis. Most critics have stressed the lyrical-poetic quality of its dialogues rather than their interactional finesse. Yet the one does not necessarily exclude the other, as I have shown (Honegger 2005) by means of a discussion of the sonnet-sequence that constitutes the very first verbal exchange between Romeo and Juliet (Oxford 1.4.206–223; Arden 1.5.92–109).[2] The main focus of this article, then, is on the complexities involved in the negotiation of love in the ensuing orchard scene in the second act. These are compared with the corresponding passages in Shakespeare's most immediate source, Arthur Brooke's *The Tragicall Historye of Romeus and Juliet* (1562),[3] contrasted with the conventions of traditional (courtly) wooing and set against the meta-comments on courtly interaction as found in Count Baldassare Castiglione's *The Book of the Courtier* (1528, English translation 1561).

2. Preliminaries

Romeo and Juliet, who meet for the first time at the feast of the Capulet family, fall in love with each other at first sight. Their first exchange of words (Oxford 1.4.206–219; Arden 1.5.92–105) adapts the form of a joint

Journal of Historical Pragmatics, Volume 7, Number 1 (2006): pp. 73–88. Copyright © 2006 John Benjamin Publishing Company.

sonnet and the two approach both a dramatic and poetic climax with the imminent completion of the sonnet. The final couplet, with its verbal parallelisms (move, prayer) and the fact that the two adjacent lines spoken by the protagonists share the same rhyme, immediately precedes and foreshadows the harmonious physical union by means of a kiss.

Romeo's lonely Petrarchism, as evidenced before in his lines about love in general and Rosaline in particular (Oxford 1.1.167ff; Arden 1.1.169ff), and also in his verses upon perceiving Juliet for the first time (Oxford 1.4.157–166; Arden 1.5.43–52), is modified and shared by Juliet in their joint sonnet. Shakespeare, by showing Juliet as taking up Romeo's metaphors of pilgrimage, has her observe one of Baldassare Castiglione's recommendations for elegant courtly conversation, namely, "so the metaphors be well applyed, and especiallye yf they be answered, and he that maketh answere continue in the self same metaphor spoken by the other" (Cox 1994: 173). Moreover, the two lovers-to-be follow Castiglione's advice of exploring each other's feelings

> with such sobermoode, and so warilye, that the woordes maye firste attempt the minde, and so doubtfullye touch her entent and will, that they maye leave her a way and a certein issue to feine the understandinge that those woordes conteine love: to the entent if he finds anye daunger, he maye draw backe and make wise to have spoken or written it to an other ende (Cox 1994: 276).

Lastly, Juliet's participation in the composition of the sonnet foreshadows her active role in the developing relationship with Romeo, which in turn may be seen as mirroring the historical changing attitude towards woman who was "no longer merely a necessary vessel for procreation but an active sexual partner" (Neely 1985: 13). As will become clear, Juliet's interactional patterns are going to be different from those of a typical Petrarchan heroine and she is the very opposite of a Petrarchan heroine in that she falls immediately in love with Romeo.

For Romeo, Petrarchan language, formerly the expression of his amorous frustration and isolation, has become the very instrument to conquer and win over the beloved lady.[4] The sonnet, as a lyrical work of art, should end with the kiss. Yet the world of Verona is not all Petrarchan conceits, nor is the play a string of sonnets. Romeo's "post-oscular" line acknowledges the fact that it is one thing to sonnetise about kissing, but another actually to do it. The imaginary curve that indicates the face-threatening potential peaks with the kiss, which constitutes a possible point of interactional transition. The dangers inherent in a kiss, even if it is prefaced by and embedded in Petrarchan language and regulated by social etiquette, are not to be underestimated. Already medieval theorists on love warned: "Li baisiers autre chose atrait."[5] And neo-platonic theory of love is also ambiguous about kissing. Castiglione's Peter Bembo voices the following warning: "For sins a kisse is a knitting together both of body and soule, it is to be feared, least the sensuall lover will be more inclined to the part of the bodye, then of the soule" (Cox 1994: 354).[6]

Romeo and Juliet could be expected to abandon their pretensions towards witticisms after the first kiss and resume their conversation on a different, more intimate level. This is not the case. We must not forget that the metaphoric language of the sonnet has been playful and ambiguous, and a man would be naïve to think himself the object of love when a lady is so courteous as to allow him to kiss her. In such a context, the (non-verbal or verbal) reaction immediately after the kiss is of crucial importance.[7] Romeo forestalls misleading interpretations of his action by framing it with the comment "Thus from my lips, by thine, my sin is purged" (Oxford 1.4.220; Arden 1.5.106), continuing this way their conversation on the same metaphorical level. This is, interactionally speaking, rather a step backwards—even if it is "reculer pour mieux sauter". Juliet seems to enjoy Romeo's playful advances and, taking the cue from him, prompts him to kiss her once more with her "Then have my lips the sin that they have took" (Oxford 1.4.221; Arden 1.5.107). It is only now, after the second kiss, that she seems to signal a readiness to abandon the pilgrim-and-saint metaphor, although she still retains a facetious tone in her "You kiss by th'book" (Oxford 1.4.223; Arden 1.5.109),[8] which completes the first quatrain of a second sonnet. Yet the witty tone cannot hide the fact that the second kiss poses something of an interactional problem. The first kiss can be accounted for within the framework of Renaissance greeting habits. The second kiss, then, is "superfluous" and legitimised only by means of the two protagonist's word-play. Unfortunately we are in a play and not in a Sidneyan sonnet sequence and the lovers' second sonnet composition is interrupted by the nurse. Juliet is whisked away to see her mother, so that the audience is expertly guided back into the more prosaic world of drama where marriage is still largely dependent on parental consent. Romeo and Juliet, before the close of what modern editions have called Act I, are to discover their respective identities, and what started with a kiss as tender dalliance turns for both into something far more serious and threatening than expected.

3. A Declaration of Love?

Anything that comes after the sonnet sequence between the two lovers-to-be at the end of the first act must look like an anticlimax. The following orchard scene, which replaces and condenses Arthur Brooke's description of Romeus's long-drawn suffering into one scene, may add to the organisation and development of the plot, yet it is, if one expects a "traditional" wooing sequence with reluctant and aloof lady and patiently suffering lover, oddly disappointing. Yet the scene's "deficiencies" are, as will be shown, more than compensated for by Shakespeare's introduction of new interactional complexities and by making Juliet a much more active protagonist than her predecessor in Arthur Brooke's *Romeus and Juliet*.

The first encounter between Romeo and Juliet and the orchard scene are separated by a sonnet spoken by the Chorus, which calls in a new era of mutual love, and the scene with Mercutio and Benvolio, that marks the return to less highly strung levels of language and interaction, providing a relaxation from the "high style" of the sonnet dialogue. Romeo's entrance, too, continues rather his former Petrarchan "luf-talkyng"[9] than the inspired language of the sonnet dialogue. Wells (1998: 915) describes him as follows: "Wandering about in Capulet's orchard trying to catch a glimpse of his new beloved, he runs through some of the standard lines in the Petrarchist's repertoire, much as a musician might warm up with some arpeggios before an important performance." Indeed, the spontaneous yet poetic language of the first encounter gives way to the former monologic exploration of Petrarchan imagery—at least as long as Romeo is not talking directly to Juliet. It is she who gets down to the reality of love and the problems that such a liaison creates, whereas Romeo is still busy searching for new oxymorons and metaphors. Her Saussurean analysis ("avant la letter," though) of the relationship between signifier and signified (Oxford 2.1.81–92; Arden 2.1.38–48) ends with her impassioned plea: "Romeo, doff thy name, / And for thy name, which is no part of thee, / Take all myself" (Oxford 2.1.90–92; Arden 2.1.47–49).[10] Romeo has overheard the entire speech hidden in the darkness of the garden, which stands in contrast to Arthur Brooke's version of the story, which features a longish monologue by Juliet (Bullough 1957: 296–297) in the seclusion of her bedroom. Romeo's eavesdropping seems to be a Shakespearean innovation. Shakespeare's Romeo, then, takes Juliet's lines as his cue, self-selects himself for the next turn[11] and steps forward, addressing Juliet with "I take thee at thy word. / Call me but love, and I'll be new baptized: / Henceforth I never will be Romeo" (Oxford 2.1.92–94; Arden 2.1.49–51). These are not bad lines, since they refer to Juliet's argument about the arbitrariness of names and signal that the speaker has overheard her speech. Unfortunately, they are lost on Juliet, who is simply too surprised to attend properly to the utterance. As a consequence, Romeo's elegant self-identification fails, too. Yet young Montague perseveres in his endeavour, and now that he has Juliet's full attention, he succeeds with his second attempt (Oxford 2.1.96–100; Arden 2.1.53–57). Again, he alludes to her preceding speech and addresses her as "dear saint" (Oxford 2.1.98; Arden 2.1.55). This form of address connects the shadowy figure in the garden with the young man at the ball and functions as the shibboleth for the two protagonists.

Yet Juliet, although clearly positively affected by Romeo's sudden entry, is in no mood to continue in the playful spirit of their last encounter. Her "Art thou not Romeo, and a Montague?" (Oxford 2.1.103; Arden 2.1.60), which Romeo tries to counter lamely with his "Neither, fair maid, if either thee dislike" (Oxford 2.1.104; Arden 2.1.61), touches upon the sore spot of his family affiliation and all it implies. The following turns (Oxford 2.1.105–127; Arden 2.1.62–84) show the two talking, at least stylistically, at cross purposes. Juliet's brief utterances, often no longer than one line, focus on concrete questions ("By whose direction found'st thou out this place?" Oxford 2.1.122; Arden 2.1.79) and dangers ("If they do see thee, they will murder thee" Oxford 2.1.113; Arden 2.1.70), whereas Romeo's answers keep up the high poetic style of his former speeches. It is only after some time that Juliet seems to have found her inner balance again. She, in contrast to her predecessor in Brooke, does not have the chance to sort things out soliloquisingly in the privacy of her bedroom before meeting again with her beloved. Romeo has committed a grave interactional sin by overhearing, albeit accidentally, what was never intended for anyone else's ears. He may be forgiven for his trespass, but he should never have gone on record with information gathered from her speech. Firstly, it is a question of tact and the discovery of Juliet's feelings severely impinges upon her interactional freedom. Secondly, a lady has to be careful not to give away her feelings before she can be certain of a man's sincerity—as Brooke's Juliet makes explicit:

(1) *Juliet*   What if his suttel brayne to fayne have taught his tong,

And so the snake that lurkes in grasse thy tender hart hash stong?

What if with frendly speache the traytor lye in wayte,

As oft the poysond hooke is hid, wraps in the pleasant bayte?

(Bullough 1957: 296, ll. 385–388)

A woman evidently has to be wary and test the sincerity of her suitor,[12] although Shakespeare's Juliet seems to be less concerned with this aspect and more troubled by the restriction of her interactional possibilities. The fact that Romeo has witnessed Juliet's soliloquy makes it impossible for her to play the traditional role of the "reluctant" or even "cruel" lady. As a consequence, the interactional equilibrium between suitor and lady has been severely disturbed. Arthur Brooke's couple can make do with the traditional role distribution of active suitor and conceding lady, but Shakespeare's complication of the plot calls for a less conventional solution. It is therefore no deliberate decision by Juliet to "refuse [. . .] to engage further in these elaborate, ritualized negotiations and exchanges of erotic power that constitute courtship" as Callaghan (1994: 81) argues. Romeo's open references to her lines has rendered their content on-record, i.e. Juliet knows that Romeo knows and that he wants her to know that he knows, so that Juliet no longer has the option of simply ignoring her self-exposure and relying on his tact. As it is, she cannot, and probably does not want to unsay her confession of love. Yet she is likewise reluctant to continue their conversation or to accept Romeo's protestations of love before having clarified some points. Her long address is of great import for the further development of their relationship:

(2) *Juliet* Thou knowest the mask of night is on my face,

Else would a maiden blush bepaint my cheek

For that which thou hast heard me speak tonight.   130

Fain would I dwell on form, fain, fain deny

What I have spoke; but farewell, compliment.

Dost thou love me? I know thou wilt say 'Ay',

And I will take thy word; yet if thou swear'st,

Thou mayst prove false. At lovers' perjuries   135

They say Jove laughs. O gentle, Romeo,

If thou dost love, pronounce it faithfully;

Or if thou thinkest I am too quickly won,

I'll frown and be perverse and say thee nay,

So thou wilt woo, but else not for the world.[13]   140

In truth, fair Montague, I am too fond,

And therefore thou mayst think my behaviour light;

But trust me, gentleman, I'll prove more true

Than those that have the coying to be strange.

I should have been more strange, I must confess,   145

But that thou overheard'st, ere I was ware,

My true-love passion. Therefore pardon me,

And not impute this yielding to light love,

Which the dark night hash so discovered.

(Oxford 2.1.128–149; Arden 2.1.85–106)

Juliet renders explicit the physical symptoms of her embarrassment in the first lines of her speech. These references function as "in-built" stage props ("night, Juliet blushes") for effects that would not be easy to bring about spontaneously. Furthermore, Juliet's lines convey to Romeo that she is a maiden who has lost considerable face due to his eavesdropping, and that the content of her soliloquy, and especially her confession of love, is now a mutually acknowledged on-record topic (Romeo now knows that she knows that he knows). The central problem of love, however, is touched upon only after she has given this metacomment on their interactional mishap which prevents her from making her confession of love in style. In the following, she pays Romeo back in kind. He is forced to listen to another "soliloquy", yet this time *his* declaration of love is taken for granted, analysed, and discussed. Whatever Romeo's interactional shortcomings, he would certainly not have cast his confession in the form of the monosyllabic, pitifully un-Petrarchan "Ay", but would certainly "fain have dwelt on form".[14] Juliet signals that they have gone beyond matters of form. It is clear to her that Romeo wants her to believe that he loves her in return. Yet although she wants to believe it, and tells him that she does so, she is aware of the danger inherent in accepting his protestation of love without further proof. Unfortunately, the traditional formats and scripts for initiating a love relationship have been rendered useless by Romeo's eavesdropping, so that she cannot "test" him by playing hard to get. Juliet alludes to this in her offer to act the part of the reluctant lady if he wishes her to do so. She knows that very often "the form is the message" and if Romeo needs more "traditional" proof of her constancy and chaste virtue—and maybe an occasion to produce some verses "To His Coy Mistress"—then he is welcome to it. Besides this, she signals that she, for her part, would prefer to do without the conventional trappings of wooing. This may be also the meaning of her request that Romeo "pronounce it [i.e. his love] faithfully" (Oxford 2.1.137; Arden 2.1.94). In brief, her speech can be interpreted as a plea to abandon the traditional interactional patterns and to talk, if not exactly business, then at least more plainly than Petrarchan lovers in general, and Romeo in particular, are wont to do.[15]

The following exchange, then, is dominated by Juliet's endeavour to reestablish her interactional sovereignty and motivate Romeo to abandon his Petrarchan effusions. Consequently, she cuts short his attempts to bring about his protestation of sincere love in style by playing on her "light" (Oxford 2.1.148; Arden 2.1.105) and "dark" (Oxford 2.1.149; Arden 2.1.106). Her critical gloss on his choice of metaphor catches him completely unawares. As yet he has had dealings only with Rosaline, who kept both her silence and her distance, and his one encounter with Juliet at the feast has been harmoniously collaborative, with her following his metaphoric lead. Juliet's unexpected interruption stops him dead in his Petrarchan tracks and he asks: "What shall I swear by?" (Oxford 2.1.155; Arden 2.1.112).[16] His second, presumably also Petrarchan attempt to swear his love does not get beyond the first five words before Juliet intervenes again, calls the entire interaction into question, and makes a move to terminate their late-night conversation:

(3) *Juliet* I have no joy of this contract tonight:

It is too rash, too unadvised, too sudden,

Too like the lightning which doth cease to be

Ere one can say 'It lightens'. Sweet, good night.

This bud of love, by summer's ripening breath,

May prove a beauteous flower when next we meet.[17]   165

Good night, good night. [. . .]

(Oxford 2.1.160–166; Arden 2.1.117–123).

This, then, is sufficient to put a stop to Romeo's poetic outpourings, even though Juliet is considerate enough to sweeten the pill of (temporary) rejection.[18] His incredulous question "O wilt thou leave me so unsatisfied?" (Oxford 2.1.168; Arden 2.1.125) marks his sudden fall from Petrarchan heights and prompts Juliet to ask for disambiguation: "What satisfaction canst thou have tonight?" (Oxford 2.1.169; Arden 2.1.126). Romeo's answer, then, finally hits the right tone. His "Th'exchange of thy love's faithful vow for mine" (Oxford 2.1.170; Arden 2.1.127) is simple, unpretentious, and has the ring of truthfulness. Furthermore, it establishes the spirit of mutuality that has been absent from their interaction in the orchard so far. Romeo's "Wouldst thou withdraw it [i.e. love's faithful vow]? For what purpose, love?"[19] (Oxford 2.1.173; Arden 2.1.130) brings about the final restitution of Juliet's interactional freedom that has been so severely infringed by his unnoticed presence in the garden. She is given the opportunity to take back her words without denying them, to return to the moment before she uttered the fateful lines and to retake her decision. It is this imaginary construct that enables Juliet to overcome the interactional impasse which has been the direct consequence of the informational imbalance created by Romeo's eavesdropping. So far, Juliet has not been able to act freely or to negotiate the terms of the interaction that has been sprung on her. The first part has been dominated by her effort to win back her interactional rights. Now that she has succeeded in doing so, she is finally able to give vent to her feelings as she wants and to dwell on form:

(4) *Juliet* My bounty is as boundless as the sea,

My love as deep; the more I give to thee,

The more I have, for both are infinite.

(Oxford 2.1.176–178; Arden 2.1.133–135)

She not only reverts to Petrarchan language,[20] but also takes up Romeo's sea image from before (Oxford 2.1.125–126; Arden 2.1.82–83) and thus signals her willingness to enter into a love-relationship with Romeo.

The harmony between the lovers is hardly re-established when the beginnings of a potential joint action are disrupted by the outside world in form of the nurse, whose interference will punctuate the remaining exchanges. When Juliet again addresses Romeo,[21] she seems to have taken the cue for her next turn from the intrusion of the outside world:

(5) *Juliet* Three words, dear Romeo, and good night indeed.   185

　　　　If that thy bent of love be honourable,

　　　　Thy purpose marriage, send me word tomorrow,

　　　　By one that I'll procure to come to thee,

　　　　Where and what time thou wilt perform the rite,

　　　　And all my fortunes at thy foot I'll lay,   190

　　　　And follow thee, my lord, throughout the world.

　Nurse (within) Madam!

　Juliet I come, anon!—But if thou meanest not well;

　　　　I do beseech thee—

　Nurse (within) Madam!   195

　Juliet By and by, I come!—

　　　　To cease thy strive and leave me to my grief.

　　　　Tomorrow I will send.

(Oxford 2.1.185–198; Arden 2.1.142–153)

Petrarchan "luf-talkyng" has rather quickly given way to no-nonsense marriage talk or, as Whittier (1989: 37) formulates it more elegantly: "She [Juliet] readily harnesses Eros in social form." We are obviously no longer in the world of chivalry where the suitor has to prove his worth and the sincerity of his love by means of long-drawn service or suitable chivalric exploits. In Shakespeare's Verona—and also in his London—it is the suitor's willingness to commit himself in marriage to his beloved that proves his honourable intentions. This is not so conspicuous in *Romeo and Juliet* because the main focus is on the first encounter and the climactic falling in love of the two protagonists, but it is nevertheless there. Juliet's linking of "honourable love" and "marriage" is, of course, a rather obvious hint at what Romeo should have done, namely to declare his love *and* to propose. Yet Romeo is too preoccupied with love to proceed immediately to the "business" part.

The text analysed in the preceding paragraphs differs considerably from the First to the Second Quartos and so does, as a result, the interpretation of the exchange. Many lines of the passage discussed above, namely lines 164 to 178, do not occur in the text of the First Quarto; Juliet's wish for a pause for thought is immediately followed by the first interruption of their night-time conversation and her offer of marriage (see Praetorius 1886: 26–27). The latter is not introduced by the preceding exchange and, as a consequence, comes rather as a surprise. The text of the Second Quarto, with its mitigating passage that re-establishes some understanding between the lovers, is therefore, from an interactional point of view, preferable.

The third and final part of the interaction between Romeo and Juliet (Oxford 2.1.204–235; Arden 2.1.158–193) is much more harmonious than the preceding ones. The important questions concerning their relationship have been discussed and agreed on, and the interactional imbalance created by Romeo's *faux pas* has been corrected. The shared metaphors derived from the world of falconry are, on a stylistic level, an expression of this re-established harmony, and after agreeing on the time for the messenger, there remains nothing much to do. Yet the two lovers are loath to part and fill in time with lines on remembering and forgetting (Oxford 2.1.216–221; Arden 2.1.170–175). This brief passage has neither dramatic interest nor poetic metaphors to recommend itself and is mostly phatic in function. It provides, in its simplicity and even-handed distribution of turns, an appropriate penultimate chord to the interactional piece that began with the first encounter at the feast. The final chord comprises Juliet's resumption of the falcon metaphor (Oxford 2.1.223–227; Arden 2.1.177–181) and ends in the couplets spoken by the lovers (Juliet: Oxford 2.1.230–231; Arden 2.1.184–185; Romeo: Oxford 2.1.232–235; Arden 2.1.186–193).[22] The "dissonance" that characterised the first part of their encounter in the orchard is counterbalanced, the two lovers part in concord, and the initial phase of their relationship comes to a conclusion.

4. Conclusion: Shakespeare at Work

We have already pointed out some of the most important differences between Shakespeare's presentation of the lovers and the one in his probable source, Brooke's *Romeus and Juliet*. There are, apart from the alterations due to the transfer from novella to drama, namely the dialogisation of all relevant information and the condensation of narrative time, two momentous changes which are not (primarily) motivated by the exigencies of adapting a narrative for stage performance. Firstly, the initial encounter between the two at the feast is cast in the form of a jointly composed sonnet. Secondly, Romeus's conventional declaration of love and his offer of marriage during the balcony scene in Arthur Brooke's text are replaced by a complex passage that comprises not only a reversal of roles but also considerable interactional complications. Shakespeare, in terms of plot organisation and dramatic structure, shifts the focus from the confession of love to the first encounter and the falling in love. The interactional climax of the first phase in their relationship is thus not identical with the actual declaration of love, but, in the framework advocated in Castiglione's *The Book of the Courtier*, would coincide with the first tentative explorations undertaken by the socially competent courtier, which then may be followed by a more direct confession of love. The first encounter and the falling in love would be, in a less condensed account, more clearly separated from the actual declaration of love by intervening events, which would allow for two independent focal points. Shakespeare's dramatic compression of the interaction between the two lovers does not favour such a solution. He packs most of the declaration's poetic and dramatic potential into the joint sonnet so that it has the impact one usually expects from the confession of love proper. Nicholas Brooke's (1968: 98) confusion of the lovers' first meeting at the feast with the ensuing betrothal in act 2 (orchard scene) and his evaluation of "betrothal" and wedding proves this point: "The betrothal [i.e. the sonnet-encounter at the feast or, as Brooke (1968: 106) also calls it, 'the dance-betrothal of Act I'] was given maximum ceremonial as the climax to Act I; the wedding is reduced to an absolute minimum in the end of Act II." It is also noteworthy that Shakespeare has not conflated the sequence of falling in love with an immediate confession, but kept them somewhat apart. This separation allows him to exploit the strengths of both sequences. The emotional impact of the first meeting is not adulterated or watered down by the admixture of elements that would detract from the elated Petrarchan mood. The two young people have as yet no idea of their respective identities so that the inception of their love is not hindered by social considerations. The discussion of such disquieting and potentially disruptive issues as family membership and the problem of how to cast their love in concrete social forms are relegated to the ensuing orchard scene. By means of the joint sonnet, Shakespeare has come as close as possible to what Barthes (1977/1990: 150) "hallucinates" about: "I hallucinate what is empirically impossible: that our two profferings [i.e. confessions of love] be made at the same time: that one does not follow the other, as if it depended on it."

Shakespeare, because he has played his strongest "emotional card" in the fashioning of the first encounter, must have felt that a conventional confession of love would offer little dramatic interest. Furthermore, from the point of view of narrative organisation it would add nothing new towards the development of either characters or plot. His decision to deviate from the traditional pattern creates new dramatic interest and opens new possibilities for protagonist characterisation and plot development. As a consequence, Juliet increasingly gains a voice of her own. Romeo's lyric praise of her beauty

(Oxford 1.4.157–166; Arden 1.5.43–52) is not yet matched by a similar speech on her part, but already their first face-to-face encounter is characterised by the fact that Juliet contributes her part to the sonnet—even though she is still largely following Romeo's lead. Her overheard soliloquy in the orchard and the ensuing conversation with Romeo then show her as a person who is able to speak her own mind, who refuses to be imposed upon by Romeo's Petrarchan rhetoric, and who fights for her right to declare her love in her own words and style. This development reaches its climax in the epithalamium, a form traditionally assigned to the bridegroom, yet here spoken by Juliet in expectation of her newly wed Romeo (Oxford 3.2.1–31; Arden 3.2.1–31). As Böschenbröker (1996: 52) notes, this reversal of conventional roles turns Juliet "zum Subjekt, das in eigener Verantwortung spricht und handelt und sich somit gleichberechtigt neben Romeo stellt" 'into a subject who speaks and acts in her own right and thus makes herself Romeo's peer'.

Notes

1. See, for example, Rudanko (1993), the numerous publications by Norman F. Blake and Brown and Gilman (1989).

2. I quote from *The Oxford Shakespeare* edition by Levenson (2000). The references to the Arden edition are to *The Arden Shakespeare* edited by Gibbons (1980). I prefer Levenson's (2000) edition of *Romeo and Juliet* because it gives the text of the Second (or "Good") Quarto (1599) and does not conflate it with the First (or "Bad") Quarto (1597), the text of which is printed in an appendix at the end of the book.

3. See Bullough (1957: 284–363) for Brooke's text.

4. See Muller (1995: 323): "Drastisch formuliert, benutzt er, wenn auch vielleicht nicht bewusst, die Sprache der Liebeslyrik der Renaissance als Mittel der Verführung."

5. Quoted from Robert de Blois's (fl. 1233–1266) *Chastoiement des dames* (Fox 1950:136, l. 127). Translation: The kiss attracts other things.

6. See Perella (1969: 143) on the influence of this concept: "There is no doubt that the soul-in-the-kiss image received its greatest impetus in the Renaissance through Castiglione's presentation, for no man of letters could be ignorant of the *Book of the Courtier.* Henceforth the conceit was destined to become one of the most abused commonplaces in the literature of love."

7. Twentieth-century iconographic convention, as evidenced in movies and TV series, has it that the ratification of a kiss's meaning occurs immediately after its completion—either with a gasping for breath and renewed kissing or, if things have not yet been properly sorted out, with a gasp followed by a clout.

8. Fritz (1999: 148) gives the translation "Ihr küsst nach allen Regeln der Kunst." Müller (1995: 322–323) interprets Juliet's comment as follows: "Für sie folgt Romeo als Liebender zu sehr literarischen Modellen und höfischen Etikettbüchern. Sein Kuss ist für sie kein echter, sondern ein literarischer Kuss." This point of view is shared by Bly (1996: 100), who calls it "a mild rebuke". Brooke (1968: 95) sees it as a rejection of Romeo's effort to continue in the same mode: "The formality which

was right, is now wrong, once the pattern is completed in its final cadence." Leisi (1997: 103), however, translates Juliet's sentence as "Ihr habt das Küssen aber raus", i.e. as a compliment.

9. Colie (1974: 140) points out: "Romeo by no means abandons sonnet-language because he has in fact fallen truly in love."

10. Juliet, who has formerly always used *you* to address Romeo, changes to *thou* in her "soliloquy" and continues in the ensuing dialogue. Her use of *thou* can be interpreted first as a sign of fear and indignation about the intrusion, but then as a sign of her affection for Romeo. See Finkenstaedt (1963: 91–173) and Stein (2003) for a discussion of the pronouns of address in the sixteenth (and seventeenth) centuries.

11. See Sacks, Schegloff, and Jefferson (1974/1998) for the organisation of turn-taking. Since Juliet intended her speech as a soliloquy, there are no proper transition relevance places.

12. See also Rychard Hyrd's (1540) translation of Juan Luis Vives's *Instruction of a Christian Woman* (1523), which gives the following warning: "Give none ear unto the lover, no more than thou wouldst do unto an enchanter or sorcerer. For he cometh pleasantly and flattering, first praising the maid, showing her how he is taken with the love of her beauty, and that he must be dead for her love, for these lovers know well enough the vainglorious minds of many, which have a great delight in their own praises, wherewith they be caught like as the birder beguileth the birds—" (quoted in Neely 1985: 12).

13. These lines seem to contradict Wells's (1998: 916) assessment of Juliet as "young and inexperienced. Unlike these men-about-town, she does not know that according to the rules of the game that Romeo is playing, you are meant to be cold and aloof when your lover reveals his wounded heart, and that you are supposed to freeze the flames of his passion with your icy disdain. Instead she tells him she is in love and asks him if he loves her. [. . .] Such simplicity is touching." A careful reading of the relevant passage also reveals that her handling of the interaction with Romeo evidences less touching simplicity than emotional sincerity under difficult conditions.

14. Declarations of love often function like performatives. It is therefore of some importance that the lover himself is able to give expression to his love in suitable words.

15. It is not by accident that she uses, among others, the form of address "fair Montague" (Oxford 2.1.141; Arden 2.1.98), thus focussing on Romeo's socio-political situation.

16. Romeo, in the same line in the First Quarto, is given yet another abortive attempt at protesting his love: "Now by" (Praetorius 1886: 26).

17. Juliet's metaphor echoes that of Romeo's father in Oxford 1.1.147–149; Arden 1.1.149–151, who compared the effect of Romeo's private suffering to a "bud bit with an envious worm / Ere he can spread his sweet leaves to the air / Or dedicate his beauty to the same."

18. Not so in the text of the First Quarto. See Praetorius (1886: 26–27).

19. The simple yet intimate form of address that Romeo uses now for Juliet, namely "love", is also indicative of the change in tone.

20. Colie (1974: 143) comments on the lovers' Petrarchan language and makes an important point: "As we look back over the lovers' utterance, we can see very plainly the problem of expression: petrarchan language, the vehicle for amorous

emotion, can be used merely as the cliché which Mercutio and Benvolio criticize; or, it can be earned by a lover's experience of the profound oppositions to which that rhetoric of oxymoron points. When Romeo and Juliet seek to express their feelings' force, they return constantly to petrarchanisms hallowed with use—but having watched their development as lovers, an audience can accept as valid the language upon which they must fall back."

21. Neither the First nor the Second Quarto has a stage direction. Circumstantial evidence makes it likely that Juliet exits and re-enters a few moments later at 2.1.185.

22. Levenson (2000: 219) follows the line-attribution of the First Quarto. The Second Quarto ascribes "*Iu.* Sleep dwel vpon thine eyes, peace in thy breast" (Greg 1949, ll.ii.187) to Juliet and has Romeo speak two additional couplets which are repeated virtually unchanged at the beginning of 2.2.

Works Cited

Barthes, Roland. 1977/1990. *A Lover's Discourse. Fragments.* (Translated from French by Richard Howard. Title of the original: *Fragments d'un discour amoureux.* 1977.) Harmondsworth: Penguin Books.

Bly, Mary. 1996. Bawdy puns and lustful virgins: The legacy of Juliet's desire in comedies of the early 1600s. In: Stanley Wells (ed.). *Romeo and Juliet and Its Afterlife.* (Shakespeare Survey 49). Cambridge: Cambridge University Press, 97–109.

Böschenbröker, Rita. 1996. Repräsentationen der Liebe in *Romeo and Juliet:* das Epithalamium. *Shakespeare Jahrbuch* 132, 44–57.

Brooke, Arthur. 1562. The Tragicall Historye of Romeus and Juliet. In: Geoffrey Bullough (ed.). 1957. *Narrative and Dramatic Sources of Shakespeare. Volume I. Early Comedies, Poems, Romeo and Juliet.* London: Routledge and Kegan Paul, 284–363.

Brooke, Nicholas. 1968. *Shakespeare's Early Tragedies.* London: Methuen.

Brown, Roger, and Albert Gilman. 1989. Politeness theory and Shakespeare's four major tragedies. *Language in Society* 18, 159–212.

Bullough, Geoffrey (ed.). 1957. *Narrative and Dramatic Sources of Shakespeare. Volume I. Early Comedies, Poems, Romeo and Juliet.* London: Routledge and Kegan Paul.

Callaghan, Dympna C. 1994. The ideology of romantic love: The case of *Romeo and Juliet.* In: Dympna C. Callaghan, Lorraine Helms and Jyotsna Singh (eds.). *The Weyward Sisters. Shakespeare and Feminist Politics.* Oxford: Blackwell, 59–101.

Colie, Rosalie L. 1974. *Shakespeare's Living Art.* Princeton: Princeton University Press.

Cox, Virginia (ed.). 1994. *Count Baldassare Castiglione: The Book of the Courtier.* (First published 1528. Translated by Sir Thomas Hoby 1552–1555, published 1561. Everyman Library). London: Dent.

Finkenstaedt, Thomas. 1963. You *and* Thou: *Studien zur Anrede im Englischen* (mit einem Exkurs zur Anrede im Deutschen). Berlin: de Gruyter.

Fox, John Howard (ed.). 1950. *Robert de Blois: Son oeuvre didactique et narrative.* Paris: Nizet.

Fritz, Ulrike (ed. and trans.). 1999. *Shakespeare: Romeo and Juliet / Romeo und Julia.* (Englisch-deutsche Studienausgabe). Tübingen: Stauffenburg.

Gibbons, Brian (ed.). 1980. *The Arden Shakespeare: Romeo and Juliet.* (Reprinted 1997.) London: Nelson.

Greg, W. W. (ed.). 1949. *Romeo and Juliet. Second Quarto, 1599.* (Shakespeare Quarto Facsimiles 6.) London: The Shakespeare Association and Sidgwickand Jackson.

Honegger, Thomas. 2005. Die Transformation der höfischen Liebe in Shakespeare's *Romeo und Julia. Jenaer Universitätsreden* 17, 201–217.

Leisi, Ernst. 1997. *Problemwörter und Problemstellen in Shakespeares Dramen*. Stauffenburg: Stauffenburg.

Levenson, Jill L. (ed.). 2000. *The Oxford Shakespeare: Romeo and Juliet*. Oxford: Oxford University Press.

Levin, Harry. 1960. Form and formality in *Romeo and Juliet. Shakespeare Quarterly* 11, 3–11.

Müller, Wolfgang G. 1995. 'Kiss me, Kate': Zur Semantik and Ästhetik der Darstellung des Kusses in der englischen Literatur. *Literaturwissenschaftliches Jahrbuch* 36, 315–337.

Neely, Carol Thomas. 1985. *Broken Nuptials in Shakespeare's Plays*. New Haven and London: Yale University Press.

Perella, Nicolas James. 1969. *The Kiss Sacred and Profane*. Berkeley and Los Angeles: University of California Press.

Praetorius, Charles (ed.). 1886. *Romeo and Juliet. The First Quarto, 1597*. (A Facsimile from the British Museum Copy C 34 k 55). London: Praetorius.

Rudanko, Juhani. 1993. *Pragmatic Approaches to Shakespeare. Essays on Othello, Coriolanus and Timon of Athens*. Lanham, New York and London: University of America Press.

Sacks, Harvey, Emanuel A. Schegloff and Gail Jefferson. 1974/1998. A simplest systematics for the organization of turn-taking for conversation. (Originally published 1974 in *Language* 50, 696–735). In: Asa Kasher (ed.). 1998. *Communication, Interaction and Discourse*. (Volume 5 of *Pragmatics: Critical Concepts*. Six volumes). London and New York: Routledge, 193–242.

Stein, Dieter. 2003. Pronominal usage in Shakespeare. In: Irma Taavitsainen and Andreas H. Jucker (eds.). *Diachronic Perspectives on Address Term Systems*. Amsterdam and Philadelphia: John Benjamins, 251–307.

Wells, Robin Headlam. 1998. Neo-Petrarchan kitsch in *Romeo and Juliet. Modern Language Review* 93, 913–933.

Whittier, Gayle. 1989. The sonnet's body and the body sonnetized in *Romeo and Juliet. Shakespeare Quarterly* 40, 27–41.

DARYL W. PALMER

Motion and Mercutio in Romeo and Juliet

There is nothing permanent that is not true, what can be true that
is uncertaine? How can that be certaine, that stands upon uncertain
grounds?[1]

It is by now a commonplace in modern scholarship that drama, particularly Tudor drama, poses questions, rehearses familiar debates, and even
speculates about mere possibilities.[2] In 1954, Madeleine Doran spelled out
some of the ways in which debate "affected the structure of Elizabethan
drama."[3] In turn, Joel B. Altman, having eloquently extended Doran's
examination, concludes that "the plays functioned as media of intellectual
and emotional exploration for minds that were accustomed to examine the
many sides of a given theme, to entertain opposing ideals, and by so exercis-
ing the understanding, to move toward some fuller apprehension of truth
that could be discerned only through the total action of the drama."[4] Altman points to Henry Medwall's *Fulgens and Lucres* (c. 1490) as an exemplar
of this practice. Although the interlude instructs and entertains, "the center
of interest has shifted from demonstration to inquiry. The action develops
not from an abstract assertion, but from a specific question: who is the
nobler man, Cornelius or Gaius?"[5] By the time William Shakespeare began
to write his plays, inquiry was an essential part of dramatic construction. So
Juliet asks, "What's in a name?"[6] *Hamlet* opens with the question: "Who's

Philosophy and Literature, Volume 30, Number 2 (October 2006): pp. 540–554. Copyright ©
2006 The Johns Hopkins University Press.

185

there?" (1.1.1), and achieves a kind of apotheosis in the figure of its hero: "To be, or not to be, that is the question . . ." (3.1.55). Everyone recognizes these familiar questions, and we know (or think we know) how to describe the most viable answers. I want to suggest, however, that this familiarity has dulled our appreciation of the drama's interrogative range. As a way of resisting this tendency, I want to argue that Shakespeare's *Romeo and Juliet* takes up an ancient conversation about *motion,* a dialog that originates with the pre-Socratics. This is not to say that the play is ultimately about motion. It obviously engages a panoply of thematic materials. I have simply chosen, in this limited space, to concentrate on the way the playwright stages his questioning as a kind of fencing lesson. My goal is to produce neither a "reading" of the play nor an allegory of philosophy, but rather to recollect the ways in which Shakespeare's drama qualifies and extends an ancient inter-rogative tradition. In so doing, I follow Stanley Cavell who maintains "that Shakespeare could not be who he is—the burden of the name of the great-est writer in the language, the creature of the greatest ordering of English —unless his writing is engaging the depth of the philosophical preoccupa-tions of his culture."[7]

Some of the most venerable documents of Western philosophy fix on the problem of motion. If we go back more than 2,300 years, we come upon Plato's *Theaetetus,* in which Socrates explains a "first principle" to the title character, namely that "the universe really is motion and nothing else."[8] A kind of history lesson in ontology and epistemology, this tentative explanation has its origins in Heraclitus or Empedocles or Protagoras or some combina-tion of the aforementioned. Perhaps the most famous expression of this ideal comes from Heraclitus: "You cannot step twice into the same river, for other waters and yet others go ever flowing on."[9] More to the point is the follow-ing declaration from the same philosopher: "Everything flows and nothing abides; everything gives way and nothing stays fixed."[10] In this spirit, Pro-tagoras declares, "All matter is in a state of flux."[11] Such precedents provide the backdrop for Socrates in the *Theaetetus* as he summarizes: "The point is that all these things are, as we were saying, in motion, but there is a quickness or slowness in their motion" (*Thea,* 156c). In this historical spirit, he identi-fies "a tradition from the ancients, who hid their meaning from the common herd in poetical figures, that Oceanus and Tethys, the source of all things, are flowing streams and nothing is at rest" (*Thea,* 180d–e).

To be sure, the dialog depends on the rehearsal of such positions, but far more important for our purpose is Plato's attempt, through the figure of Socrates, to grasp motion through dialog. More inclined toward Parmenides' distrust of motion, Socrates has, from the outset, been setting up the terms of inquiry in a form that anticipates the dramatic shape of the Renaissance play by fixing the (ineffable) object of study so that it gives up its essence, its being.

Contemporary critics and philosophers will of course raise many objections to this motive,[12] and rightly so; but in the conversation I want to trace, the motive endures dramatically. Plato even pays attention to character. From the outset, Theaetetus marks himself as a green pupil, charming and polite. The young fellow finds Socrates' talk hard to follow. He becomes wary: "Really, I am not sure, Socrates. I cannot even make out about you, whether you are stating this as something you believe or merely putting me to the test" (*Thea*, 157c). As Shakespeare will always emphasize, character emerges out of dialog. Human disposition inflects inquiry. Maturity affects analysis.

Assuming that every change is a "motion," Socrates proceeds to confront his pupil with the difficult task of studying motion only in terms of motion, change in terms of change. That which fixes undoes what we study, but how difficult to adhere to such an injunction! Later in this dialog, Theodorus complains of thinkers who attempt such a task: "Faithful to their own treatises they are literally in perpetual motion; their capacity for staying still to attend to an argument or a question or for a quiet interchange of question and answer amounts to less than nothing . . ." (*Thea*, 179e–180a). According to his plan, Plato is preparing his readers to admit that they can only have knowledge of *being*. That which is ever becoming (something other) may be perceived, but not known. Motion, if it can be probed at all, will register as perception, not knowledge, a crucial distinction for what follows because literary scholarship often conflates perception and knowledge (*Thea*, 186e).[13]

This is not to say that Shakespeare read a given dialog by Plato as a source the way he read Ovid. To approach the Renaissance is to encounter Plato in every nook and cranny. We know, in general, that early modern thinkers read Plato, but his presence was more ubiquitous than simple citation would indicate.[14] Paul F. Grendler explains that "The Renaissance drew upon a centuries-old tradition whose roots went back to Plato's *Laws* and *Republic*, as well as Christian antiquity . . ."[15] With more particular application to Shakespeare's world, Sears Jayne declares, "at no time during the Renaissance were the English people ever limited, as the myth suggests, to a single conception of Plato; rather, they knew about Plato from many different sources, and entertained several different conceptions of his work."[16] Finally, Melissa Lane describes the way the philosopher's heirs have understood their role in the conversation: Plato "was, after all, Aristotle's teacher and a key source for Ciceronian Rome and Augustinian Christianity. And this status made him a magnet in the search for originality—both as the beginning and as the inspired genius."[17]

I take this "search" to be paradigmatic for subsequent centuries as it pops up in learned books and busy streets, even among the rapiers and daggers of Elizabethan London. As J. D. Aylward puts it in *The English Master of Arms*, most Englishmen of the period wanted to associate themselves with the practice of swordplay.[18] Theater audiences relished the expert fencing of actors.[19] London buzzed with talk of Continental fencing masters who claimed followings in their schools and in print. To these masters, fencing was both physical and mental, a palpable conflict and the basis for intellectual dialog. Vincentio Saviolo illustrates this motive in his *Practice* (1595). For Saviolo, combat comes down to discernment. He complains that "There are many that when they come to fight, runne on headlong without discretion."[20] In this same spirit, Giacomo Grassi warns his readers of the need for *judgment*, noting that, "amongst divers disorderlie blowes, you might have seen some of them most gallant lie bestowed, not without evident conjecture of deepe judgment."[21] Disorder must be avoided; the point, in other words, is to approach the physicality of combat through reason honed by reading. George Silver, Saviolo's main English competitor, remarked the project's difficulty by foregrounding motion: "The mind of man a greedie hunter after truth, finding the seeming truth but chaunging, not always one, but alwayes diverse, forsakes the supposed, to find out the assured certaintie: and searching every where save where it should, meetes with all save what it would."[22] No Socrates, Silver nonetheless shares a certain skepticism with the ancient philosopher.

More confidently than Silver, Saviolo pursues his inquiry in keen prose carefully tied to illustrations. The combatants appear on a grid that suggests geometric attention to their motion. The diagram, like the words in a dialog, seems to stabilize motion and permit thoughtful evaluation. In this manner, Saviolo scrutinizes the "cut." An obviously dramatic maneuver, the cut adds a thrilling sound to motion in ways that modern directors of action films take for granted. An audience can easily appreciate a cut, and an opponent must respect the obvious wound. Such satisfactions, however, cannot be the test of a movement. In order to grasp this argument, the student will want to make the motion answerable, fixing it in some manner, questioning it, and responding to it. Saviolo does precisely this when he outlines the cut in a mathematical diagram.[23] With the aid of his illustration, the author explains the move's limited effectiveness, numbering positions so as to better fix the represented motion. In the end, he concludes that the cut may satisfy the passions, but it will not win the combat.

With this lesson and many others like it, Saviolo returns to his primary theme, warning his reader about motion inspired by "e-motion." Indeed, everything in the treatise aims at distancing the pupil from his passions. Master and pupil sit on a riverbank. Urging calm attention, this sage spokesman takes advantage of the stillness to advocate deliberate attention to speed and slowness. Not unlike Socrates, Vincent encourages his young pupil to "expounde questions."[24]

For some time now, scholars have recognized that Shakespeare and his contemporaries were reading these manuals. Indeed, as Joan Ozark Holmer explains, Saviolo's "articulation of the ethic informing the truly honorable duello . . . significantly illuminate[s] the tragic complexity of the fatal duels in *Romeo and Juliet*."[25] What has not been fully appreciated is the way the manuals' emphasis on Platonic dialectic informs the practice of questioning at the heart of Shakespeare's great love story. Depending on the drama's inquisitive tradition, Shakespeare could center his love story on scenes of combat in order to expound questions about motion because he knew that his principal players were capable swordsmen.

Juliet wants to know what is in a name. Shakespeare, in writing *Romeo and Juliet*, might well have answered, *motion*. We know that "Romeo" suggests the wandering pilgrim; but long before Shakespeare, Plato emphasized the physics of such a name. In the *Cratylus*, Socrates muses about the letter "r," suggesting that the great "imposer of names" used the letter "because, as I imagine, he had observed that the tongue was most agitated and least at rest in the pronunciation of this letter, which he therefore used in order to express motion. . . ."[26] No mere allusion, the name Romeo demands that players agitate their tongues so as to play a part in the main character's motion. Moreover, the rough "r" of Elizabethan speech would have heightened this effect. There is, after all, no rest in Romeo, and so it makes sense that his cherished friend is named Mercutio. As we have already noted, the Greeks thought of any change as motion. Mercutio embodies that sense of the word as he restlessly engages his friend's sphere of activity, even threatening to displace Romeo as the play's real interest.

All of this activity takes shape in the streets of Verona, where the play's initial questioning turns on the nobility of moving versus standing. Standing, it turns out, is a kind of obsession in this play: the words "stand" and "stands" occur some 30 times. Throughout the drama, the words signal a nexus of male identity in combat, sexual arousal, and simple motionlessness. Sampson and Gregory quickly announce the theme:

> *Gre.*: I strike quickly, being mov'd.
> *Sam.*: A dog of the house of Montague moves me.
> *Gre.*: To move is to stir, and to be valiant is to stand; therefore, if
>   thou art mov'd, thou run'st away.
> *Sam.*: A dog of that house shall move me to stand!
>
> (1.1.6–11)

With breathtaking alacrity, Shakespeare initiates his tale of "star-cross'd love" with a dialog devoted to motion. Gregory puts his faith in speed, and does not doubt that he can be moved to anger. Yet he willingly abandons this formulation in order to sport with Samson's expression of resolution. Does motion or fixity define the valiant man? More clown than philosopher, Samson chooses to stand even as he boasts of his desire for maidenheads:

> *Sam.*: Me they shall feel while I am able to stand, and 'tis known I am a pretty piece of flesh.
> *Gre.*: 'Tis well thou art not fish; if thou hadst, thou hadst been poor-John. Draw thy tool, here comes [two] of the house of Montagues."
>
> (1.1.28–32)

That all this talk of motion evolves inevitably into talk of manhood may seem forced to a modern audience, and the playing of this translation on the stage can easily elide the way that Gregory baits Samson through these stages of "thought." A pitiful imitation of Socrates, Gregory adopts that old Platonic device of the dialog, but his instruction ends in an ambiguous validation of "standing." Because of the way it merges with male sexuality, this "proof" becomes an integral part of the play's deadly orchestrations.

Of course the real assay of this discourse in *Romeo and Juliet* (as in Saviolo's treatise) will demand *"swords and bucklers"* (1.1.1SD). For this reason, Samson's battle cry deserves attention: "Draw, if you be men. Gregory, remember thy washing blow" (1.1.62–63). Primed by his partner, Samson draws his "tool," confident that he can determine his manhood by doing so. The caesura concretizes the character's recognition that his manhood is linked to "washing blows" and other sorts of codified motion.

Such is the world inhabited by Romeo, Tybalt, and Mercutio, the main interlocutors of the play. Extensions of Samson and Gregory, these young men confound all attempts to tutor them. When Mercutio rhapsodizes of Queen Mab, Romeo tries in vain to lead him home (1.4.95). For his part, Capulet fruitlessly tries to teach Tybalt about hospitality (1.5.76–81). Benvolio fails to lead Mercutio out of the hot day (3.1.1). This list goes on and on, leaving Shakespeare's audience with real doubts about the possibility of successful pedagogy and utter suspicion of all attempts to make motion answerable.

At the play's beginning, Romeo and the Friar seem to embody the old Platonic model as they discuss Romeo's new love on a "grey-ey'd morn" (2.3.1). Romeo propounds his notions with an "early tongue" (32). In this pastoral setting, the counselor challenges his young pupil's passion with an energy worthy of Socrates and Saviolo. Adopting the language of fencing that already permeates the play, the Friar expresses a certain self-confidence in his analytical abilities: "then here I hit it right— / Our Romeo hath not been in bed to-night" (41–42). In early modern England, the study of motion seems to hinge on being able to "hit it right." Having done so, the Friar presses on: "And art thou chang'd? Pronounce this sentence then: / Women may fall, when there's no strength in men" (2.3.79–80). Galvanized by the sudden appearance of Romeo's change, the teacher wants to make the motion answerable. He seizes on the passion with a question followed by a caesura, indicating the instructor's cogitation before he attempts to fix the phenomena with a legalistic phrase: "Pronounce this sentence." As in Saviolo's dialog, this pastoral pedagogy ends up being about "strength in men."

As it did in Plato's dialog, the scene also takes shape through the old tension between youth and experience as the pupil attempts to come to terms with motion: "O let us hence, I stand on sudden haste" (2.3.93). Romeo here casts himself in a comic version of the manly debate between Gregory and Samson. Shakespeare's audience would have understood what Romeo meant, but many probably laughed at the callow bawdy and the embedded contradiction. Literally, Romeo insists on haste, but his "standing" would also suggest an erection and/or a kind of standstill that frustrates haste. The typical pupil, Romeo's passion will frustrate his execution.

And what of the Friar? His wisdom fits neatly into the second line of a couplet: "Wisely and slow, they stumble that run fast" (2.3.94). In his own imperfect way, more Heraclitus than Socrates, Friar Lawrence tries to respond to this turmoil by attending to the question of speed. He urges slowness, and it remains his constant focus. A little later in the play, he insists on the due and proper speed: "Too swift arrives as tardy as too slow" (2.5.15). To be sure, the play's critics have been divided over how they view the Friar's sagacity, but I think Socrates provides the perfect measure for his advice. Instead of knowledge, the Friar deals in perception; and this focus has the ring of common sense even though it lacks knowledge. It is worth noting that praise for Friar Lawrence's mental faculties comes from the Nurse (3.3.160).

In the end, the Friar is so fearful of speed that he orchestrates standstill. When faced with Romeo's murder of Tybalt, he counsels waiting so "we can find a time" (3.3.150). (One could contextualize the Friar's taste for slowness by pointing out that the fencing community endorsed it with its formal requirements for a duel *alla stoccata*.) Sizing up the lover's situation, he concludes, "here stands all your state" (3.3.166). How appropriate then that his plan for peace involves a vial of "distilling liquor" that will leave Juliet fixed, in a state like death (4.1.95). Frightened by motion, the Friar's passion for fixity seems to poison the whole play. When Paris and Romeo each arrive at the Capulet tomb, they tell their men to "stand" aloof (5.3.1; 5.3.26), and the two lovers destroy each other. How ironic that the Friar, having discovered the carnage, misreads the motionless forms and abandons the sleeping Juliet. The Friar's absurd reason flows through a single line: "Come go, good Juliet, I dare no longer stay" (5.3.159). Unable to make motion answerable, the counselor is reduced to "Come go." At the play's end, he reckons his own part in the action with these words: "here I stand both to impeach and purge / Myself" (5.3.226–227).

At the other end of the spectrum, Tybalt buzzes about the stage, all motion and little scrutiny. Saviolo might have invoked Tybalt as the perfect illustration of the fighter doomed by his own passions. When Benvolio would part the contestants in the play's first scene, Tybalt cries, "What, drawn and talk of peace?" (1.1.66–67). The very presence of the sword and buckler in his culture seems to truncate all dialog. Nowhere is this more apparent than at the Capulet's ball, when the host must rage in order to get his attention: "What, goodman boy? I say he shall, go to! / Am I the master here or you? Go to!" (1.5.77–78). In a culture of combat that revered the role of master, Tybalt has no time for authority. When he announces that he goes "to speak to them" at the beginning of 3.1, we know that he really seeks what Mercutio offers, namely "a word and a blow" (3.1.40). The inherently bad pupil explains that, for this, "You shall find me apt enough" (3.1.41).

Mercutio, by contrast, has more of the philosopher in him, and this aspect takes shape in terms of fencing. Unafraid of motion, he can, nonetheless, step back and observe. In ways no other character in the play does, Mercutio recollects knowledge; he understands numbers and technical terms. As the Queen Mab speech brilliantly shows, he has the capacity to reflect on the nature of motion and Shakespeare indulges him with impressive set speeches: "Sometime she driveth o'er a soldier's neck, / and then dreams he of cutting foreign throats, / Of breaches, ambuscadoes, Spanish blades" (1.4.82–84). Whatever we make of Queen Mab, we may admit that she instantiates, for Mercutio, a deadly dreaming realm of perception where passion leads men to their doom. If the soldier gives into passion, we may lay the blame on Queen Mab. Mercutio's auditors cannot follow such a poetical lesson. "Peace," Romeo pleads, "peace, Mercutio, peace! / Thou talk'st of nothing" (1.4.95–96). We may hear in this complaint (and not for the only time in the play) something of Theaetetus: "Really, I am not sure, Socrates. I cannot even make out about you, whether you are stating this as something you believe or merely putting me to the test." Whereas Romeo and Tybalt embody motion, Mercutio puts motion to the test, but his pupils always fumble over the examination.

Nowhere are Mercutio's aspirations on this score more apparent than in 2.4. The scene opens with Benvolio and Mercutio discussing the whereabouts of Romeo, but it turns quickly into a fencing lesson. Mercutio expands on his theme with Tybalt as his subject: "He fights as you sing prick-song, keeps time, distance, and proportion; he rests his minim rests, one, two and the third in your bosom: the very butcher of a silk button, a duellist, a duellist; a gentleman of the very first house, of the first and second cause. Ah, the immortal *passado*, the *punto reverso*, the *hay*" (2.4.20–26). Mercutio offers a complex lesson here, laden with technical vocabulary, real and invented. His reference to "the very first house" identifies Tybalt with both a family and a school of fencing. As though he were consulting Saviolo, Mercutio sets forth the terms that always organized a critique of fencing, namely time, distance, and proportion.[27] Meanwhile, words such as *"passado," "punto reverso,"* and *"hay"* give the instructor the opportunity to demonstrate each technique, animating the pictures Saviolo made popular. Mercutio even coins the term "duellist," a feat that suggests the teacher's original mind. Yet for all of this learning and bravado, Mercutio frames his lesson in the most thoughtful of ways by returning to the Platonic concern "with due occasion, due time, due performance."[28] For Plato, a life lived among perceptions would have to aim for the "right" time, occasion, etc. Mercutio notes (rather enviously, I think) that Tybalt embodies this attention, and so finds his point "in your bosom." In ways a modern audience will find difficult to follow in performance, Mercutio aims to dazzle his auditor with a discourse as applicable to life as it is to fencing. A veritable Theaetetus, Benvolio tries to follow this brilliant account. He says, "The what?" (2.4.27). A better teacher would listen to his pupil's question, perhaps pause to recollect the matter and begin anew. Mercutio merely presses on in his pedagogical fury, halting only when he sees Romeo approach.

At this point, Mercutio spies a more intriguing pupil and commences a history lesson: "Laura to his lady was a kitchen wench . . . Dido a dowdy, Cleopatra a gipsy . . ." (39–41). When Romeo attempts to make an apology for having missed his friends the night before, noting that "in such a case as mine a man may strain courtesy," Mercutio diagnoses Romeo's strain: "That's as much as to say, such a case as yours constrains a man to bow in the hams" (50–51, 52–53). Mercutio believes that Romeo has so indulged in amorous motions that he can no longer perform the simple courtesy of a bow. Romeo catches on, and Mercutio declares, "Thou hast most kindly hit it" (55). In ways that Benvolio cannot manage, Romeo proceeds to take up this challenge; and the two exchange verbal hits until Mercutio cries, "Come between us, good Benvolio, my wits faints" (67–68). Romeo, for his part, demands more intense motion: "Switch and spurs, switch and spurs—or I'll cry a match" (69–70). Brighter than Benvolio, Romeo knows how to play, but he lacks a certain capacity for reflection. Mercutio, by contrast, has the prescience to embrace motion and draw away in the same instant. "Nay," he chides Romeo, "if our wits run the wild-goose chase, I have done; for thou hast more of the wild goose in one of thy wits than, I am sure, I have in my whole five" (71–74). In this lively exchange, we come to understand Mercutio's aspirations. Like the Friar, Mercutio wants to be a kind of pedagogue. At the same time, he envies Tybalt's passion and remains too interested in the competition to drive his point home. Mercutio wants to know if he has won the verbal duel: "Was

I with you there for the goose?" (74). Like the Friar, Mercutio fails. Romeo never learns his lesson.

In fact, Mercutio's insights into motion were probably lost on the audience members as well. As Adolph L. Soens remarked some time ago, Mercutio, who seems to fight by the Italian book after the English habit, identifies Tybalt with the "Spanish book of fence as mannered and artificial as that book of poetics by which Romeo makes love and sonnets."[29] Soens argues convincingly that Shakespeare's audience would have wanted to dislike Tybalt's brave manner even as they respected his technical expertise (Soens, p. 125). What fascinates me about this set of identifications is less their relative accuracy than their effectiveness in (apparently) fixing motion in ethnic stereotypes for the Elizabethan audience. Silver announces this combative agenda in his treatise when he complains that Englishmen "have lusted like men sicke of a strange ague, after the strange vices and devises of Italian, French, and Spanish Fencers. . . ."[30]

To his credit, Soens avoids this trap and offers a stunning description of motion that I quote at length in order to suggest a more formalistic appreciation for the way motion matters to Mercutio's death. At the beginning of 3.1, Shakespeare envisions a hot street that ensures motion. Soens explains:

> The efficient and popular Italian fencing of Mercutio contrasts in posture and motion, as well as implications with the formal, deadly, and pedantic Spanish fencing of Princox (I.v.84) Tybalt. Mercutio and Tybalt circle each other, Tybalt upright, his arm outstretched, rapier and shoulder in a line, trying to keep his point in Mercutio's face; Mercutio, crouched in stoccata, holds his rapier low, by his right knee, cocked back for a thrust. Both extend their daggers toward the opponent to parry thrusts or to beat aside a threatening rapier in preparation for a thrust.

Their motions contrast as effectively, though not so absolutely, as their postures. Tybalt dances to and fro, attempting to evade his opponent, to catch him off balance and to gain angular advantage, while Mercutio moves with wider steps (and both move a great deal) and rushes in a series of tangents to the circle whose radius is Tybalt's outstretched rapier and sword-arm. Mercutio, in other words, rushes rapidly in and out of distance, hoping to catch Tybalt unprepared, and to throw a thrust from stoccata or imbroccata (in which the sword is held, knuckles up, over the head) while Tybalt is both off balance and within distance. Both parry with the dagger as a rule, although stop thrusts combined with parries can be found in both the Italian and Spanish manuals. The difference in styles suggests the mechanics of Mercutio's death. Mercutio takes his fatal thrust, not by accident, but in a situation where the advantage is all with the Spanish style . . . (Soens, p. 126).

In ways that no other scholar has done for this scene, Soens helps us to grasp Mercutio's death as a matter of contrasting motions. For Soens, this difference is the point: Romeo's intervention puts Mercutio's fighting style at a disadvantage. More compelling still is Romeo's well-meaning yet clumsy attempt to bring all this complex motion to a standstill in the name of "reason" (3.1.62, 70). In Platonic terms, reason would be precisely what these men need, but Romeo is talking about "reason" colloquially as "cause," specifically his marriage to Juliet (Holmer, p. 182). Romeo wants to stop the motion, but lacks the reason to do so. For Holmer, this confrontation recalls Saviolo's condemnation of ill-considered quarrels spurred on by fury (Holmer, pp. 181–185).

Just as important, I contend, is Saviolo's pragmatic recognition that some of the most compromised of motions, say combats between friends and kin, do not permit analysis. For the teacher who longs for truth and justice in quarreling, certain situations nonetheless demand an end to thought. In a description that seems to anticipate the conflict in *Romeo and Juliet,* Saviolo urges his pupil to abandon reflection:

> consider that he which challengeth him, dooth not require to fight with him as a freend, but as an enemye, and that he is not to think any otherwise of his minde but as full of rancour and malice towards him: wherefore when you see one with weapons in his hand that will needs fight with you, although hee were your freend or kinseman, take him for an enemy. . . . [31]

Saviolo's account neatly exposes Romeo's error. Faced with such a predicament, Romeo appeals to the "minde" and encourages Tybalt and Mercutio "to think any otherwise," contrary to Saviolo's advice. As Holmer has noted (Holmer, p. 174), Mercutio's dying words come straight from Saviolo: "They have made worms' meat of me" (3.1.107). Only when it is too late does Romeo grasp at the master's injunction: "take him for an enemy."

Even as Shakespeare offers his audience a veritable laboratory of fencing mechanics and the geometric spectacle of Mercutio's death, the playwright spins out a mechanics of catastrophe that cannot satisfy the rational mind. Romeo's teacher sends "a friar with speed," but the messenger arrives too late (4.1.123). Romeo chooses "quick" drugs that enable him to die before Friar Lawrence arrives and Juliet awakes. A moment too late, Friar Lawrence exclaims, "how oft tonight / Have my old feet stumbled at graves!" (5.3.121–122). In time to see that the "lady stirs," the counselor determines he can "no longer stay" (5.3.147, 59). If we step back from this action, I think we can describe this early tragedy anew: Shakespeare has created a work that teases us with the possibility of making motion answerable. Who can watch such motions and not demand an inquiry? Yet with Mercutio dead, who will expound the questions?

For centuries, audiences have been mesmerized by the character that inspired Coleridge to write the following encomium:

> O! how shall I describe that exquisite ebullience and overflow of youthful life, wafted on over the laughing waves of pleasure and prosperity, as a wanton beauty that distorts the face on which she knows her lover is gazing enraptured, and wrinkles her forehead in the triumph of its smoothness! Wit ever wakeful, fancy busy and procreative as an insect, courage, an easy mind that, without cares of its own, is at once disposed to laugh away those of others, and yet to be interested in them. . . . [32]

Generations of readers have agreed with this appraisal, but what we have failed to appreciate is the pedagogical (and therefore interrogative) motive behind all this "exquisite ebullience." When Plato bequeathed his brilliant dialogs to posterity, he left behind more than questioning: the philosopher left us with the idea of the brilliant teacher whose radiance would always authenticate the asking. This is precisely the role Socrates gives to himself in the *Theaetetus*: "And the highest point of my art is the power to prove by every test whether the offspring of a young man's thought is a false phantom or instinct with life and truth" (*Thea*, 150c). For a dramatist like Shakespeare, the old conversation about motion must have held all sorts of attractions, but the implications for character must have been tantalizing. Aspiring to both embody motion and test it, Mercutio longs to be the young man's guide: he is the obvious product of Shakespeare's musing over motion, on the page, on the stage. Although his lessons never approach the rigor of Socrates, his "wit ever wakeful" energizes audiences with ambitions worthy of the ancient Greeks. Were we able to make motion answerable, we would be very close to the origins of life itself. Mercutio aspires in this direction. Perhaps *Romeo and Juliet* feels so profound because we experience this aspiration and mourn its failure.

NOTES

1. George Silver, *Paradoxes of Defence* (London, 1599), A3r, v.
2. The author would like to thank Jose Ramón Díaz-Fernández and Peter S. Donaldson for organizing *A Boundless Sea: Shakespeare's Mediterranean on Film* at the Seventh World Shakespeare Congress in Valencia, Spain, where the initial version

of this essay was presented. And special thanks to my colleague in philosophy Alan Hart for his wise reading of the work in progress.

3. Madeleine Doran, *Endeavors of Art* (Madison: University of Wisconsin Press, 1954), p. 312.

4. Joel B. Altman, *The Tudor Play of Mind* (Berkeley: University of California Press, 1978), p. 6.

5. Altman, *The Tudor Play of Mind,* p. 21.

6. William Shakespeare, *Romeo and Juliet, The Riverside Shakespeare,* 2nd ed., ed. G. Blakemore Evans (New York: Houghton Mifflin, 1997), 2.2.43.

7. Stanley Cavell, *Disowning Knowledge,* updated ed. (Cambridge: Cambridge University Press, 2003), p. 2.

8. Plato, *Theaetetus, The Collected Dialogues of Plato,* ed. Edith Hamilton and Huntington Cairns (Princeton: Princeton University Press, 1961), 156a; hereafter abbreviated *Thea.*

9. Heraclitus, *The Presocratics,* ed. Philip Wheelwright (New York: Odyssey Press, 1966), p. 71.

10. Heraclitus, *The Presocratics,* p. 70.

11. Protagoras, *The Presocratics,* p. 239.

12. See, for instance, Jacques Derrida, *Disseminations,* trans. Barbara Johnson (Chicago: University of Chicago Press, 1981), pp. 65–84.

13. On this fundamental distinction between perception and knowledge, see Gail J. Fine, "Knowledge and *LOGOS* in the *Theaetetus,*" *Philosophical Review* 88 (1979): 366–397.

14. Paul Oskar Kristeller, "Humanism," *The Cambridge History of Renaissance Philosophy,* ed. Charles B. Schmitt, et al. (Cambridge: Cambridge University Press, 1988), p. 129.

15. Paul F. Grendler, "Printing and Censorship," *The Cambridge History of Renaissance Philosophy,* p. 42.

16. Sears Jayne, *Plato in Renaissance England* (Dordrecht: Kluwer Academic Publishers, 1995), p. xiii.

17. Melissa Lane, *Plato's Progeny* (London: Duckworth, 2001), p. 9.

18. J. D. Aylward, *The English Master of Arms* (London: Routledge & Kegan Paul, 1956), pp. 17–31.

19. Andrew Gurr, *The Shakespearean Stage 1574–1642,* 3rd ed. (Cambridge: Cambridge University Press, 1992), p. 4.

20. Vincentio Saviolo, *Vincentio Saviolo His Practice* (London, 1595), I4r.

21. Giacomo Grassi, *DiGrassi His True Arte of Defence,* trans. Thomas Churchyard (London, 1594), A2r.

22. Silver, *Paradoxes of Defence,* A3v.

23. Aylward, *The English Master of Arms,* p. 58.

24. Saviolo, *Vincentio Saviolo His Practice,* B4v.

25. Joan Ozark Holmer, "'Draw, if you be Men': Saviolo's Significance for *Romeo and Juliet,*" *Shakespeare Quarterly* 45 (1994): 163; hereafter abbreviated Holmer.

26. Plato, *Cratylus,* 426 d, e.

27. On Mercutio's "debt" to Saviolo, see Holmer, p. 173.

28. Plato, *Statesman,* 284e.

29. Adolph L. Soens, "Tybalt's Spanish Fencing in *Romeo and Juliet,*" *Shakespeare Quarterly* 20 (1969): 121, 123–125; hereafter abbreviated Soens.

30. Silver, *Paradoxes of Defence*, A4v.

31. Saviolo, *Vincentio Saviolo His Practice*, E2r, v. On Saviolo's recommendation not to part combatants, see Holmer, p. 183.

32. Samuel Taylor Coleridge, *The Romantics on Shakespeare*, ed. Jonathan Bate (London: Penguin, 1992), p. 515.

Chronology

1564	William Shakespeare christened at Stratford-on-Avon on April 26.
1582	Marries Anne Hathaway in November.
1583	Daughter Susanna born, baptized on May 26.
1585	Twins Hamnet and Judith born, baptized on February 2.
1587	Shakespeare goes to London, without family.
1589–1590	*Henry VI, Part One.*
1590–1591	*Henry VI, Part Two; Henry VI, Part Three.*
1592–1593	*Richard III; The Two Gentlemen of Verona.*
1592–1593	Publication of *Venus and Adonis,* dedicated to the Earl of Southampton; *The Sonnets* probably begun.
1593	*The Comedy of Errors.*
1593–1594	Publication of *The Rape of Lucrece,* also dedicated to the Earl of Southampton; *Titus Andronicus; The Taming of the Shrew.*
1594–1595	*Love's Labour's Lost; King John; Richard II.*
1595–1596	*Romeo and Juliet; A Midsummer Night's Dream.*
1596	Son Hamnet dies; a coat of arms granted to Shakespeare's father, John.

1596–1597	*The Merchant of Venice; Henry IV, Part One;* purchases New Place in Stratford.
1597–1598	*The Merry Wives of Windsor; Henry IV Part Two.*
1598–1599	*Much Ado About Nothing.*
1599	*Henry V; Julius Cesar; As You Like It.*
1600–1601	*Hamlet.*
1601	*The Phoenix and the Turtle;* Shakespeare's father dies.
1601–1602	*Twelfth Night; Troilus and Cressida.*
1602–1603	*All's Well That Ends Well.*
1603	Death of Queen Elizabeth; James VI of Scotland becomes James I of England; Shakespeare's Company becomes the King's Men.
1604	*Measure for Measure; Othello.*
1605	*King Lear.*
1606	*Macbeth; Antony and Cleopatra.*
1607	Marriage of daughter Susanna on June 5.
1607–1608	*Coriolanus; Timon of Athens; Pericles.*
1608	Death of Shakespeare's mother.
1609	Publication, probably unauthorized, of the quarto edition of the *Sonnets.*
1609–1610	*Cymbeline.*
1610–1611	*The Winter's Tale.*
1611	*The Tempest;* Shakespeare returns to Stratford, where he will live until his death.
1612	*A Funeral Elegy.*
1612–1613	*Henry VIII;* The Globe Theatre destroyed by fire.
1613	*The Two Noble Kinsmen* (with John Fletcher).
1616	Marriage of daughter Judith on February 10; Shakespeare dies on April 23.
1623	Publication of the First Folio edition of Shakespeare's plays.

Contributors

HAROLD BLOOM is Sterling Professor of the Humanities at Yale University. He is the author of 30 books, including *Shelley's Mythmaking* (1959), *The Visionary Company* (1961), *Blake's Apocalypse* (1963), *Yeats* (1970), *A Map of Misreading* (1975), *Kabbalah and Criticism* (1975), *Agon: Toward a Theory of Revisionism* (1982), *The American Religion* (1992), *The Western Canon* (1994), and *Omens of Millennium: The Gnosis of Angels, Dreams, and Resurrection* (1996). *The Anxiety of Influence* (1973) sets forth Professor Bloom's provocative theory of the literary relationships between the great writers and their predecessors. His most recent books include *Shakespeare: The Invention of the Human* (1998), a 1998 National Book Award finalist; *How to Read and Why* (2000); *Genius: A Mosaic of One Hundred Exemplary Creative Minds* (2002); *Hamlet: Poem Unlimited* (2003); *Where Shall Wisdom Be Found?* (2004); and *Jesus and Yahweh: The Names Divine* (2005). In 1999, Professor Bloom received the prestigious American Academy of Arts and Letters Gold Medal for Criticism. He has also received the International Prize of Catalonia, the Alfonso Reyes Prize of Mexico, and the Hans Christian Andersen Bicentennial Prize of Denmark.

NORMAN F. BLAKE is a research professor in the English department and Centre for Technology and the Arts at De Montfort University, Leicester, U.K. He has published widely, focusing on Chaucer, especially the Canterbury Tales Project, William Caxton and the relation of printing to the development of standard English, and the language of Shakespeare. His recent books include *A History of the English Language* (1996) and *A Grammar of Shakespeare's Language* (2002).

TANYA POLLARD is associate professor of English at Brooklyn College. She wrote *Drugs and Theater in Early Modern England* (2005) and edited *Shakespeare's Theater: A Sourcebook* (2003).

DAVID SALTER is lecturer in English literature at the University of Edinburgh. He wrote *Holy and Noble Beasts: Encounters with Animals in Medieval Literature* (2001).

WILLIAM M. MCKIM is a retired professor of English at Northern Kentucky University. He has written articles on Shakespeare; Spenser; Baseball, Religion, and American Culture; and the poetics of aging.

ROBERT N. WATSON is former chair of the department of English and chair of the faculty of the University of California at Los Angeles College of Letters and Science, and is now associate vice-provost for Educational Innovation. His books include *Shakespeare and the Hazards of Ambition* (1984), *Ben Jonson's Parodic Strategy: Literary Imperialism in the Comedies* (1987), *Back to Nature, The Rest Is Silence: Death as Annihilation in the English Renaissance* (1995), and *The Green and the Real in the Late Renaissance* (2006).

STEPHEN DICKEY is senior lecturer in English at UCLA. He has written articles on Elizabethan drama.

JENNIFER A. LOW is associate professor of English at Florida Atlantic University. She wrote *Manhood and the Duel: Masculinity in Early Modern Drama and Culture* (2003).

LINA PERKINS WILDER is assistant professor of English at Connecticut College, where she teaches courses on Shakespeare, Milton, and the "early modern" period of English literature.

THOMAS HONEGGER is professor of English philology with special consideration of medieval studies at Freidrich-Schiller-Universität-Jena, Germany. He has written *From Phoenix To Chauntecleer: Medieval English Animal Poetry* (1996) and has edited books both on medieval language and literature and on Tolkein.

DARYL W. PALMER is associate professor of English at Regis University. He is the author of *Hospitable Performances: Dramatic Genre and Cultural Practices in Early Modern England* (1992) and *Writing Russia in the Age of Shakespeare* (2004).

Bibliography

Abbate, Alessandro. "The Text within the Text, the Screen within the Screen: Multi-Layered Representations in Michael Almereyda's *Hamlet* and Baz Luhrmann's *Romeo + Juliet*." In Gerhard Fischer and Bernhard Greiner, eds. *The Play within the Play: The Performance of Meta-Theatre and Self-Reflection.* Amsterdam, Netherlands: Rodopi, 2007, pp. 377–391.

Adams, Barry B. "The Prudence of Prince Escalus." *English Literary History* 35 (1968): 32–50.

Andreas, James. "The Neutering of *Romeo and Juliet*." In *Ideological Approaches to Shakespeare: The Practice of Theory,* ed. Robert P. Merrix. Lewiston, NY: Edwin Mellen Press, 1992.

Andrews, J. F. (ed.). *Romeo and Juliet: Critical Essays.* New York: Garland, 1993.

Belsey, Catherine. "The Name of the Rose in *Romeo and Juliet*." *Yearbook of English Studies* 23 (1993): 125–142.

Black, James. "The Visual Artistry of *Romeo and Juliet*." *SEL: Studies in English Literature, 1500–1900* 15 (1975): 245–256.

Bond, Ronald B. "Love and Lust in *Romeo and Juliet*." *Wascana Review* 15 (1980): 22–31.

Bryant, James C. "The Problematic Friar in *Romeo and Juliet*." *English Studies* 55 (1974): 340–350.

Carroll, William T. "'We Were Born to Die': *Romeo and Juliet*." *Comparative Drama* 15 (1981): 54–71.

Chang, Joseph S. M. J. "The Language of Paradox in *Romeo and Juliet*." *Shakespeare Studies* 3 (1967): 22–42.

Cribb, T. J. "The Unity of *Romeo and Juliet*." *Shakespeare Survey* 34 (1981): 93–104.

Dickey, Franklin M. *Not Wisely But Too Well: Shakespeare's Love Tragedies.* San Marino, California: Huntington Library Press, 1957.

Estrin, Barbara. *"Romeo and Juliet,* and the Art of Naming Love." *Ariel* 12 (April 1981): 31–49.

Evans, Bertrand. "The Brevity of Friar Laurence." *PMLA* 65 (1950): 841–865.

Evans, Blakemore G. Introduction to *Romeo and Juliet,* by William Shakespeare, ed. G. Blakemore Evans. Cambridge: Cambridge University Press, 1980.

Everett, Barbara. *"Romeo and Juliet:* the Nurse's Story." *Critical Quarterly* 14 (1972): 169–182.

Faber, M. D. "The Adolescent Suicide of *Romeo and Juliet." Psychoanalytic Review* 59 (1972): 169–182.

Farrell, Kirby. "Love, Death, and Patriarchy in *Romeo and Juliet."* In *Shakespeare's Personality,* ed. Norman N. Holland, Sidney Homan, and Bernard J. Paris. Berkeley: University of California Press, 1989.

García Mainar, Luis. "Shakespeare's *Romeo and Juliet* and Male Melodrama." In José Manuel González, ed. *Spanish Studies in Shakespeare and His Contemporaries. International Studies in Shakespeare and His Contemporaries.* Newark: University of Delaware Press, 2006, pp. 148–170.

Gibbons, Brian. Introduction to *Romeo and Juliet,* by William Shakespeare, ed. Brian Gibbons. *The New Arden Shakespeare,* ed. Harold F. Brooks, Harold Jenkins, and Brian Morris. London and New York: Methuen, 1980.

Gregory, Sue. "Making Shakespeare Our Contemporary: Teaching *Romeo and Juliet* at Key Stage Three." In Martin Blocksidge, ed. *Shakespeare in Education.* London: Continuum, 2005, pp. 20–39.

Hanson, Kristin. "Shakespeare's Lyric and Dramatic Metrical Styles." In B. Elan Dresher and Nila Friedberg, eds. *Formal Approaches to Poetry: Recent Development in Metrics.* Berlin, Germany: Mouton de Gruyter, 2006, pp. 111–133.

Hodgdon, Barbara, and W. B. Worthen, eds. *A Companion to Shakespeare and Performance. Blackwell Companions to Literature and Culture.* Oxford, England: Blackwell, 2005.

Holmer, Joan Ozark. "'Myself Condemned and Myself Excus'd': Tragic Effect in Romeo and *Juliet." Studies in Philology* 88 (1991): 345–362.

Kahn, Coppelia. "Coming of Age in Verona." *Modern Language Studies* 8 (1977–1978): 5–22.

Leech, Clifford. "The Moral Tragedy of *Romeo and Juliet." English Renaissance Drama: Essays in Honor of Madeleine Doran and Mark Eccles.* Henning, Standish, et al., eds. Carbondale and Edwardsville: Southern Illinois University Press, London and Amsterdam: Feffer and Simons: 1976.

Levenson, Jill L. "The Definition of Love: Shakespeare's Phrasing in *Romeo and Juliet." Shakespeare's Studies* 15 (1982): 21–36.

Levin, Harry. "Form and Formality in *Romeo and Juliet.*" *Shakespeare Quarterly* 10 (1959): 35–44.

Mahood, M. M. "*Romeo and Juliet.*" In *Shakespeare's Wordplay.* London: Methuen, 1957.

Marsh, Derick R. C. *Passion Lends Them Power: A Study of Shakespeare's Love Tragedies.* Manchester: Manchester University Press, 1976.

Mason, Harold A. *Shakespeare's Tragedies of Love.* 1970.

Moisan, Thomas E. "Rhetoric and Rehearsal of Death: the 'Lamentations' Scene in *Romeo and Juliet.*" *Shakespeare Quarterly* 34 (1983): 389–404.

Moore, Olin H. *The Legend of Romeo and Juliet.* Columbus: Ohio State University Press, 1950.

Ostrovsky, Arkady. "Shakespeare as a Founding Father of Socialist Realism: The Soviet Affair with Shakespeare." In Irena R. Makaryk, and Joseph G. Price, eds. *Shakespeare in the Worlds of Communism and Socialism.* Toronto: University of Toronto Press, 2006, pp. 56–83.

Parker, Douglas H. "Light and Dark Imagery in *Romeo and Juliet.*" *Queen's Quarterly* 75 (1968): 663–674.

Porter, Joseph A. *Shakespeare's Mercutio: His History and Drama.* Chapel Hill: University of North Carolina Press, 1988.

Reynolds, Bryan, and Janna Segal. "Fugitive Explorations in *Romeo and Juliet:* Searching for Transversality inside the Goldmine of R&Jspace." In Bryan Reynolds and Bruce Smith, eds. *Transversal Enterprises in the Drama of Shakespeare and His Contemporaries: Fugitive Explorations.* New York: Palgrave Macmillan, 2006, pp. 124–167.

Riethmüller, Albrecht. "'She Speaks, Yet She Says Nothing: What of That?' *Romeo and Juliet* in Hector Berlioz's and Leonard Bernstein's Adaptations." In Christa Jansohn, ed. *German Shakespeare Studies at the Turn of the Twenty-First Century. International Studies in Shakespeare and His Contemporaries.* Newark: University of Delaware Press, 2006, pp. 128–143.

Roe, John. "Unfinished Business: A Lover's Complaint and *Hamlet, Romeo and Juliet* and *The Rape of Lucrece.*" In Shirley Sharon-Zisser and Stephen Whitworth, eds. *Critical Essays on Shakespeare's A Lover's Complaint: Suffering Ecstasy.* Aldershot, England: Ashgate, 2006, pp. 109–120.

Ryan, Kiernan. "*Romeo and Juliet:* the Language of Tragedy." In *The Taming of the Text: Explorations in Language, Literature and Culture*, ed. Willie van Peer. London: Routledge, 1988, pp. 106–121.

Scragg, Leah. *Shakespeare's Mouldy Tales: Recurrent Plot Motifs in Shakespearean Drama.* London: Longman, 1992.

Seward, James H. *Tragic Vision in Romeo and Juliet.* Washington, D.C.: Consortium Press, 1973.

Siegal, Paul N. "Christianity and the Religion of Love in *Romeo and Juliet*." *Shakespeare Quarterly* 12 (1961): 371–392.

Soncini, Sara. "Re-Locating Shakespeare: Cultural Negotiations in Italian Dubbed Versions of *Romeo and Juliet*." In Manfred Pfister, and Ralf Hertel, eds. *Performing National Identity: Anglo-Italian Cultural Transactions*. Amsterdam, Netherlands: Rodopi, 2008, pp. 235–248.

Stamm, Rudolf. "The First Meeting of the Lovers in Shakespeare's *Romeo and Juliet*." *English Studies* 67 (1986): 2–13.

Thomas, Sidney. "The Queen Mab Speech in *Romeo and Juliet*." *Shakespeare Survey* 25 (1972): 73–80.

Utterback, Raymond V. "The Death of Mercutio." *Shakespeare Quarterly* 24, No. 2 (Spring 1973): 105–116.

Wall, Wendy. "De-Generation: Editions, Offspring, and *Romeo and Juliet*." In Peter Holland and Stephen Orgel, eds. *From Performance to Print in Shakespeare's England*. Basingstoke, England: Palgrave Macmillan, 2006, pp. 152–170.

Wallace, Nathaniel. "Cultural Tropology in *Romeo and Juliet*." *Studies in Philology* 88 (1991): 329–344.

Waters, Douglas. *Christian Settings in Shakespeare's Tragedies*. London: Associated University Presses, 1994.

Watts, Cedric. *Romeo and Juliet*. Boston: Twayne, 1991.

West, William N. "Mercutio's Bad Language." Bryan Reynolds and William N. West, eds. *Rematerializing Shakespeare: Authority and Representation on the Early Modern English Stage*. New York: Palgrave Macmillan, 2005, pp. 115–129.

Williamson, Marilyn L. "Romeo and Death." *Shakespeare Studies* 14 (1981): 129–137.

Young, Bruce W. "Haste, Consent, and Age at Marriage: Some Implications of Social History in *Romeo and Juliet*." *Iowa State Journal of Research* 62 (1988): 459–474.

Acknowledgments

Norman F. Blake. "On Shakespeare's Informal Language," *Journal of Historical Pragmatics*, Volume 3, Number 2 (2002): pp. 179–204. Copyright © 2002 John Benjamin Publishing Company. Reprinted by permission of the publisher.

Tanya Pollard. "'A Thing Like Death': Sleeping Potions and Poisons in *Romeo and Juliet* and *Antony and Cleopatra*," *Renaissance Drama*, Volume 32 (2003): pp. 95–121. Copyright © 2003 Northwestern University Press. Reprinted by permission of the publisher and the author.

David Salter. "Shakespeare and Catholicism: The Franciscan Connection," *Cahiers Élisabéthains: Late Medieval and Renaissance Studies*, Volume 66 (Autumn 2004): pp. 9–22. Copyright © 2004 David Salter. Reprinted by permission of the author.

William M. McKim. "Romeo's 'Death-markt' Imagination and its Tragic Consequences," *Kentucky Philological Review*, Volume 20, Numbers 4–5 (March 2005): pp. 38–45. Copyright © 2005 Kentucky Philological Association. Reprinted by permission of the publisher.

Robert N. Watson and Stephen Dickey. "Wherefore Art Thou Tereu? Juliet and the Legacy of Rape," *Renaissance Quarterly*, Volume 58, Number 1 (Spring 2005): pp. 127–156. Copyright © 2005 Northwestern University Press. Reprinted by permission of the publisher and the authors.

Jennifer A. Low. "'Bodied Forth': Spectator, Stage, and Actor in the Early Modern Theater," *Comparative Drama*, Volume 39, Number 1 (Spring 2005): pp. 1–29. Copyright © 2005 Western Michigan University. Reprinted by permission of the publisher and the author.

Lina Perkins Wilder. "Toward a Shakespearean 'Memory Theater': Romeo, the Apothecary, and the Performance of Memory," *Shakespeare Quarterly*, Volume 56, Number 2 (Summer 2005): pp. 156–175. Copyright © 2005 The Johns Hopkins University Press. Reprinted by permission of the publisher and the author.

Thomas Honegger. "'Wouldst thou withdraw love's faithful vow?' The Negotiation of Love in the Orchard Scene (*Romeo and Juliet* Act II)," *Journal of Historical Pragmatics*, Volume 7, Number 1 (2006): pp. 73–88. Copyright © 2006 John Benjamin Publishing Company. Reprinted by permission of the publisher and the author.

Daryl W. Palmer. "Motion and Mercutio in *Romeo and Juliet*," *Philosophy and Literature*, Volume 30, Number 2 (October 2006): pp. 540–554. Copyright © 2006 The Johns Hopkins University Press. Reprinted by permission of the publisher and the author.

Index